From Here to Anyw'

16 days, 16 countries, 16 bud'
cheapskat'

ne

First English edition published in 2016 by Smart Travel Publishing

Cover design by Ace Graphics

ASIN: B01CO39ZJW
ISBN-13: 978-1530433414
ISBN-10: 153043341X

Smart, Jason J
From Here to Anywhere

For Pat, who left us far too early
To Isla, who joined us with a squeal of delight
And to Curtis Brown, a fellow traveller and devotee of all things
unusual

THE ROUTE:

1. Manchester, UK
2. Moss, Norway
3. Novy Dwor Mazowiecki, Poland
4. Nykoping, Sweden
5. Bremen, Germany
6. Riga, Latvia
7. Bergamo, Italy
8. Bratislava, Slovakia
9. Charleroi, Belgium
10. Carcassonne, France
11. Eindhoven, The Netherlands
12. Belgrade, Serbia
13. Athen, Greece
14. Larnaca, Cyprus
15. Budapest, Hungary
16. Dublin, Ireland

Contents

Day 1. Moss, Norway

Manchester – Oslo Rygge: Ryanair £24

I suspect nobody outside Norway has heard of the town of Moss. And why would they? Moss is a small coastal settlement sixty kilometres south of the capital, Oslo, with nothing of note except a few factories, a small harbour and a museum.

Locally, I suppose, Moss's paper mills make it somewhat famous among the people who live in the region. And perhaps some of its factories ought to be more well-known, especially the one that manufactures key cards for international hotel chains. The town's biggest draw is the Moss Industrial Museum. Inside this illustrious establishment, exhibitions of milling and papermaking equipment abound. The museum's website claims it also runs workshops enabling local children to make their own paper. When I read that the museum was full of Norwegian glass, I vowed to visit it myself, in order to prove it wasn't as boring as it sounded.

Oddly enough, Moss had once hit the world's headlines. In 2006, a fireball from space exploded above the town, sending fragments downwards like heavenly fireworks. Unfortunately, the townsfolk of Moss didn't notice. They were all asleep. The next morning, a few eagle-eyed locals noted that one meteorite had hit a tree, singeing a few branches. Another had landed in field. A third had hit someone's fence, knocking it over. The people of Moss looked skywards and scratched their heads.

A few days later, another fireball exploded over Moss. This time, a meteorite crashed through someone's roof. This was more like it and, even though it didn't injure anyone, it was of sufficient interest to make the news. Over in America – a nation full of space rock enthusiasts – the story broke a day later. Almost immediately, there was a mad rush to book flights to Scandinavia. And so, for a brief few days in the summer of 2006, Moss became the meteorite capital of the world. One collector, an American called Michael Farmer, later said: 'The name Moss is no joke. Every inch of the ground is covered with a thick carpet of moss plants. It made the search for meteorites difficult'.

But there had to be more to Moss than an industrial museum, a few space rocks and a healthy growth of moss. If there was, then I would do my best to find it.

2

My low-cost adventure began at Manchester Airport on a rainy, overcast July morning. My wife, Angela, dropped me off outside Terminal 3 and wished me luck. "You're mad, you know," she said again as I hefted my packed-to-capacity hand luggage from the back of the car. "Two weeks of going to all those different countries and airports. You are sure you want to go ahead with this? It's not too late to change your mind."

I smiled, putting on a brave face, but inwardly grimacing. I hated airports, I hated air travel, and to endure sixteen separate flights in just over two weeks sounded like the antics of an unhinged mind. I said my goodbyes, grabbed a quick kiss and was off. At the entrance, I turned to see my wife staring. She looked worried. I waved, she waved back, and then I entered the airport, the first of many over the next couple of weeks.

I'd travelled through Manchester Airport plenty of times before. Because of my familiarity, I knew exactly where the Ryanair baggage-drop desks were. I didn't need to go to them, of course, because I only had hand luggage, but I still wanted to have a look at my fellow low-cost passengers.

Mobs of people with suitcases were lining up at the counters. Boarding cards were at the ready, diligently printed out because no one wanted to fall foul of Ryanair's draconian seventy-euro fee for getting the check-in agent to print it out for them. I strained my neck to look at some boarding cards belonging to a group of scraped-back-haired young women wearing short skirts and tiny tops. They were flying to Malaga. The family behind them were jetting off to Barcelona. I sneakily looked at a few more boarding cards: none said Oslo Rygge.

A few families were glancing at their suitcases, some with real fear. They knew that if their bags were even just one kilogram overweight, then Ryanair's extra baggage policy would be enforced, policed harshly by the ever-vigilant Ryanair staff. This was the real reason I'd sought out the Ryanair desks; I was hoping to see a check-in meltdown or, better still, a Jeremy Kyle-type fracas.

I moved closer to the front, staying on the outside edge of the tape-barrier. A family of four were at the head of one line: dad, mum and teenage girls. The girls sported long false eyelashes and dramatic fake tans. Dad's suitcase had just gone on the weighing scale and he was staring at the electronic display awaiting its judgment. A second later, he spun around to face his family. "Get in!" he yelped in a Scouse accent, raising a fist to the air. "Dead on twenty! Get in there!" His wife's went on next and she was exactly on twenty too. The two girls were just as precise.

They were lucky. A tattooed young man at the next counter plonked his suitcase on the scales and groaned when it was over the limit. His pal thought it hilarious, cackling like a slack-jawed simpleton. A few passengers watched as he removed his case, laid it on the floor and unzipped it. After some rummaging, he removed a pair of jeans and rolled them up, stuffing them into his bag of duty free. Next, he pulled out a few pairs of socks and squeezed them into his jeans pockets, and then handed his pal some to do the same thing. Finally, he hoisted his bag back on the belt but the girl in charge shook her head. He lifted it back off and started going through the same process again, this time wrapping a pair of jeans around his waist, which I thought was a clever move. He handed his pal a heavy-duty T-shirt to wrap around his. This done, the suitcase was hoisted back on the scales and finally passed muster. The boys walked off towards security, jubilant at their resourcefulness. In their place, an old couple dragged their luggage forward.

As for me, I'd had enough of the baggage desks for one day and decided to brave the next segment of airport hell: security.

3

Many people who have flown from Manchester Airport will probably agree it is one of the worst airports in the world. Sure, it looks nice, and is perfectly clean with plenty of duty free shops, cafes and bars, but as an organization concerned with the rapid and efficient transit of passengers it ought to be ashamed of itself.

First, there was the farcical walk up and down the crazy zigzag barriers, passing the same faces with every turn in the queue. In the distance was the Corner of Mystery. From afar, it offered hope, perhaps even salvation from the misery of the logjam, but it was an illusion. Instead of deliverance, it was a portal to Hades. Around the corner, I faced the queue to end all queues. It was Dante's version of Hell: a humungous room of people in a never-ending parade of queuing, unzipping luggage and removing belts while uniformed minions tormented them.

From somewhere a Mancunian accent was asking whether anyone was departing before 12.50pm. I looked at my watch; it was ten past twelve. The voice belonged to a portly middle-aged man carrying a walkie-talkie. A young couple in front of me told him their flight was due to depart at 12.45. The man nodded, checked their boarding passes and then directed them towards the fast-track lane. Normally, to get into the fast-track lane, a passenger had to pay a £10 fee, but this couple had hit the jackpot for free.

I moved forward. There had to be over two hundred people in the queue, but at least the end was in sight: the security belts. That's when I noticed the barriers in front of me. They were splitting my single queue into three separate ones. A few minutes later, I had to make a decision: left, right or middle. I opted for the middle, and immediately regretted my choice when both lines either side moved forward with a surge. I gritted my teeth and seethed.

Twenty minutes later, I was still seething, even though I was getting closer to the security belts. A large, thirty-something woman was at the front of my line, her suitcase open on the table. The man in uniform was finding all sorts of things: a litre bottle of water, a collection of liquids (none of which were in the required plastic bag) and, worst of all, a pair of hair straighteners. Didn't she know that hair straighteners (and hairdryers longer than twenty centimetres) were a serious aviation hazard unless they were in a tray of their own? Someone could wallop the captain with one and blow-dry the co-pilot with the other.

The security official held the woman's straighteners up and shook his head. He gestured to a large sign on the wall. It showed a picture of some hair straighteners sitting inside a separate security tray. The woman read it and apologised. Finally, she got through, and my queue shorted to one hundred and forty-eight people.

I removed my watch and emptied my pockets of anything that might set off the scanner. Most people weren't bothering and this made me simmer. They waited until they were at the desk and then removed things, thereby delaying everyone behind them.

I felt like screaming in rage, and I hadn't even set foot on an aeroplane yet. How was I going to survive the next couple of weeks, doing this every single day? I would probably kill someone, starting with the buffoon at the front of the line right now. He was a middle-aged man clutching his boarding pass as if it was his most prized possession.

"Any metallic objects in your pocket, sir?" asked the man in charge of the scanner.

"Eh?"

"Any coins? Mobile phone? Car keys?"

The man padded his pockets, and then produced a wallet. He checked again and came up with a few coins.

"Belt?" asked the security official. He was probably used to such behaviour every day, but I was not. I felt like rushing to the man and shaking him until every metal object fell to the floor; his tattooed neck put me off, though.

The man removed his belt, but we were not finished with his tomfoolery. Despite watching everyone else go through the same process before him, the man had a large canister of Lynx deodorant in his hand luggage, a prohibited item if ever there was one. The man in uniform removed it from the bag and discarded it in a large bin filled with similar items. The idiot moved through and his wife went next. I shuffled miserably forward.

4

I escaped security twenty minutes before boarding.

My hand luggage was doing my head in. It had cost ten pounds from eBay, which, at the time, I had thought a bargain due to its wheels and retractable handle. But what the bag's manufacturer had failed to disclose was that it could not stand up of its own accord. Whenever I let go of the handle, it flopped to the floor like a bag of bricks. When it did it for the fourth time, I felt like stamping it to death. I was on the journey from hell with the most annoying piece of luggage as company. I picked it up and wandered towards the gate, stopping to grab a ham and cheese sandwich on the way. When the pimpled boy behind the counter told me the price, I almost threw it back.

"£4.99?" I scoffed. "Has it got caviar in it?"

"I know, mate," the teenager replied. "It's a rip off. But what can you do?"

I fished for my wallet as my bag dropped to the floor. I gave it a kick while it was down and, after grabbing my sandwich, dragged it towards the gate, which was in the midst of a Nordic punk invasion. About twenty-five Norwegian punks, male and female, were already waiting for the Ryanair flight to Oslo-Rygge. Instead of standing in the considerable queue (a legacy from the old world of Ryanair, before allocated seating became the norm), they were sitting down, chatting as they smoothed the spikes on their colourful heads. I sat down near them with my sandwich, carefully balancing the luggage on the next seat.

One woman a few seats along had a shock of luminous blue hair. Locks of azure spilled over her pink tie-dyed leopard-print T-shirt. The man next to her preferred darker hues, wearing a black T-shirt emblazoned with a skull and crossbones. Above it was the name of a band: UK Subs, one of the pioneers of the early UK punk movement.

Two younger men sitting across from me sported massive spiked Mohicans, their hair defying gravity, exploding vertically from their scalps. One of them caught me looking. I smiled and he smiled back.

"I take it you've been to see a punk band?" I asked.

"Yah. Rebellion Festival in Blackpool. It was amazing. Some of my favourite bands: No FX, Stiff Little Fingers and Police Bastard."

"Police Bastard? I've never heard of them?"

"No? Well they are a famous English hard-core punk band."

I didn't know what to say to that and so asked him what he thought of Blackpool.

"Blackpool is not such a nice place."

I nodded, concurring with his assessment. The seaside town had lost its lustre many decades previously; nowadays it was the domain of low-budget stag and hen party weekends. But I was surprised to find out that the Lancashire seaside town was also a hotbed of studs and spikes.

As I finished my sandwich, the punks decided to join the queue, leaving me one of the few remaining passengers sitting. I waited until the line died down to manageable levels and then sauntered to the gate, daring the Ryanair check-in staff to query my bag's dimensions. I had measured it diligently at least ten times before my journey. They looked at it but didn't say anything. A minute later, I said farewell to England for the next fifteen days, and walked out to the aircraft. As I traipsed across the tarmac, I thought back to how my plan to conquer Europe by low-cost airlines had begun.

I blame Skyscanner.

Ever since I had downloaded the app onto my iPad, I couldn't help but mess around with its flight planning software. The best thing was the app's ability to find the cheapest one-way flight to anywhere in the world. All I had to do was type in a departure airport and date, set the destination to 'everywhere' and then press search. It really was that simple.

For example, Skyscanner told me I could take off from Rome and fly to Geneva for £36, and that included taxes and airport fees. Even cheaper was a flight to Brussels for only £30. But then a cheaper flight appeared. For ten pounds, I could fly to a place I'd never heard of: Memmingen in Germany. It left at 6.40am, which was a little early for my liking, but for a tenner, I'd certainly be prepared to give it a go. And which airline was responsible for these flights? Ryanair, of course.

For amusement, I had typed Manchester Airport in as the departure airport. Ten seconds later, the results were in. The top five cheapest flights were under £30, all with Ryanair. Taking the number one spot was a flight to Oslo, coming in at £24, the same price as a curry from our local takeaway. I typed Oslo into Skyscanner and repeated the search, this time a day later. The app came up with a flight to Warsaw for £7. It was ridiculously cheap. Seven quid was less than a couple of drinks at the pub. How on earth, I wondered, could an airline make any money with prices like that? Maybe it was an error, so I skipped to the Ryanair website to check the price there. But no, there it was: Oslo to Warsaw for £7. I almost booked it there and then.

Now of course, these flights were basic, bare bones travel tickets. But for seven pounds, I should not expect any frills and nor would I receive any. Indeed, if I wanted to take a suitcase, then I'd have to pay a premium and if I wanted to choose my seat, I would need to pay a further supplement. Should I decide to eat a hearty meal on board, I'd need to take a credit card. But if all I wanted was a seat on an aeroplane, then it was ridiculously cheap.

I typed Warsaw into Skyscanner, a spark of an idea forming in my brain. The app did its magic and displayed a flight to Stockholm for £14, again with Ryanair. But then I noticed something: the airport was not Stockholm Arlanda, the city's main airport. Instead, it was Stockholm Skavsta, a much smaller airport a hundred kilometres south of the Swedish capital. It was the same story with the airports in Warsaw and Oslo. Instead of Oslo Gardermoen, Ryanair's cheap flight was to Oslo Rygge. But who cared? My brain clicked into overdrive as I formulated a sketchy plan.

6

The idea was potentially an exciting one. I'd start at Manchester Airport and fly to the cheapest destination, which was looking like Norway, then, the next day, fly to the cheapest place again, and so on and so on. I went back to Skyscanner to see where the cheapest flight from Stockholm Skavsta might take me, and that's when I discovered a problem with my plan. The cheapest flight was back to Warsaw Modlin.

I had to make some rules if the plan were to stand a chance of working, and the simplest way to achieve this was by making each new destination a different country. This would avoid the scenario of a never-ending arc between two cities. The cheapest flight to a different country was a Ryanair flight to Bremen in Germany for eighteen pounds. Then I thought of another potential pitfall. If the airport I flew into was miles away from the actual city bearing its name (as in Oslo, Stockholm and Warsaw), then doing any sightseeing might prove tricky in the short period of time I had at my disposal. One solution was to visit the town or city closest to the airport. To test whether this was viable, I typed Stockholm Skavsta into Google. It told me that the airport was near the Swedish town of Nyköping. I looked at the images that popped up. Nyköping had a rippling little river, some Scandinavian-looking buildings and a cobbled central square: Nyköping looked *nice*.

Before I planned any more of the trip, I decided to swing it past my wife. Even though she was used to me going on foreign trips by myself, I wanted to see what she thought about my latest idea. After I had outlined the plan, going over the basic principles of the journey, i.e. a trip around Europe, going to a different country every day by the cheapest flight possible, I awaited her verdict. Angela looked at me as if I was mad. Then she asked why I had to fly every day. "Why not spend a couple of days in each place?"

"Because I get to visit lots of places in the shortest time possible."

Angela considered this. "How long are you thinking of going for?"

"I'm not sure. Maybe a week..."

Angela scoffed. "A week! You'll never last a week. All those airports, check-in queues, cramped seats: you'll go mad. Have you forgotten you hate airports? Remember the luggage belt incident on the last flight? And you're thinking of doing this for seven days in a row?" She shook her head at the absurdity of the notion.

The incident to which she was referring involved a horrendously long wait at the luggage carousel in Manchester after a flight back from Moscow. One hour and twenty minutes we had waited, until an airport official had informed us that our luggage was actually on a different belt. I had composed a letter of complaint to the airport (on my phone using the airport's free Wi-Fi) even before we reached the car park.

"I won't be taking any luggage this time," I told Angela. "Ryanair charges extra for it. I'll just take hand luggage and fill my pockets with everything else."

"What about hotels?"

"What about them?"

"Well if you're booking the cheapest flights, are you also going to stay in the cheapest hotels you can find? I'd like to see you try that."

I had already considered this idea. And then scrapped it straightaway. The thought of bedding down in a fleapit and sharing a dank bathroom with a backpacker filled me with dread. I'd done all that in my twenties. No, I would not be skimping on hotels. I told Angela this.

I returned to my iPad. The idea of the trip was starting to excite me. To visit a different city each day, at the whim of whatever budget airline was cheapest, sounded special. I typed Bremen into Skyscanner. The cheapest flight to a different country was Riga, Latvia for £27. I started making notes on a scrap of paper, jotting down flight times and dates. After half an hour, I shook my head when I arrived at another dead end.

Dead ends were airports with only a return flight to the same destination or else a hellishly expensive flight that went against the whole reason for attempting the trip in the first place. I retraced my steps and chose another destination, and then after a couple of hours of furious planning, I found I had a workable itinerary. The only problem was that the initial week had morphed into sixteen days.

What the hell, I thought and, before I could stop myself, I booked the first one: Manchester to Oslo Rygge, for £24. Then I booked the next one and then the one after that. Before long, my inbox started filling with airline confirmations. Within the hour, I'd booked all sixteen flights. The total cost, including taxes, came to £437, which was less than one return flight from Manchester to Gibraltar.

Once the initial rush of adrenaline had settled, I sat back and fretted. Had I been rash booking all these flights? What if one was cancelled? What if I missed one? What if there were no hotels in Nyköping? What about my passport? Where was it? But with another *bing* in my inbox, there was nothing I could do about it now; the flights were booked and I was heading to Europe in eight weeks' time. My trip, from *here to anywhere*, promised to take me to places such as Athens, Budapest and Riga – all great destinations. But before I got to any of those, I had to get to Moss.

The Ryanair Boeing 737 was almost full, with only a couple of seats vacant. Oslo Rygge was clearly a popular Ryanair destination. I wondered how many of my fellow passengers would be going to Moss as opposed to Oslo.

My allocated seat was on the aisle at the very back of the blue and bile-coloured cabin. Having an aisle seat was handy because it meant I would be one of the first to leave when we landed. However, because I had delayed my boarding until the last minute, there was no room for my bag in the overhead bin. I had to house the thing between my knees.

A teenage girl was sitting in the middle seat next to me. She was listening to music. To her left, by the window, was a white-haired man. He was doing a crossword. Six or seven rows ahead of us were a few members of the punk contingent, easily recognisable due to their Mohicans reaching halfway to the overhead panels. I stopped gazing about and tried to find a comfortable position around my hand luggage. I twisted my torso and then angled my left foot so that it curved under the seat in front. My right foot was sticking out in the aisle – there was nowhere else for it to go. It was the only way to gain any semblance of comfort. The one consolation was that the person in front would not be reclining their seat during the flight: Ryanair's seats offered no such luxury.

The intercom crackled into life. "This is your captain speaking," said the deep Irish voice from the flight deck, "and I'd like to welcome aboard this Ryanair service to Rygge. Weather en route will be calm, but when we get to Rygge, the forecast is for a little wind. We'll let you know more before we get there. Flight time today should be about one hour and thirty minutes."

Everyone buckled up while the cabin crew disappeared. As we pushed back from the gate dead on time, I heard two male cabin crewmembers talking behind me. They were sitting in their secret little compartment at the rear. One was Irish; the other sounded Eastern European.

"Four red bulls," stated the Irish man.

I could hear a few clinking sounds. "Yes. Four."

"Twelve cappuccinos."

Again, a rummaging sound. "Yes, twelve."

Unlike most cabin crew who probably did doing nothing during taxi, these two were doing a stock take.

"Five diet cokes."

"Yes."

"Three Pringles."

There was a pause. "No, only two."

"Are you sure?"

"Yes. One, two. Look."

Both men rummaged this time, but I didn't know whether they located the errant cylinder of crisps because both of them burst forward to start the safety demonstration. Two female colleagues were doing the same thing at the front. More or less as soon as they had finished, the co-pilot came over the intercom telling them to take their seats for take-off. All four did and the men behind me continued with their stocktake until the noise from the jets buried their voices.

8

The transition from ground to air was smooth and, more or less as soon as we were airborne, the cabin crew set to work again. The two men who had been stocktaking, together with the young women up front, were toiling like demons. First, they came down the aisle with menus, which only a few people took, mainly because most passengers had brought their own food. In fact, one man sitting opposite had brought a first-class packed lunch along for the ride, complete with soup, bread and flask of coffee. The girl next to me was already eating some homemade sandwiches. Fair play to them, I thought; Ryanair's meals were almost the same price as the flight.

In the interim between giving out the menus and taking the orders, the cabin crew tried to sell some scratch cards, but no one bought any. After that, they wheeled the service trolley along. As for me, I put my earphones on, turned my music up and tried to blot everything out.

"Okay, folks," said the captain an hour later. I removed my earphones and tuned into his voice. "The update on the weather is that the landing is going to be a little bumpy. There's going to be a bit of crosswind on approach, and you might even spot the occasional flash of lightning. Nothing to worry about, of course."

Ryanair 3224 began its descent ten minutes later. As it did, we hit a thick cloud layer, which proved bumpy as hell. Soon after, a sudden lurch through a turbulent air pocket caused a few whimpers. When a jolt knocked us further downward, someone yelped. Even the cabin crew looked worried. The girl next to me was gripping her armrest and so was the old gent near the window. I glanced out and saw we were skimming the underside of the extensive layer of cloud. One second it was grey; the next it was conifers and lakes. The wings were flapping like a goose on take-off. Down we went.

Just when I thought things couldn't get any worse, the plane nosedived, causing the engines to flare as if we were going to crash. Ahead of me, I could see a red Mohican juddering back and forth as the aircraft's fuselage buffeted like a pea in a pan of boiling water. Then we straightened out and, quite suddenly, the air became smooth. Then, before I had chance to ponder this, the wheels touched down with a sudden thump. Instead of staying put, though, we bounced back up like a kangaroo. In that instant, a woman screamed. It was the loudest, most horrifically piercing scream I'd ever heard, the type of scream an actress makes when she wakes up to find a vampire hovering over her exposed neck. Then we hit the runway again and stayed on it this time. The cabin was deathly silent.

A trumpet sounded, signalling we had arrived on time. "Welcome to Rygge Airport," said a member of the cabin crew, "where the local time is five past four in the afternoon. We hope you had a pleasant flight with Ryanair today, and we look forward to you flying with us again."

9

As soon as the airport processed us, a few people trickled outside to their cars or towards whoever had come to pick them up. Most others made their way to a bus stop where a large white coach was waiting. It said Oslo on the front. The punks belonged to this group, and so did everyone else apart from me. Just as I suspected, I was the only person going to Moss.

I wandered over to a taxi driver, a black man in his late forties. I asked him whether he knew about any buses that went to Moss and he surprised me by nodding. "It leaves from over there." He pointed behind him. "But you'll be waiting a long time; it does not leave until five pm." The man's English was accented but excellent.

I looked at my watch. It was twenty past four. Could I be bothered waiting for almost three quarters of an hour, only to be dropped off at the Moss bus station – wherever that was – and then have to find the hotel? A taxi could deliver me to the hotel door in less than fifteen minutes. The driver knew what I was thinking and answered before I even asked the question. "Two hundred and fifty krone to Moss. Standard fare."

Two hundred and fifty Norwegian krone was close to £25, a hefty fare to pay for such a short journey. I mulled it over. The extra minutes would mean more time to see the industrial museum and maybe even leave some to spare to seek out mossy outcrops, but twenty-five quid was a big slice of my Norwegian budget.

I watched the big white bus pulling away to Oslo. Its departure made up my mind. I nodded and jumped into the quietest taxi in the world: its hybrid engine purred as we set off. The only sound was the swishing of the wiper blades. "Do you know anyone in Moss?" the driver asked.

"No. I'm just visiting."

"Visiting Moss…?" He looked incredulous.

I smiled. "I've been to Oslo before, but I've never been to Moss." I changed the subject. "Do you live there?"

The man nodded. "With my wife." He switched off his windscreen wipers. The final remnants of the storm were clearing up.

"It must be freezing in winter. Lots of snow, I bet?"

"Yes, of course. Winter is bad, maybe minus twenty, twenty-one, but in the north it is much worse. When I first moved to Norway, twenty years ago, the only job I could find was in a chicken factory. It was so cold that my hands used to freeze in the factory. The winters were terrible. I hated it, minus forty degrees was normal. It was so cold that, on some days, we had to stay inside our home – no work! You know, if you try pouring water when it is that cold, it freezes before it reaches the ground. I couldn't stand the chicken factory and I couldn't stand the cold, so I moved south."

"So you moved to Norway twenty years ago…?" I asked, curious. We were slowing down at a roundabout on the outskirts of Moss. The buildings by the side of the road were all wooden with sloping roofs.

"Yes, from Somalia. But I go back to Mogadishu every year with my wife to escape the winter. We see our parents and grandparents, and enjoy living in temperatures of thirty-two degrees."

"I've seen photos of Mogadishu. Tropical beaches, palm trees, beautiful mosques. But that was before the war."

"Yes. It is still dangerous now. Too risky for foreigners to visit. Too many people with weapons and bombs. And the corruption is bad, but that is because of the Italians. They corrupted all their African colonies: Somalia, Eritrea, and Libya."

We drove in silence for a minute until we rounded a corner and came upon the main street of Moss. A few shops, a pizza joint, a hairdresser and something called the Parkteatret, which turned out to be a small music theatre, lined the road. A woman carrying an umbrella was walking a dog. She didn't really need the umbrella as the rain had almost stopped.

I asked the driver a question. "Were you here when the meteorites fell?"

"Meteorites?"

"In 2006 some space rocks dropped from the sky over Moss."

"Really? I don't remember."

I didn't have time to question him further because we came to a stop outside the Moss Hotel, a three-story, lemon-coloured building with a fetching tower at one end. It looked like something from a gothic horror film. The Moss Hotel was one of a pair of similarly-priced hotels in the town (the other was the Mitt Hotel) and the reason I'd opted for Moss was its name. In England, it would be the last hotel anyone would want to stay in; it sounded dank and musty. I arranged with the taxi driver to pick me up the next day and paid him his fare. I grabbed my luggage and headed to the hotel.

10

As I entered the lobby of the Moss Hotel, the late Cilla Black's hit song, *Surprise, Surprise,* was playing through the in-house speakers. It was an apt tune because the kindly woman behind the counter asked whether I wanted to pay by card or cash.

"I thought I'd already paid," I said.

The woman checked her computer. "No, it says here your credit card only guaranteed the room. You still need to pay. This happens a lot."

I fished out my reservation and, sure enough, the woman was right: it was pay on arrival. Buggeration, I lamented. Thank Christ I was in Norway for one day. Any more than that, and I'd be bankrupt. As it stood, her machine walloped my credit card for 1190 kroner, almost £120, for what would end up as the most expensive hotel of the trip. As I listened to Cilla singing, I hated the song with a sudden vengeance.

The Moss Hotel was quite nice, though, and contained no clumps of moss as far as I could tell. It was a bit old-fashioned, but then again, it was two hundred years old. After depositing my things in the room, I went for a wander outside. The hotel stood in the centre of Moss, opposite a red-brick church with a single copper-green spire. I walked over to it, and stood by a fountain in its courtyard, which was noisily gushing water from its innards. I surveyed Moss from my central position, and decided the town appeared leafy but largely unremarkable. It looked safe enough, though, and so I left the church grounds and headed along a parade of high street stores, which had already closed for the day. The only place open was a small café popular with the local Moss teenagers. They paid me no heed as I passed, more interested in their sneaky cigarettes than a visitor from across the water. Further on, I stopped to study my map in order to locate the number one tourist attraction in Moss, namely the Industrial Museum.

The museum was in the northern part of town, a five-minute walk away. When I arrived, I found its doors closed for the day. It wasn't surprising, given the time, but still annoying. With my flight leaving for Poland the next day, there would be no time to visit it now. The paper-making equipment and glassware would have to remain an enigma. With a brooding sky that threatened more rain, I decided to walk to the harbour instead.

11

I turned left, passing something called the Bingo Hall, its sign being one of the few written in English. Instead of the blue-rinse brigade, a twenty-something man entered, making me wonder whether *bingo* meant something else in Norwegian. I walked past a large advertisement for an upcoming music festival called the Moss Folkfest. Instead of Hillbillies, they had *Hellbillies*, who were just one of the acts performing. They were in good company, because 70s chart wonders, Boney M, a folk band if ever there was one, were also playing.

I found the harbour area (which was mainly a mooring place for pleasure boats) at the bottom of a slight hill. It had taken some finding due to its location behind a set of apartment buildings. The apartments were modern and tastefully designed, with Scandinavian glass panelling and pine-covered balconies. An elderly woman, almost on the top floor, was standing on one, staring out across the bay. The sea she was gazing at was dark and cold, brooding under a gunmetal sky. Across the other side of the inlet was a series of quaint wooden houses, most painted white, with red and black roofs. Behind them, conifer-covered hills rose towards the clouds.

I walked to the edge of the water to watch some seagulls resting on one of the pleasure boats tied along the side. One gull saw me and started squawking and flapping its wings in consternation. That's when I noticed two men with their backs to me, standing at the end of a long wooden pier. They were both fishing, their lines submerged in the swirl beneath them. They must have heard the gull, because they turned and studied me for a moment. After deciding I wasn't a boat thief, they swivelled back to the grey sea.

I ambled along the marina front, passing close to the only large ship in the harbour. It was a huge red tanker with FEED STAVANGER written on its side. I took a photo and then found myself walking back into town, heading towards a white building that looked like a silo. An articulated truck was leaving its premises; when it had gone, I stopped to take a photo of the factory. A pair of dog walkers noticed me and looked to see where my camera was pointing. I could tell they were nonplussed because, after all, I had just taken a photo of a large industrial building. I lowered my camera and shook my head. Was Moss so devoid of sights that I was now taking photos of factories? I put my camera away and headed back up the hill so I could find a supermarket to buy some food. With the price of my room still a sore point, I did not want to blow the rest of my budget on a meal in a Norwegian restaurant.

12

I placed two half-stale bread rolls, a thin packet of pork, a bottle of Diet Coke, a sachet of sliced cheese, a banana and a bottle of beer on the checkout belt and waited. When the teenager pointed at the price on her electronic till, I checked to see whether I'd mistakenly picked up some gold bullion. But no, my basic groceries were costing me 350 kroner, about £35. That was the weekly shopping bill for some families in the UK, and I wondered how anyone could live in Norway with these prices. I would be destitute within a month. I packed them in a bag and walked back to the hotel.

"Finished sightseeing?" asked the lady who had checked me into the Moss Hotel a couple of hours previously.

"I think so. Nothing much is open. Besides," I gestured outside, "it looks like it's about to rain."

The woman peered out of the window. "Did you manage to see the Norwegian Lady?"

I raised my eyebrows. "I'm not sure…"

"I think you did not. You would know if you had seen the Norwegian Lady. The statue is near the ferry terminal, a ten-minute walk from here. You should go."

"I might do after I've eaten something." Suddenly, a thought struck me. "Do you remember any meteorites falling over Moss a few years ago?"

She thought for a moment. "You know, now you mention it, I do seem to remember something. I think a few fell on the outskirts of town, or maybe in the woods. I can't really remember. It was a long time ago."

"Do you know what happened to them? Did they end up in a museum or something?"

"I don't know what happened to them. Maybe they were sent for testing. Is that why you are in Moss – to look for meteorites?"

I shook my head. "I was just wondering about them, that's all."

The woman nodded and returned to her computer and so I headed to my room to eat my supermarket banquet. Thirty minutes later, I was outside, on my way to see the Norwegian Lady.

13

The Norwegian Lady was in the opposite direction to where I'd been before, in an area of Moss close to the North Sea. On the way, a line of trucks passed me, heading towards a large ferry at the end of a large pier. With spots of drizzle falling, I crossed a small bridge towards the statue. It was at the end of a wooded canal path.

I am the Norwegian Lady, and I stand here to wish all men of the sea, safe return home, the placard on her statue read. Over five decades old, the nine-foot tall bronze statue showed a young woman gazing out into the expanse of open water before her. She was tall and proud and, thousands of miles away, across the Atlantic Ocean, an identical statue was staring back from a windswept beach in Virginia, USA. Both ladies commemorated a dreadful shipwreck from 1891.

In that year, on Good Friday no less, a ship sailing from Florida to Moss encountered a terrible storm, a storm so bad that the stricken ship had to abandon its journey and head towards the American coast. It almost made it, but, when it was three hundred metres from landfall, a second storm struck. This new force of water and wind was too much for the ailing ship. First, the rigging collapsed, damaged beyond repair, and then the mast broke off and tumbled into the lifeboats. With the only way of saving themselves now out of action, eight of the seventeen people on board, all of them Norwegians, drowned.

A few days later, the ship's wooden figurehead washed ashore. The owner of a local hotel dragged it to safety and then stood it up.

The Norwegian Lady, as the townsfolk later dubbed her, stood for the next sixty-two years, staring out across the Atlantic, until a hurricane badly damaged it in 1953. A decade later, bronze statues replaced the wooden one, this time on both sides of the Atlantic. The statue I was staring at was one of these.

I took a photo and then spied two Norwegian women stripping down to their swimming costumes. Neither seemed to mind that it was cold and drizzly. I watched as they neatly folded their clothes into a pile and walked to the end of a long pier. One of them climbed down some steps and then jumped into the North Sea with a splash. Her friend soon followed, and I could see their heads bobbing in the cold grey water. I fleetingly wondered if they were mad. Was there so little to do in Moss that people turned to swimming in the sea? Feeling a little bit like a voyeur, I turned tail, passing the statue as I made my way back to the hotel.

An hour later, I was consuming the remainder of my pork, cheese and bread when the heavens finally opened. A sheet of rain lashed against the windowpane as the wind howled along the street. Later, as I climbed into bed, I could hear the tempest still raging, a tumultuous cacophony of rattling rafters and incessant window beating. But I had survived my first day in Europe and, despite the apparent lack of things to do in Moss, had rather enjoyed myself. Even the storm could not subdue my sense of adventure. I wondered what Poland would have to offer.

Top row: A large silo in Moss; Moss harbour
Middle row: The Norwegian Lady; Moss Church; A boat in Moss
Bottom row: Some of the punks on the flight; Moss town centre

Day 2. Nowy Dwor Mazowiecki, Poland

Oslo Rygge – Warsaw Modlin: Ryanair £7

The taxi driver was waiting outside the Moss Hotel at the agreed time. Due to the lingering drizzle, I made a run for it and threw my luggage in the back. Then I jumped into the front passenger seat. "Do you know something?" I said as we set off. "This taxi fare is triple the cost of my flight."

The taxi driver guffawed. "Norway is *expensive*. In Mogadishu, this journey would cost five dollars. For the crazy money you are paying, you could travel across the whole of Somalia. But you might get shot; that is the payoff."

"How much would a taxi to Oslo cost?"

"It is a fixed price of 1150 krone, which is about £110. There is a British man who flies here every two weeks, and I drive him to Oslo. He never takes the bus or hires a car; he only travels with me. I charge 2300 krone for the round trip! He tells me his business pays for it so he does not care."

"Wow."

"So tell me, my friend, what did you think of Moss?"

I looked outside at the Norwegian countryside we were passing; mainly farmers' fields. "It was okay. But there's not much to do. Even the industrial museum was closed."

The driver nodded sagely. "That's why people go to Oslo."

We arrived at Rygge Airport ten minutes later and I prepared myself for the second Ryanair flight in less than twenty-four hours. I said goodbye to the taxi driver and entered the small terminal. I was through to departures in no time at all.

The gate area was full, with only a few seats to spare, so I loitered near a window. Outside, the weather was brooding and grey. A mass of thick cloud hung over the airport, occasionally releasing torrents of rain that hammered against the roof. Every now and again, almighty booms, followed by bright flashes, caused the rain to stop briefly, as if the droplets were fearful they might anger their more sinister siblings. But then, after a few seconds of relative serenity, the deluge resumed with even more force.

I looked at the long queue for the Warsaw Modlin flight. It was absurd; the incoming aircraft had not even landed. In fact, I wondered whether it would even arrive with the weather as it was. Fifteen minutes later, a tinny announcement came over the system saying the Warsaw flight was about to board. Board what, I hazarded? A bus? But with the announcement, a rush of new people surged to join the line.

Flash! Boom! The proximity of the thunder made it sound as if the storm was directly overhead the airport. More rain lashed down, battering the roof like never before. And then, like a phoenix descending, a Ryanair flight emerged from the cloud and landed. A colossal arc of surface water sprayed in its wake.

I looked at my watch. The time was 11.13 am. My flight to Warsaw Modlin was due to depart at 11.45, which left thirty-two minutes. As soon as the Boeing 737 stopped at the gate, the ground-based machinery sprang into rapid action.

Within thirty seconds, a Shell fuelling truck arrived, as did an empty luggage train. Less than a minute later, the mobile steps arrived and were anchored into position at both the front and rear doors. At 11.19, the aircraft's doors opened and, thirty seconds after that, the first passengers started making their way down the steps. The aircraft had only been on the stand for six minutes.

I was watching a masterclass of organisation, where every cog in the Ryanair machine was working without fault. At 11.25, just eight minutes after pulling in at the gate, all the arriving passengers were gone, and most of the departing ones were waiting to board. At 11.27, one of the pilots began to walk around the aircraft, checking the wings, engines and wheels. Two minutes later, the first new passengers began climbing the steps just as the ground crew offloaded the incoming baggage. By 11.30, the plane had been fuelled and filled with a new set of luggage. I shook my head and joined the back of the, by now, short line. Soon after, I was strapped into my seat waiting for my flight to Poland. When we left the stand, I checked my watch. It was 11.44, one minute ahead of the posted departure time. Utter magnificence.

2

Take-off was smooth, despite the storm. I was sitting in the aisle again, next to another teenage girl. She was playing a game on her phone. Once more, the cabin crew were working full pelt, giving out menus, trying to flog scratch cards and duty free, serving food and drinks here and there: busy, busy, busy, with no let up for a second.

To pass the time, I flicked through the *Let's Go with Ryanair* magazine that one member of the cabin crew had given me when I'd boarded. There was a letter supposedly written by Mick O'Leary, the colourful boss of Ryanair, thanking me for flying his airline and telling me how great his planes were. The next page offered a whole load of statistics about the airline: mainly how punctual Ryanair was. The previous month, 87% of its flights left on time, which compared favourably to British Airways' 83% on-time record.

A few pages later, there was a photo of a bikini-clad blonde girl pouting on a beach in Crete. She was a 29-year-old Spaniard posing for the latest Ryanair Cabin Crew Charity Calendar. When asked what she liked best about working for Ryanair, she said: 'Dealing with people every day'. I wondered whether that was the truth.

One hour and thirty minutes after taking off from Norway, a trumpet flurry sounded from the speakers as we touched down in Warsaw Modlin. The jaunty little tune managed to annoy me after just two seconds. Thankfully, someone switched it off as we trundled towards the terminal. Outside, the weather was sunny, with an almost cloudless sky. Poland looked inviting, especially since the flight had only cost seven pounds: the cheapest of any on my jaunt across Europe.

Since we were the only aircraft at the airport, the staff processed us without delay, and less than fifteen minutes after landing, I was out the other side with a small wad of Polish zlotys in my wallet. The vast majority of my fellow passengers boarded the bus bound for Warsaw, forty kilometres to the south. Not me, though; I was sitting inside a hotel shuttle bus bound for Nowy Dwor Mazowiecki, the nearest town to the airport. I was the only passenger, and the driver looked like he doubled up as the hotel handyman; he had a screwdriver next to the gear stick and paint covered his jeans.

He didn't seem to want to talk, and so I stared outside instead. Past the airport perimeter was a cemetery lined with simple wooden crosses, then a series of rundown, redbrick apartment blocks that reminded me of a rough council estate in England. As we headed further into town, we passed a large supermarket covered in steel shutters, giving it the look of a Cold War prison. At the entrance, two men sat on a wall with cans of beer. An old woman with purple hair emerged from the shop carrying a bag of carrots.

Where the hell was I? Novi Dwor Mazowiecki looked like a sump estate. It was two thirty in the afternoon, mid-week, and all I could see were women pushing prams, men doing nothing in particular (except drinking cheap lager) and children playing on randomly located seesaws. At the end of a depressing road that looked like it belonged in a Stalinist version of the 1950s, we came to another redbrick building with large arched windows. We stopped in front of it. Finally the driver spoke. "Royal Hotel. Get out now."

3

The Royal Hotel was great, despite the boorishness of the driver. It even had a couple of miniature horses wandering around an enclosure near an outdoor bar. The room was just what I needed, too, even if the hotel safe was at floor height, meaning I had to crouch down to set the code. I put my passport, laptop and remaining Norwegian money in it, pressed the code and locked it all up. Then I gazed out of the window and saw the shuttle-bus driver cutting the grass with a mower. It was time to see the sights of the town.

Beyond the hotel grounds, I passed the same ugly apartment blocks I'd seen on the way in. Two young women were sitting on the doorstep of one, smoking cigarettes. From somewhere came the sound of two dogs in battle. Ahead of me was the Cold War supermarket. I decided to scope it out from the empty bus stop across the road.

The supermarket was a large, flat topped, two storey building clad in corrugated steel. Its exterior bore no advertisements: just the word MARKET in large red letters. The only way in and out was from two doors that formed the entrance, and yet, despite its unappealing look, it had a steady flow of customers. The two beer drinkers I'd seen on the way in were still sitting on the wall. Both were studying the entrance, their shaven heads making them look like prime degenerates. As if on cue, one of them took a gulp of his cheap Polish lager. An old man walked past them and went inside. A minute later, a woman came out, lighting a cigarette as she did so. The two men stood up and left with her. I decided to move on.

The road took me past more redbrick buildings. They reminded me of army barracks. A few more citizens of Nowy Dwor Mazowiecki appeared on the side lines: a granny with a stooped back; a barrel chested man in a football shirt; a young woman pushing a pram. No one glared at me, or even glanced in my direction and, so I concluded that, despite its rough and ready appearance, Novi Dwor Mazowiecki was perfectly safe. Or maybe they thought I was one of them. When I passed a white statue of the Virgin Mary surrounded by flowers, I was cheered slightly. A woman and a little girl were standing by it, the woman watching while the girl laid a bloom. I carried on walking.

To my right was a small overgrown park. Thick trees blocked most of the view so I continued along the road, following a gentle curve that seemed to be traversing the edge of the town. The traffic was light, made up of only a few cars and, more commonly, bicycles. Evidently, Novi Dwor Mazowiecki's flat terrain lent itself to pedal power. Finally, the trees cleared to reveal what looked like a war memorial. Two stone soldiers stood on small plinths, each flanked by a cannon. Next to them was a tall stone column engraved with the words: Heroic defenders of Modlin Fortress who died for the Fatherlands 1939.

In September of that year, Germany had invaded Poland. The country soon capitulated except for its last defensive outpost: Modlin Fortress. In the resulting eighteen-day siege, the Germans threw in everything they had and killed two thousand people. Once they had ejected the Poles, the Germans used the fortress buildings as barracks, a hospital and a training centre. The Royal Hotel had once been an industrial-sized military laundrette. One nasty little section became a small concentration camp. In it, they shackled, tortured and ultimately murdered 20,000 people. To service the complex, the Germans built an airstrip, which eventually morphed into Warsaw Modlin Airport, the place I'd arrived into.

Back on the main road, I spied a sign saying Museum. With sightseeing opportunities so scant in Nowy Dwor Mazowiecki, I headed towards the small rectangular building. A bald old man with a white handlebar moustache was standing outside watching me. Not knowing whether he was in charge or a loitering local, I stopped and said hello. He studied me but said nothing. I shrugged and entered the building from a side door. As I stepped inside, I turned and saw the old man staring after me. He was like a character from *Scooby Doo*.

Inside the building was a small café devoid of customers. A bull of a man in his thirties sat behind the counter. He seemed unaware of my presence, looking down at something, presumably a book or his phone.

"Hello," I said to attract his attention,

The man spun around surprised. "Eh?"

"Hello, is this a museum?"

He looked me up and down and then nodded. Maybe this was the old timer's son, I thought. The man emerged from behind the counter. "Come," he said, his voice booming and deep. He walked towards a door on the other side of the cafe and opened it. I followed close behind. After shouting something in Polish, a young man appeared. He looked like a student. The cafe henchman returned to his station behind the counter.

"Hello," said the newcomer, shaking my hand. "My Engleesh is ... not so good. I very sorry. But I am museum ... man."

I followed him through the door into a thin corridor of exhibits, which in turn led off into a series of smaller rooms. We stopped by a display of old Polish army uniforms. "Are these from the war?" I asked. The signs were in Polish.

The man smiled and shrugged. "I sorry. I not understand. Engleesh not good..."

After a few seconds of awkward silence, I made a move towards another exhibit, this one showing a machine gun. The man followed me but then decided to sit down on a stool further along. He looked at me apologetically.

I stopped in front of a female dummy dressed in combat fatigues. Her pose looked wrong because she looked too flirty to be a soldier. She should've been wearing a crop top and hot pants. Her bright red lipstick and eye make-up were also at odds with the uniform, and then I realised why. She actually was a shop mannequin, as were the other figures in the museum. The museum had bought a job lot of cheap mannequins and had simply kitted them out in troop costumes. With a final spin around the remaining exhibits, I thanked the young man and exited through the deserted cafe.

Outside, the strange old man was still there. He had produced a pushbike from somewhere and looked like he was mending the chain. When he sensed my presence, he stopped and studied me with open suspicion. I stopped a metre away and smiled. "Do you know where Modlin Fortress is?"

The man's eyes furrowed. He shook his head and returned to his bike.

4

I was eager to see the remaining sections of Modlin Fortress but I couldn't find a single sign pointing to where they might be. Instead, I carried on through the town until I came to some large but low-level structures that resembled battery hen sheds. There were rows of them, all on my left-hand side, some partially hidden by copses of trees, but most sitting along an overgrown pathway. If they contained chickens, I did not know – I definitely couldn't hear any – but the lack of people, together with a few broken windows, suggested the sheds were now derelict. I walked towards one, but found all access points blocked with barbed wire. Then I came to a yellow sign. TEREN WOJSKOWY, it read, which I later found out meant MILITARY AREA.

I heard voices. I looked up to see a couple of civilian men on the roof of a nearby shed. Both were unaware of me, busy with blowtorches and heavy tools. Whether they were repairing the roof or trying to break in, I couldn't be sure, but I decided to leave them to it. I found the main road and walked until I ended up at the end of the town. There was only countryside ahead of me and so I retraced my steps until I spied a track through a forest. I felt sure that the fortress had to be in that direction.

At first, it was like walking along a nature trail. Butterflies fluttered around the foliage on both sides of the path, birds chirped in the trees and agile red dragonflies hovered like miniature helicopters over flowers. Then I heard a rustling sound and stopped dead in my tracks. When I didn't hear it again, I concluded it must have been a bird, or perhaps a mouse, so carried on until the sound of the traffic behind me ebbed to nothing. I found myself in deeper forest. Now the trees were reaching into the trail, casting brooding shadows at my feet. I traversed a sharp bend and came to an overgrown section of track that ended at a huge redbrick building.

It was obviously part of the fortress, but, like the chicken sheds, it looked abandoned and broken. Cracked windows, crumbling brickwork and creepers gave the whole place a sorry and neglected feel. A red squirrel darted out from somewhere, ran across my path and then disappeared into the trees. A fly buzzed at my head as I walked towards a sign. The words were in Polish – probably warnings. I turned around, and followed the trail back through an even darker area of forest.

Some new rustling seemed more sinister, some hoots ominous. Then I had an alarming thought: Poland had wolves, didn't it? And bears? My God! I was alone in a forest surrounded by things that wanted to eat me. I stopped to listen, but the forest sounded perfectly normal. I listened some more and heard only a bird singing. I swallowed hard and then resumed walking, this time at a quicker pace, aware that my crunching footsteps would be a beacon to any hungry beast lurking nearby. Then I forced myself to calm down and that's when I realised I could hear a car engine. Below me, on the other side of a thick line of trees, was a road, and beyond that, a river. I found a clearing, which led to a series of broken metal steps. I escaped the forest.

5

My face was itchy. I absently scratched it and found a large spot just in front of my ear. Another one (even more ridiculously tickly than the first) was on the back of my neck. And then I found a third on my actual ear. So I had been attacked in the forest after all: by mosquitoes. I tried to leave the spots alone, but the itching was maddening. I decided to get closer to the river to take my mind off them.

A man had his penis out. A middle-aged gent wearing thick green wellies was urinating into some bushes about five metres away. He obviously thought he was alone. When he saw me, he looked shocked, but he was powerless to do anything apart from hold on to his Polish sausage. I was about to smile at him but realised how odd this would seem, so turned to look at a few ducks paddling around in the water. Rivers always looked peaceful, especially on warm summer days, even with a massive bridge to my left, thundering and shaking with a steady stream of traffic, and a man watering the vegetation to my right. I glanced back towards the man, who was now heading further along the riverbank. He sat down and dipped his rod into the water.

I was thinking of sitting down myself, but, if I did, I felt I might doze off. If that happened, then my quest to see as much of the town as possible would fail miserably. And I had not seen anything of note so far. Hoping there was more to Nowy Dwor Mazowiecki than a tiny museum, I said goodbye to the ducks, clambered up the embankment and decided to see what was on the other side of the bridge.

The bridge doubled up as a railway crossing. Its tracks followed a path below the main section, running parallel to it. With cars and trucks zooming past, I marched along the roadside verge until I reached the middle. There I stopped to gaze down at the river from my lofty position, noticing a tall redbrick tower I'd not seen before. That had to be part of the fortress, I reckoned. I strained my eyes looking for any trail that might lead to it, but all I saw was thick woodland. I took a photo anyway.

A tinkling bell caused me to turn around. A cyclist was bearing down on me, a young woman carrying a shopping bag over one handlebar. I pressed my back against the crash barrier, sucked in my stomach and allowed her to whizz by. "*Dziękuje*," she said as she passed, *thank you*. She seemed perilously close to the traffic.

At the other end of the bridge was a road sign telling me that Warsaw was straight ahead and that Nowy Dwor Mazowiecki's *centrum* was to my left. When a fork in the road appeared, I took the left-hand one.

Unlike the eighteenth century redbrick buildings around my hotel, the commercial heart of Nowy Dwor Mazowiecki was stuck in a 1970s time warp. The shop fronts were faded and dated, the apartment blocks resembled Milton Keynes from forty years previously, but, on the plus side, it had a few bars, a pretty park and a well-kept church.

As I made my way along the main street, I passed some small terraced houses. Suddenly, a door opened. An old man emerged wearing black underpants and slippers. He stood in his doorway, exposing his blubber-filled belly to all and sundry while he smoked a cigarette. Further on, I noticed an ice cream parlour and decided to treat myself.

Two women in white aprons and hairnets looked at me as I approached their counter. I quickly established that neither could speak English, so to make myself understood, I pointed at the large plastic ice cream on the counter, then raised one finger. This brought about some whispered discussion. Finally one of the women, the younger of the two, spoke. What she said sounded like this: *so smack chess*. It probably wasn't, but with no understanding of Polish, I raised one finger again, smiled disarmingly and pointed at the plastic ice cream again. The women conferred once more, and then burst out laughing. The older one was laughing so much she had to go into a side room, where I could hear her cackling. Her younger colleague regarded me, trying her hardest not to laugh. I felt highly embarrassed but could not fathom what they were finding so amusing.

The first woman reappeared with a miniature ice cream. She wasn't openly laughing anymore but still looked highly tickled. It appeared she had snapped off the bottom section of a regular cone and then dolloped a bit of white and pink ice cream on top. Instead of handing it over, the woman pointed to both sides, twisting the tiny cone in her fingers as she showed me the two colours.

Ah, I thought, she wants me to choose a flavour. I opted for plain vanilla and the woman nodded, returning a minute later with a full size ice cream. Transaction complete, I took my treat to the park.

A few people were sitting in the park, most of them pensioners. An elderly woman shuffled by wearing a thick coat despite the warm temperature. She exited the park near a store called Planet Alkoholi and then disappeared along a side street. I found an empty park bench to relax on for a few minutes.

The park was haunted. The ghost of Traugott Schulze, a nineteenth century pastor, wandered it at night, his ethereal form slinking around the dark flowerbeds and creeping by shadowy trees. There are three accounts of how the pastor died.

The first tells the story of Pastor Schulze giving a church service while bedlam ran amok outside. Rampaging insurgents were terrorising Nowy Dwor Mazowiecki and eventually found the church. The Pastor tried to shoo them off in the name of the Lord, but the braying mob burst in and gave Schulze a stark choice: join the uprising or else they would beat him to within an inch of his life. Being a man of the cloth, the pastor refused to fight, and so the mob dragged him outside, tied him to a post and did as they promised, giving Schulze such a beating that he remained mentally unstable for the rest of his life. Such was his state of mind that he could no longer fulfil his role as pastor and therefore died in a state of Godless limbo. He had no choice but to become a spectre of the night.

Account two had a similar theme. This time, unknown assailants kidnapped Pastor Schulze from his home, gave him the ultimatum and then, when he refused to join their riot, they tied him up and then dragged him around town for a short while. Only then did they give him a beating, which, again, left him mentally ill.

The third version is the most bizarre. In this one, the pastor was at home, possibly in bed, when he heard someone knocking on his door. Believing insurgents had come for him, Schulze fled from his window, naked. When the townsfolk heard all the commotion, and then saw a naked priest scuttling around the market place, they grabbed him, tied him to a post and gave him a good beating, resulting in, of course, mental illness.

With a final mouthful of ice-cream cone, I stood up and walked to a taxi. It was getting late and I wanted to be back at the hotel before dark.

7

The next morning, with a couple of hours to kill before my next flight, I decided to find the main section of the fortress once and for all. I asked Olga the hotel receptionist where it was.

"The fortress is … well … all around," she told me. "It is hard for me to say …"

That made sense, I thought. I'd assumed the main fortress to be a clump of buildings close together, but maybe the whole area around the hotel was the fortress. Nevertheless, I showed Olga a photo of the tower I'd taken from the bridge the previous day.

"Ah, yes. That is the Red Tower. I will show you." She produced a small map from her counter and opened it up. She drew a route for me, which would take about fifteen minutes, she reckoned. I thanked Olga and set off.

Just outside the hotel grounds, I ambled past the same rough-looking apartment blocks, hearing the same unseen dogs barking in the distance. Even though it was only nine thirty in the morning, a man was sipping from a can of lager. He was walking a dog, heading towards the Cold War supermarket. I passed the statue of Mary, noticing the flowers the little girl had placed, and then found a woodland path I'd somehow missed the day before. I crossed the road towards it, finding myself walking through thick trees and meadows. At the end of the trail was a large redbrick building. In the middle was a wide archway blocked by a metal grille. On either side of the archway were long stretches of barrack-type buildings, all of them abandoned and decaying. Both stretched into the woodland beyond.

Behind the arch was the top of the Red Tower. I walked across the gravel, unsurprised to find the grille locked and secure. With no way in, I decided to investigate the barracks instead. Almost every window was boarded up; those that weren't were smashed and dark. They were too high to see into anyway. I rounded a bend and saw the Red Tower. It was still behind the main building and I could see no way in. And that's when I heard the crunching of footsteps.

Two security guards were walking towards me at speed. One of them was shouting in Polish, gesturing that I should turn around and leave. I smiled and pointed at the tower, making it clear I wanted to climb it by doing a walking mime with my fingers.

The men looked at the tower and shook their heads. Then the first man shouted at me again and, though the language was foreign to me, the meaning was clear: get lost or face the consequences. I nodded and turned around. As I joined the woodland trial back to the town, I snatched a glance at the security men. Both were watching me. Why the heavy-handed approach? Was the fortress under renovation? Was there something more sinister going on? To be honest, I didn't care anymore, and felt annoyed by the actions of the guards, and irritated with myself for coming to Nowy Dwor Mazowiecki in the first place. There was simply nothing to do or see.

8

To finish off my sightseeing extravaganza of Nowy Dwor Mazowiecki, I decided to visit the supermarket. As I suspected, the place was bursting with booze. One section was dedicated to bottles of vodka, all at incredibly cheap prices.

Apart from two women at the checkouts, the only other people inside the large supermarket were a woman and a little girl. Both were looking at some cheese. Just then, a man walked in, jangling with an armful of beer bottles. He looked like he'd just woken up: grey stubble and sunken eyes. He noticed me looking at him so I pretended I was studying at some sausages. He took his booty to a checkout, and one of the women counted them up. In return, he received a handful of change. With this, he bought two cans of Polish lager.

I decided there and then that this was my cue to get out of the supermarket and Nowy Dwor Mazowiecki as a whole. The town seemed broken and in major decline. I guessed the reason was simple. Any young Pole who had the means to do so had already left. Maybe they worked in the capital or perhaps they had taken advantage of Ryanair's low fares and gone to a different country. The people left in town were those who couldn't leave: mothers with young children; old age pensioners, and men without job prospects. Faced with the same set of circumstances, I think I would've turned to drink, too. I returned to the hotel to pack and prepare myself for my next flight. My only hope was that Sweden would offer some respite from the gloom of Poland.

*Top row: The large supermarket near my hotel; A flirty shop
mannequin dressed as a soldier
Middle row: Memorial to Polish troops lost in the Battle of Modlin;
The Red Tower; Planet Alkoholi – a fine shop if ever there was one!
Bottom row: Nowy Dwor Mazowieki town centre and park; Housing
in town (former army barracks)*

Day 3. Nyköping, Sweden

Warsaw Modlin – Stockholm Skavsta: Ryanair £14

Back to Scandinavia.

Boarding at Warsaw-Modlin went as smoothly as ever and the only issue was the lack of room in the overhead luggage bins. With every space packed with cheap Polish duty free, my luggage went beneath my knees, jammed under the seat in front. I took pleasure in jamming it in with my foot as punishment for it falling over twice at the airport.

"Good afternoon from the flight deck," said the captain in a European accent. "Due to a missed air traffic slot, we are going to be delayed by twenty minutes." The pilot sounded pained, and well he might be. A delay of twenty minutes was going to cost him dearly. The knock-on effect would be enormous down the line somewhere. A few groans were audible around the cabin.

Five minutes later, he came back on. "Good news! Air traffic control has moved our slot forward considerably. We should be pushing back in the next few minutes." This cheered everybody up and, when the plane started moving, we cheered even more. Soon we were taking off, turning gently northwards through the calm and sunny skies above Nowy Dwor Mazowiecki.

2

As the scratch cards came past, I noticed the man across the aisle looking at some photos on his phone. Being a nosy parker, I manoeuvred myself into a position where I could look too. The photos were surprising: they were of the man baring his chest. In one photo, he was flexing his biceps, offering a huge cheesy grin for the camera. A third photo showed him arm wrestling another bare-chested man. Both of them looked oiled up.

Even though we'd been airborne less than fifteen minutes, the girl next to me decided she needed the toilet. It was always annoying when this happened, and I made a show of unbuckling my belt, and then standing up in the cramped cabin so she could squeeze past. As she did so, she looked apologetic, which made me feel like a bit of a cad. And that was when a baby started screaming two rows ahead. It pierced my eardrums and rippled my eyelids. The more its mother tried to shush it, the louder the infant got. The man across from them actually stuck his fingers in his ears. He looked ridiculous. But with the screeching enveloping my very core, I did the same thing too.

When we landed, the trumpet sounded again, and a few people clapped. It was half past three in the afternoon and, as I walked through the small terminal building, I noticed a sign telling me that Nyköping (pronounced like neo-shopping) was only seven minutes away by bus. I went outside to the local bus stop to catch it while everyone else made their way to the Stockholm bus.

I peered at the small timetable. The bus was due in half an hour, so I sat down and listened to some music. Twenty minutes later, the Stockholm bus departed, leaving me as the only passenger in the vicinity. Fifteen minutes after that, another troop of passengers exited the terminal and made a beeline for the Stockholm bus stop. Except for two people who didn't: a pair of Ryanair cabin crew who joined me at my bus stop. According to their name badges, the young blonde woman was from Lithuania and the young dark-haired man was from Spain. Because of their respective tongues, they were conversing in English, and so I listened in as they discussed alcohol. The young man was talking about his eternal quest for the perfect spirit.

"Have you tried *tuica*?" said the woman from Lithuania. "I was in Bucharest a few weeks ago, buying a gift for someone. I didn't know what to get and the duty free owner showed me a bottle of tuica. He said I could try some. It was *so* nice! He said most people add chocolate milk to it because then it tastes like a chocolate bar – only an alcoholic one."

The man smiled. "Sounds good. So were you a little tipsy for the flight?"

The girl glanced at me, checking I wasn't listening. As far as they were concerned, I was listening to music. "No…well, maybe a little. But it was so nice and I bought a bottle. I ended up drinking it all myself. At home, of course. But I'll tell you something. Tuica comes in plastic bottles. You know what that means?"

The man nodded. "They do not weigh much."

"Exactly. My luggage was not heavy."

Half past four came and there was no sign of the Nyköping bus. Five minutes later, when it still hadn't turned up, the man checked the timetable and then his watch. "Just our luck," he said to his colleague. "We land early and the bus is late."

The blonde woman removed her heels. She replaced them with some flat shoes from her luggage. And then, after an hour of waiting at the infernal bus stop – longer than the time it took to reach Stockholm – a big green local bus finally pulled up.

3

Nyköping is actually one of the oldest cities in Sweden. It has a population of around 30,000, and its main industry is manufacturing. Recently, though, its tourist board has been trying to lure visitors in with the promise of 'a river that winds through the city … where you can stroll along cultural streets and stop at historical sites.'

Outside, we were passing a few green and yellow agricultural fields with occasional conifers and red farmhouses thrown in. As the only tourist on the bus, I pondered Nyköping's efforts at attracting tourists and could only surmise it hadn't been very successful. That said, as we approached the outskirts of town, Nyköping looked well-kept and almost grand. A set of wooden buildings looked pleasingly *Scandinavian*: all sloping roofs and pastel painted exteriors. The citizens of Nyköping seemed jollier too. I spied a young couple walking hand in hand, the woman laughing at something her companion had said. Maybe the town would turn out all right.

The green bus stopped in the town centre next to a small bus station. The nearby buildings looked nondescript but unthreatening. I grabbed my bag, thanked the driver and stepped outside.

I wondered where to go. I had the address of the hotel, but no map. I had stupidly assumed there would be a line of taxis at the bus station, but there were none. While I sniffed the air for clues as to my whereabouts, the blonde Ryanair girl climbed off the bus, leaving her colleague behind. She waved at him and then made her way towards a small park behind the bus station.

I unzipped a compartment in my luggage to find the hotel's details. As I did so, my case clattered to the ground. I left it there and read the printed sheet. The Mercure Hotel Nyköping was in a part of the town called Gumsbackevägen, which I couldn't even pronounce. There was a little map on the page, but it was too small to read, apart from telling me the hotel was near something called Trafficplatz Kungsladugården, which was no use at all. Breaking one of the major rules in my travelling handbook, I turned on data roaming on my phone and opened the Google Maps app, grimacing at the potential cost. I typed in the name of the hotel and the map told me it was a 23-minute walk away. It would be after 5pm by the time I reached it. That would leave hardly any time to see what the town had to offer. Sighing, I studied the route, finding it simple to memorise. Straight across the park, turn left along a main road and then keep going until I reached the hotel. I turned off data roaming and set off.

The park consisted of a small area of grass, a few trees and a set of benches. Some teenagers were lurking around one of the benches, slyly puffing on cigarettes as they pretended to kick a ball around. The main road turned out to be a busy dual carriageway, and dragging my stupid bag along the hard shoulder made me curse Nyköping and its lack of taxis. The wheels of my Ryanair-approved luggage felt like they were going to come off at any second, which would mean hauling the damned thing by its seams. The ground beneath me wasn't helping either: it was rough gravel. And the people passing by in their cars added to the misery. All were staring, wondering why a man was walking along a highway with a small suitcase. I ignored them and stepped up the pace, eventually arriving at the Mercure Hotel dripping with sweat. Instead of taking twenty-three minutes, it had taken fifteen. I sounded my own trumpet in triumph, even though close to an hour and a half had elapsed since my flight had landed in Sweden.

4

The hotel was out of town (in one of those places that has a McDonald's, a car dealership and a petrol station), but redeemed itself massively when I discovered a free evening meal was included in the room price.

"An evening meal?" I said to the young receptionist who had just told me this news.

The woman smiled. "Yes sir. But it is only a buffet. Swedish meatballs and roast potatoes. Nothing special."

Meatballs sounded fine by me. Nyköping had just gained an extra point. In all my travels, no other hotel had ever offered a complimentary evening meal. As soon as I'd deposited my bag in the room, I was back in the elevator to take advantage of it.

"I'm sorry, sir," said the receptionist, "the buffet does not start until six." That was twenty minutes away. I decided to order a drink instead.

Sixty-five Swedish kroner later, which was about six quid, I sat down with my Swedish lager to wait things out. When the buffet kicked into life, the meatballs were tasty and the potatoes filling. Meal finished, I pondered whether I could be bothered undertaking the lengthy walk back into town. Now that I was full of meatballs and beer, I suddenly felt I needed to relax. But if I didn't get into Nyköping tonight, then I probably wouldn't have time the next day, not with a flight to Bremen in Germany to catch in the morning. That was the problem with seeing Europe on a day-to-day basis; it didn't leave much time to actually see the sights. I got up and walked outside.

Without my luggage, the walk into town was less fraught, and it gave me a chance to take in my surroundings more. Opposite the hotel was a huge cornfield, the crops almost glowing yellow in the evening sun. I walked along a footpath by the side of the main road, passing a scrap yard I had not noticed on the way in. It catered for caravans and boats: a strange combination, I thought.

When the town came into view, I was impressed. Compared to Nowy Dwor Mazowiecki, Nyköping was postcard pretty. A couple of spires jutted up above some neat townhouses. The latter belonged in a brochure called *Homely Homes for Swedes*.

Due to it being late, many shops were closed. That didn't bother me one bit, and I enjoyed having the high street more or less to myself. I arrived at the main square, which was deliciously appealing, dominated by a trio of buildings. The first was large, blocky and white. It had a blue and yellow Swedish flag rippling outside the entrance. It was the Stadshus, City Hall, the most modern of the trio. If IKEA had designed it, I would not have been surprised.

The next building, the tourist office, looked older. It featured a stately yellow and white exterior, topped with a red brick roof. It looked like someone had draped giant layers of icing over some marzipan arches. A tall steeple sat on the top. It was definitely the nicest building of the three, especially with the potted plants outside. Opposite was Saint Nicholas' Church. I was tempted to climb its spire but then spotted some sort of tower behind it, so decided to try that instead.

I followed a little pathway, climbing some steps through a line of trees. Then I noticed the devil worshippers. They were sitting on the ground in a circle with their shaven heads and cigarettes, chanting incantations to Satan. I slipped past them, unnoticed, and regarded the group from further up the hill. They were in fact just a group of teenagers, laughing and joking as they passed around a joint.

Above me was the tower. It was sitting on top of a craggy piece of rock that looked dangerous to climb. I took a photo of the wooden structure (which I later found out was the bell tower for the church lower down) and then wondered what to do next. I didn't fancy clambering over the rocks and, besides, it would probably be closed anyway. I decided to head further into town.

5

I found a quiet spot overlooking a small river. In the middle of the water was a statue of swallows in flight, water spraying from the base. I decided to ring my wife and tell her about how nice Nyköping was. It had exactly the right ingredients a foreign town should have: a series of appealing buildings, a peaceful river, a large central square that looked clean and well-kept and, best of all, a feeling of complete safety. The only thing going against it was the Scandinavian prices. Everything was double the cost of Poland.

Angela sounded impressed when I told her all this. "So it's a better place than where you were yesterday?"

"Much better. It's in a different league; there's no comparison. You'd love it here, that's all I can say. And right now, I'm staring at some ducklings paddling about in a river. In Poland, the only things to stare at were empty beer cans and red bricks."

Angela asked me how I was doing for clean clothes.

"I'm not desperate yet, but I'm thinking of washing some socks in the sink when I get back tonight. Then I'll use the hairdryer on them. Maybe the same with a T-shirt."

Angela laughed. "A hairdryer will never dry a T-shirt. You need to hang it up somewhere."

Ten minutes later, I was on my way to a castle. Nyköping Castle was just along the river on a small grassy hill. It wasn't very big, and it didn't really seem like a castle in the traditional sense. Instead of battlements and fortifications, it looked like a white farmhouse sitting above a large dry stone wall. In fact, had there not been a sign telling me it was a castle, I would have walked past it without a second glance.

Nevertheless, I found its entrance, but, as I expected, the castle was closed for the day. If it was open, I would have gone in to see its exhibits. Some in particular were of interest to me – those detailing the castle's most famous event: the Nyköping Banquet.

6

On a cold December evening in 1317, foul deeds were afoot inside the castle walls. King Birger of Sweden had invited guests from all over his land to celebrate Christmas with him and his wife. But as well as the promise of a scrumptious meal, the king was planning other things, as we shall soon discover.

Two of the invited guests were the king's younger brothers, Duke Valdemar and Duke Eric. People considered Eric to be bold and intelligent, and Valdemar, a skilful warrior. Their invitation was a cause of apprehension for some in the kingdom, though, for it was common knowledge that the king despised both siblings ever since they had imprisoned him a few years previously.

King Birger was all smiles and handshakes when they arrived, pretending to let bygones be bygones. He welcomed Eric and Valdemar into his castle, but asked that the Dukes' entourage stay in lodgings further in the town, claiming a lack of room in the castle. The Dukes took this in good faith and were soon enjoying the hospitality of their older brother. Food was consumed with gusto and drinks were toasted to their new friendship.

In the middle of the night, the dastardly deed took place. One of the king's trusted henchmen, together with a posse of crossbow-wielding troops, stormed the Dukes' sleeping quarters. The brothers' senses dulled by wine and slumber meant the troops easily overpowered and manacled them. Then they carried them down to the castle dungeons. After nailing their hands to heavy wooden stocks, and wrapping clasps around their necks, the brothers were chained to the dungeon walls. When the king came to see them a few hours later, he revelled in their torment and agony. As he locked their dungeon door for the last time, he made a show of throwing the large iron key into the river outside. With their imprisonment now permanent, King Birger decreed that both men die of starvation.

I studied the peaceful-looking castle, wondering where the Dukes' dungeon might have been. I concluded it had to be in the lower sections, perhaps even underground. I tried to imagine what the brothers' final days were like, but the resulting images were too dreadful to contemplate and so I stared into the river instead. In the nineteenth century, underneath its ripples, someone had found a large medieval key. Many believed it to be the key to the dungeon.

I looked at my watch. It was getting late and I still needed to see the harbour. I left the scene of the terrible banquet and walked to the main road.

7

Nyköping Harbour looked like it belonged on a postcard, especially the row of gorgeous buildings set back along a boardwalk. One looked like an eighteenth-century storehouse, which indeed it was, but, instead of servicing trading ships from the Baltic, it now served food and drink to the happy citizens of Nyköping. Further down, a lime green wooden building with a sloping roof and wooden veranda reminded me of a Wild West tavern. I could picture a sheriff kicking open its doors to eject a drunken reveller. It had once been the town's port office.

Two men emerged from the green building laughing uproariously at something. Both were in their late forties and rosy-cheeked, sporting similar black leather jackets. With their barrel-chests, high foreheads and thick bushy moustaches, they could have been Vikings, except their mode of transport was not a longboat – it was a Volvo, though neither seemed inclined to drive it. They were showing it off in a classic car convention.

The convention was going at the far end of the boardwalk, with around sixty old Volvos and Saabs parked in close proximity. Some of them appeared to be recent models, but most looked old, as if they belonged in a war film. The convention was popular among the townsfolk, and the local burger stand was doing a roaring trade, as were all the bars further along. There was even a brass band playing. I stopped at one car, an old cream-coloured Volvo with circular headlights and shiny silver bumper. A middle-aged woman in a white pullover saw me looking and came over. At first, she addressed me in Swedish but quickly switched to faultless English.

"This Volvo is a great car, isn't she?" the woman said, referring to the vehicle as a person, as many car lovers did. "I've owned her for five years now."

I pretended to study the grille. I knew absolutely nothing about cars, but ran my finger along the chrome, as if I was an expert in all things vehicular. I looked at the tyres next, nodding thoughtfully, then felt I ought to say something and so asked how old the car was.

"She is a 1968 model. An old car but still younger than me. More beautiful too!" The woman laughed at her own joke.

I walked further along the boardwalk. Billy Ray Cyrus's hit, *Achy Breaky Heart,* was blasting out from some outdoor speakers while a troupe of women did some line dancing on a small temporary stage. They were quite good too, keeping their steps and hip swaying in time to the country and western beat. Across from them was a narrow wooden bridge connecting the mainland to some jetties. A collection of tall-masted yachts were moored there. Closer to shore was a series of lily pads. It was a beautiful setting and, with the sun going down, casting the sky and water in gorgeous shades of blue, I felt truly happy.

I glanced at my watch again and saw that I'd been sightseeing for close to three hours. And during that time, I had thoroughly enjoyed myself. Of the three places I'd visited on my trip so far, Nyköping was easily the best. I walked back along the boardwalk and hit the road that would lead me back to the hotel. The walk back was a time for reflection, and the main realisation I made was that I ought to congratulate Ryanair for delivering me to somewhere so pleasing. Nyköping was a place I would actually come back to. But for now, I had to wash some clothes and look towards the next port of call on my journey: Bremen, Germany.

Top row: Heading into town; Nyköping harbour
Middle row: An old Volvo; One of the buildings in the central square
Bottom row: Turrets and spires of the town centre; The old port office

Day 4. Bremen, Germany

Stockholm Skavsta – Bremen: Ryanair £18

The next morning, I couldn't be bothered walking back along the highway to reach the bus station, so I got the hotel receptionist to order me a taxi. It was expensive but easier on the shins. Besides, today's flight was only costing me eighteen quid and so I could afford to be extravagant. The car drove me through the same rolling wheat fields and patches of coniferous forest I'd seen the previous afternoon.

When I arrived at the airport, I discovered I had miscalculated my arrival time badly because I was far too early. It was so early, in fact, that the two Ryanair baggage drop desks were unmanned. Everyone was waiting in a square-shaped holding pen with their luggage.

This didn't affect me, of course, but when I spied a café at the other side of the room, I decided to grab a drink so I could watch how the Swedes conducted themselves during check-in.

As I sat down with my latte, I noticed the same female cabin crew girl from yesterday. She was back in her blue uniform and heels, heading into departures for another day of no-frills flying. I looked at the monitor above the baggage desks: it was still blank, but just then, the display changed. It said the desks were now accepting passengers. No one else had noticed. With about fifty people waiting with their bags, I wondered what would happen when they did. My question was answered a couple of seconds later when a young blonde-haired man nonchalantly moved toward the desk, trying not to attract any attention. His efforts failed because another man noticed and, within seconds, the charge was on. Sweden might conjure images of blonde folk lounging about in steam rooms, but not so when a Ryanair flight is concerned. The Viking horde was on the move and there was no stopping them. I drained my coffee and headed for security.

I didn't realise that Swedes liked their beer so much. It was half an hour later, and I was in the small departure lounge. Almost every adult, male and female, had pints of lager in front of them. The few people who were not guzzling booze were traipsing around the scant duty free shops or else queuing up. The Malta flight, which was due to leave before mine, already had a huge line of people, most of them with massive hand-held luggage. Some bags were so oversized that I was sure the Ryanair staff would notice but, as far as I could tell, if a passenger could drag a piece of luggage towards the gate without it digging furrows into the floor, then it would probably pass muster.

I wandered to another cafe, looking at the items on offer, scoping out the sandwiches in particular. I was on the lookout for any white stuff that might be in them. I have a fear of mayonnaise, and it is a justified fear. A year previously, I had sent some blood to a laboratory to have it tested for food allergies and intolerances. It cost two hundred quid, but when the results came through the letterbox a few weeks later, they stated I was intolerant to all sorts of things. Wheat was on the list, as was yeast, milk, cheese, butter and hops. These were classified as CODE ORANGE ingredients, meaning I had to beware. But topping the inventory of intolerance was the common egg. Both the yolk and egg white were considered CODE RED foodstuff. Do not pass go, do not consume, do not let your taste buds encounter a single molecule, or else all bets are off. In fact, if I ever ate anything with egg in it, my face and head would erupt in a cruel and lingering acne-type breakout.

So I cut eggs out of my diet, which was harder than it sounded. Egg is in all sorts of things: cakes, biscuits and, of course, mayonnaise. That was why I was studying the inside of the sandwiches at Stockholm-Skavsta Airport. But it was sometimes hard to tell. The white stuff could be cheese or sour cream.

"Hi," I said to the young man with the trendy hair standing behind the counter. I pointed at a ham and cheese sandwich. "Does this contain mayonnaise?"

He picked it up and studied it. "I don't think so. But hang on, I'll check." He shouted over to his colleague, another young man in an apron.

The newcomer took the sandwich and peered at the contents. "It is not mayonnaise," he told me. "It is sauce."

"Sauce," I asked. "What type of sauce?"

"Maybe...cream sauce."

I decided there and then that I didn't want the sandwich. I simply couldn't risk it. I told them I wanted a banana instead. They looked at me as if I was mad.

3

The Malta flight departed, leaving the Ryanair passengers bound for Bremen and another set waiting for a Wizz Air flight to Warsaw. Wizz Air was a Hungarian low-cost airline very similar to Ryanair, and one that I'd be using the following week.

To kill time, I traipsed around the departure lounge, passing the same duty free shops and the same people as I started a second circuit. None of the shops held any interest for me. So this is what it feels like to be goldfish, I realised as I began my third spin. I decided to sit down to eat my banana; that would pass a few more minutes. This was the most difficult thing about air travel – waiting to fly. It was perilously boring.

So what did I know about Bremen? I knew it was in Germany, and that it had been heavily bombed during the Second World War, but that was it. For instance, I had no idea where in Germany it was, or what there was to see. I didn't even know if it was in the former East Germany or West Germany (it was in the West), but I would find out soon enough, I thought. I sat and waited for the announcement to board.

When it finally came, the Swedes drained their lagers and rushed to queue up. Like before, I waited in my seat so I could join at the last moment.

I looked over at a large purple and pink sign. It was for Wizz Air priority passengers: those who had paid a little extra to board the aircraft first. About twenty people were queuing for an aircraft that had not even landed yet. I shook my head at the madness of it all.

As was the norm, my randomly allocated seat was on the aisle. And once again, the flight was almost full. An elderly couple were sitting next to me, both poring over a crossword puzzle.

A man on the other side of the aisle, one row ahead, was a large blond-haired Viking. He had smuggled contraband aboard, and was swigging from a can of lager while the cabin crew gave their safety demonstration. Later, at cruising altitude, he produced another can of beer, and then when he had finished that, bought a third from the in-flight service, all of which explained why he became the first person I'd seen so far, on four different Ryanair flights, to buy a scratch card. When he didn't win anything, he sat back and burped.

When the trolley came past, I stopped the uniformed young woman and bought a coffee. I wanted milk with it and she handed me a tiny little pot with a foil lid. As I peeled it off, an arc of white liquid spurted across the aisle and splattered the leg of the Viking. His reaction was immediate – a look of annoyance as he brushed his trousers.

"Sorry," I muttered.

He ignored me and shook his head. I felt like squeezing the remainder of the milk over his long, blond locks, but the fear of receiving a pasting put me off. I finished my coffee just as an announcement came about the impending descent. And then, before I could grow truly bored, we landed with the trumpets from hell sounding soon after. I had arrived in my fourth country in as many days. But this time, Bremen Airport actually meant Bremen and not some sideshow village.

4

My routine was well honed by now. After passing border control, I walked through the green – nothing to declare – route and arrived into the arrivals terminal. There I scoped out an ATM to withdraw some cash. As I did, my bag clattered to the floor. Pocketing a hundred euros, I picked the luggage up and then looked for signs telling me how to get into the city centre. I couldn't see any and so decided to go outside and take things from there. I found a line of taxis waiting. The price to my hotel was twenty-five euros.

I considered this. A quarter of my money gone on a taxi. Still, it was a fraction cheaper than the taxi in Moss. "Is there a bus I can catch?" I asked the driver.

The man shrugged. "Not a bus. But there is a tram." He pointed in some vague direction and then carried on reading his newspaper. I thanked him and wandered off.

I walked past the taxis to the end of the road but couldn't see any sign of a tram stop. I could see a bus, however. It was outside the Holiday Inn. It turned out to be their private shuttle bus. I decided to ask for help inside the hotel. The receptionist couldn't have been more helpful. Even though she knew I was not a guest of the hotel, she produced a map, showed me where I was, and then told me where to go, even handing me a little slip of paper with a tram timetable on it. She then marked where my hotel was. I thanked her profusely and went outside.

Around the corner was the tram spot, already busy with seasoned Ryanair customers. A tram was heading towards them and so I picked up my luggage and ran for it. I got there just as the doors opened and, after checking it was the correct tram, I jumped aboard, pleased with myself for making it in time. And then I realised I didn't have a ticket. But, as the doors whooshed closed, I realised there was nothing I could do about it.

A few minutes later, we stopped at another tram stop. A new set of passengers jumped aboard and I watched them carefully. None seemed to have any tickets. But that did not mean they had not paid for the journey. Perhaps they had *Oyster*-type cards, or day passes hidden somewhere about their person. I grew worried. What if an inspector came aboard? What if there was some sort of barrier system in downtown Bremen? I cursed myself for rushing headlong into the tram.

In the end, I needn't have worried. The tram arrived in central Bremen about eight minutes later, and I escaped into the busy streets with everyone else, savouring the fact I had got away with not having a ticket. With the map the woman at the Holiday Inn had given me, I quickly found my hotel. It was dead bang in the centre.

5

The time was almost six p.m. and I was hungry. I found a sausage stand around the corner from the hotel and bought a long meaty treat, devouring it in seconds. German sausages always tasted great. Bremen was massive; it was a real city and it had hordes of tourists to prove it. There was even a tourist train snaking its way through the central square. As it trundled around, I joined the hundreds of people standing, gawping, pointing or taking photographs of the beautiful central market square, home to the town hall, a set of medieval guild houses and a large blocky building covered in glass and aluminium. It was the parliament building and looked at odds with the other architecture in the square, because all the others were gorgeous. The best buildings were the guild houses, a row of them taking up one end of the square. They stood side-by-side, with high pointed roofs and ornate little windows. Collectively, their individual styles formed a terrace of postcard-prettiness. In their day, they had been a wine merchant's house, a wine store and an apothecary. Today they are a bank, a restaurant and a medical centre.

Not far from there, a man was playing a guitar. He was standing underneath a large statue with another man, who was playing a small woodwind instrument. Their tune was a standard twelve-bar blues number, and a few families with small children were watching them. I'd busked once. At university, a friend and I had perched ourselves on a wall in the main pedestrian shopping arcade of downtown Bradford. For the next hour and half we strummed our acoustic guitars like mad, neither of us daring to sing. By the end of our performance, we had made enough cash to pay for a few drinks in the pub, the sole purpose for the endeavour. One thing I distinctly remember, though, was that the only people who had given us any money were parents with small kids. The children seemed mesmerised by the guitars, forcing the adults to pay out of guilt. The children of Bremen were just as fascinated, and I smiled at how much money this pair were making, adding my own contribution to their sizeable fund.

The statue was of Roland, a first century soldier. Judging by his effigy, his weapons of choice were a magic sword and an ivory horn. Roland's heroic deeds had been immortalised in historic yarns and minstrel music, passed up through the ages for centuries. When he battled a giant and killed him with a precise stab wound to its navel, Roland became a symbol of independence across Germany, and many towns and cities erected statues of him in their marketplaces. Bremen, famous across Germany for its freethinking ways, was one of these towns. I stared up at the stone cast Roland, which was now over six hundred years old. Roland's stonemasons had depicted him with a friendly smile and thick wavy hair. Built from sturdy limestone, he had weathered the elements well.

Behind the square was another monument. It showed four animals standing on top of one another. At the bottom was a donkey; then a dog, a cat, with a rooster on the very top. Smiling tourists were waiting patiently to have their pictures taken next to it. Later I learned the sculpture was in honour of a famous Brothers Grimm tale, whereby the four animals, tired of their owners treating them badly, decided to up sticks and move to Bremen. Once upon their long journey, they decided to rest their weary paws, hooves and feet in an abandoned farmhouse. There was one problem, though: upon inspection of the house, the animals discovered a set of thieves residing inside. They quickly came up with a plan. They would wait until nightfall and then scare the men away. Later, with moonlight silhouetting their form, the animals jumped onto each other's backs and made the noisiest racket they could. When the thieves opened the door, they saw a black creature barking, hissing, snorting and screeching. Believing it to be some sort of monster, they fled. The animals tittered to themselves, jumped off each other's backs and moved in. They ended up liking the farm so much that they lived there happily ever after. Or something like that.

6

Schnoor is the only part of Bremen that has kept its medieval flavour. The reason for this is twofold. Firstly, in the years following the Great War, Bremen underwent a great revival, but Schnoor's web of narrow lanes and cobbled passageways were deemed too difficult to alter, and so they were left alone. Although this ultimately proved fortuitous, at the time it meant a steady decline into fester and ruin. Schnoor became so bad that the only people who lived there were the poorest and most destitute of souls.

In 1944, the lack of development in Schnoor proved to be its second saviour. Allied aircraft ignored it completely with their barrage of bombs. Over twelve thousand of them rained down on the city, leaving most of Bremen as rubble and dust. Schnoor was left intact. Afterwards, during the great clean up, the people of Bremen recognised Schnoor for what it now was: a preserved piece of medieval history in the heart of their city.

I found the slender streets of Schnoor full of eager sightseers and trinket shoppers. Tiny handicraft shops filled the lower floors of thin, gabled cottages. Many sold ornaments, bags or paper models kits. An intricate version of Bremen's town hall sat in one window, all made from thin card. Next to it was a paper model of Dubai's Burj

Al Arab. Just then, my phone rang. It was my wife Angela asking how things were going.

"Good," I answered, finding a quiet alcove to stand in, well away from the flow of the crowd. "The weather's good, Bremen is safe and I'm wandering around a medieval street."

"So it's better than where you were yesterday?"

"I'm not sure. But it's way better than Moss and Nowy Dwor Mazowiecki. Where I am right now is full of little cafes and shops. Exactly the sort of places you like."

"Sounds lovely. But the reason I'm ringing is to tell you about a free app you need to download. My brother was telling me about it. It's called Maps.me and it's a Sat Nav-type thing, but you can use it offline. He said you download the app and then pick which countries you want."

"What's it called again?"

She told me.

"And it's free? Are you sure?"

"That's what Andrew said. He told me he used it in Peru and it worked when he didn't have any Wi-Fi."

I thanked my wife for the top tip and memorised the name of the app. After saying goodbye, I left Schnoor to head back to the hotel, wandering a riverfront promenade popular with late evening boat tours. Plenty of people were queuing up for them. I didn't have time for a boat tour, and so I left the boats behind, noticing a homeless man, thin and gaunt, wandering around a grassy embankment near the river's edge. He was picking up pieces of litter to assess their worth. First, an old cigarette lighter was inspected and deemed worthy of his pocket, then an empty plastic bottle was picked up. The man opened a discarded McDonald's carton but, after peering inside, he threw it back down on the grass. I gave him a couple of euros.

Close to the hotel, I came across another homeless man, this one sporting a white goatee beard and black cap. He was sitting on a rough piece of cloth with two dogs on either side of him. The man was feeding one dog, then the other, a few crisps from a small packet. Both animals waited patiently for their turn. I walked past him and dropped a few more euros in his hat.

7

Early the next morning, with only a couple of hours before I had to head to the airport again, I was up early in search of more Bremen sights. Bremen, I was discovering, was one of those cities where everybody waited for the green man to flash before they would attempt to cross, even with an empty road in front of them. With time so short, I couldn't wait and crossed to the sound of sharp breaths and tuts.

The town planners of Bremen had come up with a masterstroke by the river. Instead of building right up to it, they had kept large areas on both sides free of construction. So expansive and tree laden were these areas that, if I ignored the sound of car engines, I could've been in the countryside.

I was following my new Sat Nav app. I'd downloaded it the previous evening, adding maps of all the countries I would be visiting on my trip. The Bremen one was reassuringly detailed, and I was following a route it had plotted to a windmill, amazed it could work out my journey without the aid of Wi-Fi. After passing a few ducks and then an empty park bench, I spied it in the distance. It was a big one too, with red and white stationary sails. It was Bremen's last windmill; the rest had been lost to fire, war and thievery. Instead of grinding corn, it was now a café.

Nearby was a park bench. Four homeless people, two men and two women, were sitting on it, glugging from large brown bottles of beer, despite it being only seven thirty in the morning. A collection of empties lay scattered on the ground by their feet. The foursome seemed in good spirits as I passed them, laughing and joking with one another. One man noticed me and waved. When I waved back, he smiled, revealing a set of brown teeth.

I walked back to the central square, which was starting to get busy. I wanted to find something to climb so I could get a good aerial view of the city. The town hall seemed my best bet, especially since it had some upper storey windows looking out from the pointed gables. I found the entrance to the town hall easily enough but, instead of finding an elevator or even a staircase, I found a photo exhibition. They were mainly black and white stills of people I didn't know, doing nothing in particular. One showed a man in a top hat standing with a cane. The caption didn't help – it was in German.

I circled the large lower floor looking for a way up, but as far as I could tell, there was nothing. I walked up to a young woman sitting behind a desk by the entrance to ask whether I could climb one of the church spires next door.

The girl looked confused. "Yes, it is possible. But this is not a church, you know. This is the town hall."

I nodded. "I know this is the town hall. I'm just asking whether I will be able to climb the church spire."

"I see. So anyway, you must go to the building along from here with a cross on the top. A church is a building where people pray to God."

She thought I was a fool, and I could hardly blame her. I thanked her, turned tail and fled.

8

Bremen Cathedral was a massive, twin-spired structure that was over 1200 years old. I walked through the main entrance and found a booth selling tickets to climb one of the spires. After paying the one-euro fee, the grizzly woman behind the counter pointed me towards a heavy wooden door. When I opened it, it revealed a narrow stone staircase. Round and round I went, getting ever more out of breath, but I couldn't stop because I could hear some people coming up from behind. Then I heard a noise above me. Some people were coming down. I stopped, hugged the central pillar and sucked my stomach in as they squeezed past.

At the top, I could see why the ticket was only one euro: the view was abysmal. Massive metal grilles blocked most of Bremen, and the Cathedral's second spire blocked everything else. When the family of four behind me saw the view, they looked as disappointed as me.

Back in the market square, under the shadow of the great cathedral, I found the Spitting Stone. It was larger and darker than the other stones around it, and easy to see due to the tour groups surrounding it. It was famous in Bremen because a woman called Gesche Gottfried had been beheaded there in1831. Her crimes were so horrendous that the people of the city used to spit on the stone every time they passed, thus the name.

In her younger days, Gesche Gottfried was reportedly beautiful, and carried herself with an easy manner. Because of these attributes, she had no shortage of male admirers. Eventually, though, she settled down with one man and had three children with him. Everything was fine for a while, until Gesche's husband contracted a short illness. He died soon after. When doctors investigated, they scratched their heads in confusion. How he died was a mystery, and so they recorded it as natural causes. It wasn't a mystery to Gottfried, though. She knew exactly what had happened: she had poisoned her husband to death with rat poison.

And thus began a dreadful tale of murder and intrigue, a reign of terror that would last for the next fifteen years, shocking the residents of Bremen to the core.

9

With husband number one safely dispatched in a satisfactory manner, Gesche Gottfried set her sights on a well-to-do wine merchant called Michael Christoph. She didn't want to poison him (at least not at first); she merely wanted his money. She set forth to woo him to the altar but standing in her way were Gottfried's parents and her own three children, all of whom despised the new man in her life. As a result, Gottfried put her wedding plans on hold and started poisoning them instead. First to die was Gottfried's mother, who, after a period of vomiting, severe abdominal cramps and excessive salivation, passed away in May 1815. The following week, Gottfried's two daughters died, again from a 'mystery' illness that had caused agonising stomach cramps and diarrhoea. Both had eaten slices of their grandmother's funeral cake, which their own mother had smothered in rat poison. Gottfried's father was inconsolable with the sudden loss of all these relatives, but he didn't mourn for long, because Gottfried laced some soup with rat poison, dispatching him soon after. By September, she had poisoned her young son too. That was five murders in the space of just four months. And, as a bonus, Gottfried received a healthy inheritance from her parents' estate.

The people of Bremen could not believe such tragedy had struck the poor woman. And what made things worse was that the townsfolk had witnessed Gottfried nursing her family in their dying days, acting selflessly while a 'cloud of misfortune' followed her every move. People began to call Gottfried the Angel of Bremen, praying for the poor woman in their churches, and did not mind when she finally married the wine merchant, Michael Christoph.

The first time Michael Christoph was served rat poison was on his wedding night. His new bride had mixed a little bit into his favourite drink, almond milk. It was enough to make him feel unwell, but not enough to fell him. Day after day, though, with more and more poison making it into his food and drink, he started showing the first signs of illness. When she upped the dose, he developed debilitating stomach cramps and ended up bedbound. While Gottfried nursed him towards death, her brother, Johan, unexpectedly turned up at the house.

Johann had returned to Bremen following a period in the army. When he demanded his share of their parents' inheritance, Gottfried invited him to discuss it over dinner. The meal was shellfish, marinated in mouse butter, the trade name for rat poison in those times. Despite this, Johann suspected nothing and ate the lot. He died soon after. Poor Gottfried, the townsfolk harked, all her family dead and a sickly husband at death's door. When would the misery end?

Thirteen months later, Michael Christoph finally succumbed to the poison. That was eight victims in less than four years. And still the authorities did not suspect foul play. But with her double-fold inheritance, Gottfried settled down to enjoy life and, for the next six years, she enjoyed a murder-free existence.

Fate turned when a new suitor appeared on the scene. Paul Thomas Zimmermann was so smitten with Gottfried's beauty that he proposed almost immediately. She accepted his offer and bought some new packets of mouse butter to go with her engagement ring. When her fiancé grew ill, 38-year-old Gottfried asked him to sign a will bequeathing everything to her should something happen. He scrawled his signature and she served him her signature dish. He died soon after, in June 1823. Gottfried was now a rich woman. Around this time, one of her friends started annoying her, but not enough for Gottfried to kill her. Instead, she gave the woman a few mild doses of rat poison, a sufficient amount to cause a major stomach upset and gangrene to her extremities. She ended up in hospital where surgeons removed her hands and feet.

To pass the time, Gottfried had music lessons. They stopped when she poisoned the teacher, a woman called Anna Meyerholz. By December 1825, she murdered one of her neighbours too, taking her tally to eleven murders. The following twelve months was a quiet year for Gottfried, with only her landlady adding to the total, but the following year, she decided to go for the jackpot in the Great German Arsenic Bake-Off.

Gottfried invited Johann Rumpff around for something to eat. Rumpff was her murdered landlady's widower. He accepted, even though he suspected his wife's death had something to do with Gottfried. On the night of the meal, Rumpff acted as if nothing was wrong, chatting away amicably, but all the while, surreptitiously moving his food around with his fork. His efforts paid off, mainly due to Gottfried's carelessness. Instead of mashing up the rat poison, as she had diligently done in the past, she had sprinkled it over his broth and salad leaves. Rumpff noticed the white specs and, without her noticing, collected a few. Then he claimed he wasn't hungry and made his excuses and left. A few days later, he showed the granules to a doctor friend, who promised to look at them.

In the meantime, Gottfried busied herself with some more poisonings. Becoming gung-ho in her middle age, she poisoned two people at the same time, a friend called Beta, and that woman's daughter, Elise. Both died just two days apart. Thinking it best to leave town, Gottfried gathered her things and moved to Hanover. There she met her next victim, a suitor called Friedrich Kleine.

After rustling up another batch of Nanny Gottfried's Special Sauerkraut and Red Cabbage Pie, she fed it to Kleine, who ate it with delight. When he began suffering stomach cramps, and was consigned to bed, Gottfried began her nursing.

Meanwhile, back in Bremen, the doctor did some checks and discovered the white granules were arsenic. He informed the police. After some furious investigation, police found Gottfried living in Hanover. They arrested her but it was too late for Kleine: he was at death's door. He died in hospital a few days later. Friedrich Kleine turned out to be Gottfried's fifteenth and final victim.

The authorities took Gottfried to Bremen and threw her in prison. There they discovered something unsettling. Underneath her thick make-up and thirteen corsets (so many were needed in order to give her the voluptuous figure she needed to entice men), she was skeleton-like. With this physical unmasking came a mental cleansing, where she admitted to all her crimes openly, even saying there might be more victims she had forgotten about. For the next two years, she languished in prison until the night of her forth-third birthday. Flaming torches illuminated Bremen's market square as guards led Gottfried to the execution spot under the twin spires of the cathedral. With the crowd jeering, baying for blood, the town's executioner raised his axe. A second later, he beheaded Gesche

Gottfried, one of Germany's most notorious serial killers, in what would turn out to be Bremen's last public execution.

10

I could hear the melody of a tinkling glockenspiel. The wind was carrying the chimes across the cobbles of the square. The sound was coming from a building at Number 4 Böttcherstraße, otherwise known as the Glockenspiel House.

Böttcherstraße is one of the more famous streets in Bremen, due to its unusual architecture. In 1920s, a coffee baron bought the entire street, which, at the time, mostly consisted of barrel making workshops. He levelled them and allowed a forward-thinking architect to change the face, quite literally, of the whole thoroughfare. Instead of dull storefronts, the short winding street wowed the citizens of Bremen with its art galleries, chic restaurants, small museums, craft workshops and the aforementioned Glockenspiel House. When Allied bombers dropped their loads over Bremen in 1944, most of Böttcherstraße was destroyed. It took a decade for the town to restore it to its former glory.

I bought an overpriced coffee near the cathedral and then followed Böttcherstraße until I arrived at Number 4. It wasn't difficult to find due to the assembled crowd. It was almost 9 o'clock. One man had a thick, waxed moustache, flip-flops and a special hat with a peacock feather. He looked like the Pied Piper. At first, I thought he was part of the glockenspiel show, but he was a spectator like everyone else.

The Glockenspiel House sat above a compact little square. A busy café offered the best view, but it was so full that I stood in the middle of the tiny area. No one was interested in lattes and cappuccinos, though; everyone was gazing up at the triangular roof section – more specifically, at the *carillon*, the 30 porcelain bells that would produce the sound.

As the hour struck, a simple melody began again. The pleasing sound reminded me of my childhood, of randomly bashing glockenspiels and xylophones in school music lessons. But this tune was not random: it was a very precise melody, but one I didn't recognise. As the glockenspiels ran through ostinatos and major-key melodies, cameras flashed, whirred and clicked. Then a series of wooden panels on the side of the Glockenspiel House rotated. The panels revealed wooden carvings embossed with gold. They depicted famous seamen, pilots and explorers. I recognised Charles Lindbergh and Christopher Columbus, and the designer of the Zeppelin. With more people crowding the already crammed square, I took a photo and looked at my watch. It was that time again: time to pack and prepare for another low-cost flight to another country.

Top row: The central market square is simply beautiful; A windmill in downtown Bremen
Middle row: Schnoor district; The animals from a Brothers Grimm' tale; The Glockenspiel House
Bottom row: The Roland Statue; Bremen town hall

Day 5. Riga, Latvia

Bremen – Riga: Ryanair £27

As a rough estimate, ninety percent of the passengers queuing for the Riga flight were Latvian. I couldn't be sure, of course, but the Slavic features, the non-German accents and the amount of wife-beater, sleeveless T-shirts were the clues.

I was observing the queue from my seat a few metres away. Why, I wondered for the millionth time, were people lining up before the plane had even arrived at the airport? It wasn't as if they had to rush on board to bag the best seat anymore. The only reason I could think of was they wanted to get their luggage in the overhead bins. Ridiculous. And why did Eastern European men prefer sleeveless T-shirts? It turned a perfectly ordinary-looking man into a thug.

I regarded my luggage. For some reason it was behaving itself today. Maybe it was the shifting position of the clothes inside. I'd stuffed the zipped compartment with dirty washing, which had possibly caused the centre of gravity to move lower. It now stood up of its own accord. That reminded me: when I got to Riga, I needed to do more washing; I was running low on clean clothes.

I'd been to Riga a few years previously. It was before Latvia had adopted the euro, and so everything had been cheap. The capital of Latvia had impressed me so much it had kicked off a quest to visit every former Soviet republic. I was looking forward to seeing how things had changed.

A Ryanair employee came over the speakers. "We would like to call all passengers for Ryanair Flight 3602 to Riga. Those with small children may use the priority line."

The queue of passengers shuffled forward. Some with kids barged their way to the front. Five minutes later, the general call to board came.

Once inside the cabin, I checked my seat number (by the window this time) and gestured to a woman and a young girl, sitting in the aisle and middle seats, that I wanted to sit down. After stuffing my bag into the overhead bin, I offered to sit on the aisle if the woman and the girl wanted to shuffle along. The woman either didn't understand or wanted to remain on the end, because she sighed. Instead of stepping into the aisle, as most people did, she simply stood up in front of her seat. Her daughter did the same thing, forcing me to furiously fumble and manoeuvre myself along.

Finally, I sat down and secured my seatbelt. Mum and daughter took their seats and, judging from mum's expression, the whole episode had annoyed her greatly. Well, it didn't matter now, I was in my seat and that was that. Besides, I'd offered to sit in the aisle. What else was I supposed to do?

While the last remaining passengers took their seats, a member of the cabin crew made an announcement I'd never heard before. "Please can we ask that all passengers check their seat numbers before sitting down? This can be found on the top right of your boarding card."

What sort of imbecile didn't understand that rule? Surely, people had the gumption to look at their boarding cards to find their allocated seat. And if they didn't, then they should not be allowed out by themselves. I shook my head at the incompetence of some passengers. A minute later, there was a tap on my shoulder. It was a member of the cabin crew. Standing behind her was a man holding a baby. "Please can I see your boarding card?" she asked me.

I passed it over.

"Your seat is here, sir," she said, pointing at the window seat in the row behind.

Damn and blast, I lamented. I was the fool! And now I had to face the humiliation of moving. Everyone would know I was the imbecile the cabin crew had warned them about. Once again, the woman, daughter and I did the shuffle dance of annoyance. I sat down in my new seat, shamefaced and hot under the collar. I buckled my seat for the second time in five minutes.

Now accustomed to Ryanair's punctuality, I was not surprised when the aircraft left the stand within one minute of the posted departure time. Soon we were in the air for the hour and a half flight eastward. I ignored the food trolley, the perfume trolley and the scratch cards, but what I couldn't ignore was the number of people who all knew each other. A moustachioed man saw a friend sitting halfway along the cabin, booming a hearty hello his way. A young woman wandering to the toilet noticed a long lost neighbour with a baby. She stopped by the woman's seat to gossip and pinch cheeks. A man wearing a white wife-beater shirt walked down the aisle and did a double take at me. At first, I thought he was going to beat me, but he was looking at the man in the next seat. He reached over and shook hands, Latvian pouring from his mouth. It was as if the same Latvian village had somehow rendezvoused aboard the same Ryanair flight.

"Ladies and gentleman, this is your captain from the flight deck," said an Irish accent. "We'll soon begin our descent into Riga International where the weather conditions are clear and calm. We should have you on the stand a few minutes early." He was right; twenty minutes later, we were trundling along a Latvian taxiway. As the round of applause died down, I could hear the dulcet tones of a triumphant trumpet playing out over the speakers.

It didn't take long to clear the airport. Outside, after spending ten minutes of fruitless wandering trying to search out a bus, I gave up and jumped in a taxi. I showed the old geezer in the driving seat the address of my hotel and he nodded. Off we set. As we left the airport perimeter, I tried to engage him in conversation.

"No English," he barked.

I nodded, irritated by his casual rebuke. Maybe it was because he was sick of Englishmen visiting his city and causing trouble. I couldn't blame him if that was the reason. Ever since low cost airlines had invaded Riga, young Brits had flocked to the Baltics. In 2008, things came to a head when the Latvian interior minister described British tourists as 'dirty, hoggish people'. His comment followed the arrest of a drunken 34-year old British man caught urinating on Latvia's most revered memorial – the Freedom Monument.

The taxi hit a traffic jam outside of Riga's old town. That was when I noticed some business cards inside a small plastic holder on the dashboard. They were for an establishment called the Blow Lounge and featured scantily clad young women on the front. A few minutes later, the short ride from the airport ended and I was outside my hotel.

3

Shortly after dropping my things in my room, I crossed a busy road opposite my hotel. I was on my way to the former Zeppelin hangars (now the expansive Central Market). As I neared the massive curved buildings, I found the area in front of them awash with locals wearing sailors' caps. But these were not bona fide naval headwear: they were shop-bought caps a child might wear at the seaside. One middle-aged man, sporting a porn star moustache, had a golden anchor and double braid sewn into his cap. It lay jauntily across his head while a cigarette dangled beneath the moustache. He looked ridiculous, like an extra from the Village People. I absently scratched my own freshly sprouted beard, the first I'd ever grown. It was born out of pure laziness, and I intended to keep it for the duration of my trip. I wondered whether to purchase a cap to go with it.

As well as the sailor-capped folk, a number of tourists were watching an Inca gentleman playing panpipes. He had all the gear – stripy poncho, black hat and patterned headband – as he played his authentic sounding Peruvian ditty. I carried on past him, negotiating my way around an enormous array of strawberry and blackberry stalls. Then I arrived at the entrance of the massive market.

Cheese of every description was on offer inside the humungous market hall. Blocks of white, thick slices of yellow, gigantic slabs of

~ 74 ~

orange, bewildering arrays of blue-veined cheese and lumps of it floating in liquid were available to buy. If a shopper tired of the cheese, then large drums of cooking oil, piled high on counters, were available to purchase. And people were doing so with enthusiasm. I passed a woman in a headscarf who had just bought an industrial-sized vat of oil. She was rolling it toward the exit.

Towering above my head was the vast skeletal frame of the hangar. It made me visualise just how huge the Zeppelin balloons must have been. To fill this massive market hall meant it had to be *big*. Some of the mighty balloons had stretched hundreds of feet long and towered one hundred feet high. Riga's Zeppelins had been used as reconnaissance aircraft in the Baltic Sea region.

I left the cheese hangar and entered the next one. It was full of stalls selling honey (in actual honeycombs), jars of hemp butter, loaves of rye bread and plates of salted mushrooms. Further in were stalls peddling amber jewellery. Amber was popular in the Baltics, and the items for sale in the Central Market included beaded necklaces, translucent stones and silver wristbands engraved with the distinctive fossilised orange tree resin. Next up were the meat stalls. Every part of an animal was for sale: skin, innards, tongues and full pig snouts. I stopped by a glass display brimming with sausages. Fat ones, thin ones, curled-up ones and long straight ones were for sale. In charge of the stall was a stout woman wearing a blue apron. She stood watching me, as if daring me to buy something. I didn't and continued with my walk, entering the final hangar.

The smell hit my nostrils even before I stepped through: the pungent aroma of fish. Once inside, I surveyed the wares while my nose adjusted to the smell. Women in headscarves were haggling over salmon fillets or bartering over pots of cheap caviar. Other women were buying trout, or pointing at aquariums, trying to get the best deal on large, silvery live fish. One woman was buying a large flat fish that was so ugly I couldn't believe it edible. I stopped by the stall to look at it, but the battle-axe in charge glared with her lumpy eye. When I raised my camera to take a picture of some fried eels instead, she bared her teeth. I lowered my camera and fled.

Back in the old town, I saw another advertisement for Latvia's national drink, *Riga Black Balsam*. From my previous visit, I knew that balsam was a hideous concoction of vodka and herbs that every tourist shop in Riga sold in opaque brown bottles. I decided to buy a couple of bottles as gifts for people back home.

Two teenagers, one male, one female, stood behind the long counter in one shop. He had short dark hair; she had the full, long blond Scandinavian look. Behind them were rows of Black Balsam, large and small. As I walked to the counter, both burst out laughing. It was like the ice cream shop in Nowy Dwor Mazowiecki all over again, especially when the young man had to take leave. The blond girl tried her best to stifle her amusement, but when I said I wanted two small bottles of Riga Black Balsam, a small giggle escaped her mouth. Even so, she busied herself with my order, while I surreptitiously checked my trousers for gaping flies, my chin for tomato ketchup and my hair for random flotsam. All were in order; so what could be so funny? Maybe it was my beard. Maybe it made me look like some sort of Baltic inbred. Whatever the reason, I paid the money, grabbed my bottles and went in search of Riga's sights.

4

Riga was a different city compared to the one I'd visited during a cold February winter. Gone were icicles hanging from windowpanes, gone were the mounds of snow piled against walls and, instead of fur coats and cosy Russian hats, the locals preferred T-shirts and shorts.

I turned right, walking past the Laima Clock. It was a kitschy timepiece, located on the corner of Brivibas Bulvaris. First installed in the 1920s, the clock's large brown letters spelled out the name of Latvia's largest confectionery company, Laima. The time on the clock at the top matched the time on my watch: five minutes before the hourly changing of the guard at the Freedom Monument.

The monument was just along from the clock, the place where a stupid British man had once urinated. Heading toward it was a gaggle of tourists following a guide holding up a rolled-up newspaper. As they scurried over the cobbles to keep up, it seemed the Pied Piper was in town. I made my way towards the monument myself, looking upward at Mother Latvia standing atop her huge stone plinth. She was thrusting her green coppery arms vertically upwards as she held three golden stars. She represented freedom fighters who had lost their lives in the Latvian War of Independence of 1918. At her base, two young guards were standing to attention. As far as I could tell, their only movement was from their eyes, which flicked this way and that. How they could keep their bodies still for so long was beyond me. I would be useless at the job: I couldn't keep still for five minutes.

The Latvian Guard of Honour first began their sentry duties in 1935, just after the completion of the monument. Their role ended five years later with Soviet occupation. But in 1992, following the country's newfound independence, the guards of honour were reinstated, resuming their hourly vigil beneath Mother Latvia. The only time soldiers did not attend to this duty was when temperatures were below minus ten degrees Celsius.

With a few minutes to go before the changing of the guard ceremony began, I took up station on a wall overlooking a small park. I tried to stifle a small yawn. After five days of non-stop travel, I was beginning to feel a little weary. I wondered how I would be feeling by the end of Day Ten. A thin river ran through the park, home to a few ducks.

Suddenly, the crowd behind me stirred. From the side of the monument, some new guards appeared. They loitered for a minute and then, with a perfectly timed slow-motion march, they trooped to the front of the statue and began a protracted about-turn manoeuvre involving perfectly choreographed arm swinging and leg kicks. When they reached the stationary guards, they all swapped position. The old guards marched off in perfectly matched timing until they were almost hidden from view. There, they started walking normally back to their base. The crowd dispersed and so did I.

I found myself wandering, often the best thing to do in a new city, until I stumbled upon another tour group assembled next to something called the Powder Tower. The tower was a medieval round tower with a spiky conical roof.

"It originally functioned as part of Riga's defensive line in the thirteenth century," the female guide told them, "but, actually, this construction is much younger, dating from around 1650." I tuned out the voice and walked towards a young woman sitting in the shade of the tower. Kitted out in medieval costume, she was plucking some type of medieval instrument. Whatever it was, it sounded great, a mixture of a glockenspiel and a harpsichord. With the sun shining and a tune wafting over the cobbles, I smiled to myself. Ryanair had delivered me into one of the most beautiful cities in Europe. After dropping a few coins onto the girl's cloth, I headed deeper into the old town.

5

I stopped to take a picture of Riga's narrowest street when the Americans came. The old couple saw my camera and correctly deduced I was a fellow tourist.

"You speak English, son?" asked the roly-poly grey-haired gent in a southern accent, curling his vowels like a character from the *Dukes of Hazard*. He was bald on top and actually looked like the actor who had played Boss Hogg. His wife was short and stick-like; she held a guidebook of *The Baltics* in her hand.

I nodded.

The man smiled. "Can you point us in the direction of the Radisson? We seem to be lost."

The Radisson was a tall hotel just past the Freedom Monument. I knew where it was because the last time I'd been to Riga, that's where Angela and I had stayed. I couldn't see it now; it was hidden by the buildings of the old town. I powered up my new phone app and typed in the name of the hotel. Then I pressed the button to change the map into an arrow. It pointed behind me. I then decided to do a good deed of the day.

"I'll show you," I told the Americans. "It's not far."

They gleefully accepted and so I took the couple on a left-and-right route that followed the arrow until we emerged onto a main road near the Laima Clock. The Radisson was visible behind the Freedom Monument.

Both thanked me profusely, even offering me money for my service. I waved the ten-euro note away, telling them to enjoy the rest of their time in Riga. As they toddled off, I felt a wave of euphoria wash over me. The simple act of kindness I'd shown was having the strangest effect on me. It was as if I had won a prize or something. I turned in the opposite direction and found I had a spring in my step. It felt good to do something unbidden and worthwhile for a stranger. There and then, I made a pact with myself that, from now on, in every new country I visited, I would do a good deed of the day. That settled, I retraced my steps into the old town where I found another tour group, this one made up of pensioners. They were blocking most of a cramped street

"The white building on the right is the oldest of the three," the young female guide intoned in accented but perfectly understandable English. "It dates from 1490. Note how tiny the windows are on the upper level."

The slack-jawed pensioners all looked upward en masse. I did too.

The guide continued. "That was because citizens in medieval Riga were taxed on the amount of sunlight entering their homes."

The tiny openings looked barely large enough to allow sunlight in at all. Certainly, no one living in them would have been able to stare out with enjoyment. They might as well have not bothered having windows at all. My eyes moved to the left, at a yellow building with larger windows and a much fancier door, and then at the end of the terrace where a thin green building stood. It was so narrow that its door took up much of its width. The buildings, collectively, were called the Three Brothers.

"The yellow and green houses are not so old," the guide told her old-age pensioner audience. "Come, let me show you the narrowest street in Riga."

I stayed put, wanting to take a photo of the Three Brothers without human obstacles in the way. I had to be quick, though, because another tour group was on the way. Afterwards, I lowered my gaze to a stout man sporting a handlebar moustache. Thick bushy moustaches were popular in the Baltics. He was sitting on a small plastic chair waiting for the next tour group. When it arrived, he stubbed out his cigarette and picked up a large brass instrument. Then he began a hearty tune full of cheek-blowing gusto. When the new guide started talking about the three buildings, I took this as my cue to leave.

6

I found a large wooden horse that drunken Brits had once tried to assault. Wearing only their socks, the group had mounted the beast while another pal filmed the fun. When police swooped, they arrested and fined each of the drunkards ninety euros. The horse had survived its defilement and was enjoying itself down the side of St. Peter's, my current destination. A little girl was sitting on the horse now, ably assisted by her father. I headed past them to the entrance of the church. After paying the hefty nine-euro fee, a church employee directed me towards a lift that would take me to the viewing platform.

I followed a Chinese couple to the lift. Already waiting were a trio of elderly German men and a young couple with a boy aged about three. Then a couple of teenage girls joined us. Polite nods ensued before private conversation resumed. When the elevator door pinged open, a gaggle of tourists emerged and filtered past us.

Sitting on a tiny stool inside the lift was a teenage boy. He beckoned us in. Once the sardine can was full, all conversation ceased immediately. As everyone stood awkwardly shoulder to shoulder, the teenager pressed a button on the panel and returned to his phone to watch a movie.

The elevator began its ponderous ascent, reaching a maximum speed of 1mph as it tried to win the title of the World's Slowest Lift. I dared a glance at my fellow passengers and caught the eye of one of the Germans. He nodded and I smiled. Then I fixed my gaze on the electronic display. It reminded me of a funny article I'd once read about lift etiquette. It suggested things *not* to do, including staring at a fellow passenger without blinking, playing the harmonica, and soaking everyone's shoes with a water pistol.

At the halfway stage of the journey, the worst thing that can occur in a lift happened. Someone broke wind. The smell was horrendous and immediate. I almost gagged but could not let my stoic expression change. That was one of the rules. But one person did not understand the rules.

"Mummy, it smells in here," said the young boy.

I was aghast. He had spoken aloud what no one should dare. His mother looked mortified, but dad did what I'd have done in the same situation: he pretended he didn't know what his son was talking about and told him to be quiet. I had my suspicions about one of the Germans, but kept these thoughts to myself while I held my breath. While we all digested the gravity of the situation, simultaneously observing everyone for signs of guilt, the elevator jumped, staggered and lurched to a stop. The Chinese woman squealed in terror and so did the little boy. But the doors opened and we were free to escape the elevator of terror.

The platform we found ourselves on was circular and cramped. The view was great, though: I could see the red roofs of the old town, the golden dome of Nativity Cathedral (the largest Orthodox Church in the Baltics) and the Radisson Hotel beyond it. I circled the tiny platform, sidestepping everyone else in my attempt to find the perfect view. I found it on the far side: a panorama of grandiose buildings, and curving arcs belonging to the Central Market. Running through the middle of it all was the River Daugava, a wide expanse of deep blue that had begun its journey in the foothills of Western Russia. Riga looked beautiful. It was definitely turning into my favourite city of the trip so far.

7

One of the most popular gathering points in the old town is the main square. Tourists were everywhere, admiring the ornate red and white building or listening to a trio of musicians standing next to a statue in the centre. A clutch of tour guides loitered near the statue too, their small flags telling passers-by what language they offered: German, Russian and English. The statue was of Ronald, the same man I'd seen in Bremen's central square. This time he had a long white mane but still clutched a similar large shield and sword. According to legend, the length of his weapon was how all things in Latvia were once measured. The musicians finished their piece, a classical tune that pleased their audience. The tinkle of coins dropping in their case carried across the square.

I gazed at the distinctive red and white building. It was the House of the Blackheads, a relative newcomer to Riga's old town, despite its medieval appearance. When the Germans bombed Latvia during World War Two, their explosives demolished most of the original building. The Soviets finished the job during their occupation by blowing up the remaining walls. It was fifty years before the people of Riga commissioned a rebuild. Construction workers used the original plans of the House of the Blackheads to recreate the marvel I was now admiring. It looked as if it belonged in a theme park dedicated to King Arthur or inside a snow globe. Spindly spikes, carved statues, ornately decorated windows and the golden weather vanes on the top made it the most magnificent and photogenic building in Riga. The large blue-and-gold clock just added the icing on the cake. If Moscow had Saint Basil's, then Riga had the House of the Blackheads.

8

I was walking along a side street near the square when I saw an old woman dancing in the middle of the pavement across the road from me. At first I thought the pensioner was drunk, but then I noticed the towel on the ground. She was actually performing for money. In all my travels, I'd never witnessed an old lady trying to disco dance to a silent tune only she could hear. She looked ridiculous – pathetic, even – and I wondered what circumstances had led her to this. I crossed over and dropped a one-euro coin onto the towel. It joined a ten-cent coin. Her eyes flickered briefly in my direction but then became lost again. She flung her arms as she continued with her performance.

The other side of the river was a busy hotbed of tram and bus stops. I was heading to a tall spike in the distance. It looked like some sort of Soviet monument. After passing a railway museum and a bowling alley, the pain in my feet made me stop. They had been hurting for a while now, but the pounding I was currently giving them had evidently proved too much. I leaned against a tree and lifted each foot in turn to offer some relief from the blisters. It didn't really work and I had no choice but to carry on walking.

But it was worth it in the end. The spike revealed itself to be the central piece of the Soviet Victory Monument. As well as the jutting obelisk, a collection of Soviet statues stood at both ends. One side featured three angular-faced Red Army soldiers, all pulling proud gestures as they punched the air with their oversized fists. The statue at the other end was even better: Mother Russia. She was reaching skywards with unrestrained heroism. I loved it, and even the weeds poking through the rusting floor work could not dampen my enjoyment of the monument. Even better was that I was the only tourist there.

Later I learned that the Soviets had built the memorial in 1985 to commemorate their liberation of Latvia during the Second World War. It was a contentious issue then and still is today. Latvia's ethnic Russians see the monument as a sacred site for their brave and heroic countrymen. Latvians see it differently: a reminder of the old regime – deportation, imprisonment and repression. Things came to a head in 1997 when a Latvian nationalist group tried to blow the thing up. They failed and ended up blowing up two of their members instead.

9

In a pub in central Riga that evening, I ordered an Aldaris beer and sat at the bar. My feet were still hurting and I intended to sit still for an hour or so. As I was eyeing my fellow drinkers, most of whom seemed to be tourists, a man walked up to the bar and ordered a drink. He was thick set with bullish shoulders, brown hair and bright blue eyes. He was aged about forty. When he got his drink, he took a seat next to mine, cradling his vodka. Then he glanced in my direction and said something.

"Sorry," I replied.

The man switched to English. "Where you from?"

I told him, and he swirled his drink around. He looked inebriated, but not drunk. "Tell me, what do you think of Riga?"

"It's great. One of my favourite cities in Europe. There's so much to see and do."

The man didn't comment on that, but introduced himself as Pavel, an ethnic Russian. His face looked weather-beaten and dour. Maybe he was younger than forty, but a hard life had taken its toll. He downed his vodka in one and called the barman over. He spoke quickly to him and the barman nodded and returned with two glasses of vodka: one for him and one for me.

I didn't normally drink spirits but thanked Pavel for his generosity. He raised his glass to mine and downed it in one. He was a true Russian. I took a sip but Pavel scowled. "Drink in one, and then breathe through nose, not mouth."

I downed the white liquid, feeling the immediate burn in my throat. Then I breathed out through my nose. It didn't feel any different from breathing out through my mouth. As the pain subsided, Pavel ordered another round.

"No," I protested. "I have my beer."

"Nyet. Once vodka start, forget other drink."

After we'd downed another round of vodkas, things calmed down a bit. Pavel told me he worked in a factory that manufactured paint. He was the manager. "It dull work but it pay for my children's education." He told me he had learned English during a brief stint working in Chicago. "I was staying with my cousin but he did not want me there. After two years, I came back to Europe."

When Pavel discovered I'd been to Moscow, he nodded appreciatively. "My grandparents were born there. I've been many times. Now that is a beautiful city."

The conversation turned to how Russians felt about living in Latvia. Over forty percent of Riga's population were Russian, making them a sizeable minority. Pavel shook his head. "The government is trying to ban Russian language? Soon it will be illegal to order vodka if I ask for it in Russian." Speaking of vodka, I felt it only fair I should order a third round. Pavel would have none of it, saying I was his guest. A new drink appeared in front of me, my Aldaris now abandoned and growing warm. He said, "Already my children have lessons in Latvian language. They find this difficult to understand. But what can they do?"

I commiserated.

Pavel and I downed our third vodkas simultaneously. "In the newspaper not long ago, I read that a petition started for ethnic Russians to be put into concentration camps. Can you believe that?"

"Really? Concentration camps?" It hardly seemed credible.

"Bullshit, that's all it is. But it does tell you what some Latvians think of us, even though we were born here. They believe Putin is going to invade the Baltics like he has done in Crimea."

"Do you think that will happen?"

"Nyet. Latvia is part of NATO. Putin will not mess with NATO. It is just more bullshit from the Latvians."

Pavel looked like he was going to buy another round and I stopped him just in time. I lied and said I had a flight to catch and I didn't want to be late for it. He nodded and after we'd shaken hands, he returned his attention to the bar. I left him to his vodka and returned to the hotel, where I began packing. I found my little bottles of Riga Black Balsam and cracked one open as a nightcap. I took a sharp swig and coughed like a twenty-a-day man. I grimaced at the taste, but it wasn't as bad as I imagined it would be. It even had a slight coffee aftertaste, mixed with maybe a little marzipan and cough medicine for added spice. I took another swig and put it inside a clear plastic bag containing my liquids. It all went in the luggage.

So that was the fifth city finished, and the best one so far. Tomorrow would see me flying south west across Europe to a city not far from the Italian Alps. With vodka and balsam swishing around my stomach, I finished my packing and went to bed.

Top row: The Three Brothers; Mother Latvia standing atop the Freedom Monument; Soviet Victory Monument
Middle row: Laima Clock; House of the Blackheads with the spire of Saint Peter's on the left
Bottom row: Latvian Guard of Honour; The Powder Tower; View of Riga showing the Central Market and the River Daugava

Day 6. Bergamo, Italy

Riga – Milan Bergamo: Ryanair £35

I awoke to the shrill beeping of my alarm, which was a good thing because I had a flight to catch and |I'd have slept in otherwise. I showered, dressed and started filling my luggage with the various articles I'd left drying all over the room. My socks were dangling over the TV screen and a shirt was hanging in the bathroom.

Not even bothering with breakfast, I thought about finding a bus stop in the centre of town, but then got the hotel to order a taxi. My feet could not take the extra pounding of walking anywhere. Ten minutes later, I was speeding through the old town and thinking about the day ahead. I was flying to Milan with Ryanair, except their version of Milan meant Bergamo, a city forty kilometres away.

Riga Airport security was fine except for a purple-haired passenger carrying a mobile hairdressing salon inside her hand luggage. She even had a pot of cream that was so large that the man who found it held it up as if it were a chalice. When he informed her she couldn't take it through, the woman started arguing. Only the intervention of a second security official calmed things down. The woman accepted the loss and carried on through the metal detector.

It reminded me of a woman in China I'd read about. She had been about to fly with a $120 bottle of cognac stuffed in her hand luggage. When the airport staff told her she couldn't take it, she took drastic action. She grabbed the bottle, downed the lot. and collapsed to the floor. When the police arrived, they refused to let the sloshed woman travel and put her in a wheelchair instead, where she promptly fell asleep. Seven hours later, she woke up. After thanking the police for their assistance, she was released to her waiting, and highly embarrassed, family.

In departures, I calmed down following the annoyance of security. I always did, especially with a coffee in my hand. My flight was due to leave in forty minutes, which meant about fifteen minutes of relaxation before I'd have to find the gate. Many people, I knew, arrived at the airport a full three hours before their flight. Airports peddle the theory that three hours is the perfect amount of time to arrive before a flight. They say that this will allow passengers to have enough time to clear security and check-in. This is utter nonsense. Even the most hellish check-in counters will only delay a passenger for thirty minutes. Security will take the same time. So that's an hour at most. That leaves two hours to simply hang around inside the departure lounge. This is a good result for airport managers – they want passengers to kill time in their departure terminals. Without the income generated from the shops, restaurants and bars, airports would go bankrupt.

I finished my coffee just as the Ryanair Bergamo flight was called. I waited a full five minutes and then grabbed my luggage and walked to the gate. When I arrived, I noticed a Ryanair employee wandering along the line, putting yellow stickers on people's hand luggage. From what I could gather, the flight was full and so some people's hand luggage would have to go in the hold, free of charge. The Ryanair gate agent seemed to be looking for anyone with larger bags. He stopped at one passenger with a large rucksack. He gave it a yellow sticker and then informed the woman whose it was that she could collect it from the dreaded luggage carousel at the other end.

I joined the (by now) short line where my bag was given the once over. I fully expected to receive a yellow sticker, but the agent waved me through. I walked out to the aircraft and climbed the steps. When I found my seat, I was extra vigilant that it was the correct one, not wanting a repeat of the previous day's debacle. Soon after I'd buckled up, a crackling noise came through the intercom. It was an announcement from the flight deck that we were almost ready for departure. It was time to take off on my sixth flight in six days.

2

The face taunted me. Its mouth jeered and the eyes mocked.

Then it was gone.

Three seconds later, it was back. Knowing I was powerless to do anything, it ridiculed me. I tried to ignore the face, hoping it would go away, but it wouldn't. Like some terrible jack-in-the-box, it grinned and then sniggered.

I looked at the small boy and sighed. He was about three, and was standing on the chair in front so he could look back at me. When he'd first begun his antics, I tried smiling, hoping it would allay his behaviour. When this failed, I'd tried ignoring the little bastard, all to no avail. He wasn't bothering to look at the woman next to me because she was asleep. The man in the aisle seat next to her was deep in his novel. I was the focus of the boy's attention.

Why wasn't his mother doing anything? She was sitting next to him, clearly aware her son was annoying the person behind. In the end, he sat back down, but only because the fasten seatbelt sign chimed. I looked outside as we began our descent towards Italy.

As the Alps slipped in and out of view through the clouds, we flew into some turbulent air before entering the layer of white itself. The buffeting was immediate, something that always happened in dense cloud. After one particularly bad jolt, I was pleased to hear the boy in front yelp. Finally, he was getting a taste of his own sour medicine. When we cleared the cloud base, a large town appeared. Wondering whether it was Milan, Bergamo or somewhere else entirely, all I could do was wait for the landing, which arrived ten minutes later. I waited for the fanfare of trumpets and a rapturous round of applause. I wasn't disappointed.

3

Unlike in Riga, finding the airport bus was simple. A large sun-drenched sign told me that the stand for buses to Bergamo was on the far left. The other eight stands were for buses to Milan.

Twelve people were waiting for the Bergamo bus to arrive. Two of them were English. They were a middle-aged couple from the

Midlands who seemed flustered on how to purchase their tickets. I could hear them discussing their options. I'd already bought mine inside the terminal, but directed the couple to a machine at the other end of the bus stop.

"Thanks, pal," the man said. "Just to check, though, this is the bus for Milan, right?"

I shook my head. "This is for Bergamo. For Milan, you need to go over there." I pointed at a nearby Terravision bus, which said that a one-way ticket to Milan was five euros.

"Bloody wife's fault for this. Thanks again." They both toddled off with their cases.

The Bergamo bus came but there was nowhere for my luggage, so it ended up on my knee. We set off and, twenty minutes later, the bus stopped near a train station. Six passengers alighted, leaving four people still aboard, including me. With the bus going nowhere for the time being, I powered up my new mapping app and saw the hotel was a kilometre away. The question was, should I get off now or wait for the next stop, wherever that might be? I decided to alight now and manhandled the luggage off the bus with me.

Large groups of youths were hanging around by the train station. None paid me any attention as I clattered past, dragging the luggage past pizza shops, ice-cream emporiums and black men selling sunglasses from blankets. I walked by a bearded homeless man curled up near a tree. Other homeless men were sitting on a wall to my right. They were guzzling from beer bottles, and all seemed in high cheer, laughing rowdily at something. I walked on towards the hotel.

4

I quickly discovered that, unlike Moss or Nowy Dwor Mazowiecki, plenty of tourists actually come to Bergamo to *see* Bergamo, especially its old town. It was perched on some rocky high ground some distance away from my hotel. After throwing my luggage in my room, I grabbed my camera, my phone and was back out the door.

The sky looked uncomfortably overcast: a brooding swirl of grey that hovered over the horizon like an ominous presence. The cloud explained the high humidity in the air. I felt sticky and uncomfortable. Regardless, I walked up the slight gradient that formed a boulevard called Viale Papa Giovanni XXIII.

On the summit of a huge hill ahead of me was the medieval town of Bergamo: *Citta Alta*, the Upper City. It had the hallmarks of a grand European settlement: fetching pastel-coloured townhouses, sloping terracotta roofs and a series of beige towers and dramatic spires rising from the delightfully higgledy-piggledy outline. I decided there and then I liked Bergamo.

I liked it even more when I rounded a bend and saw that I wouldn't have to climb the hill using my own steam. A funicular railway offered a far more comfortable option. For less than two euros, I found myself standing inside the cramped compartment with a bunch of other tourists. The rules of funicular journeys were the same as elevators, I soon discovered.

The carriage deposited us in a square at the base of the upper town. It wasn't particularly large or even pretty, consisting mainly of cafes and souvenir shops. My fellow funicular passengers milled around, wondering which direction to choose. After a few seconds, most chose to go along an alleyway tucked between some tall buildings straight ahead. After a brief sniff of the air to get my bearings, I joined them.

Gelatos, souvenir shops (selling postcards, toy cars, jars of candy and Zippo lighters), tempting pizzerias and tiny cafes edged the narrow cobbled passageway. Families pushing prams and old folk doddering about with camcorders meant the route was a bottleneck. I failed to sidestep one old dear and almost collapsed into a shop. And then a car came from behind.

The elderly woman behind the wheel cared not a jot for the pedestrians she was inconveniencing, beeping her horn to move them to the side. She slid past me, but a thick jam of people soon forced her to stop. She gunned the accelerator to deliver a terrifying blast of engine noise to vent her anger. The crowd scattered immediately, and so she moved off again, this time at less than a walking pace. I had visions of the woman miscalculating her brake-accelerator combination and causing carnage. In the UK, there were always news stories about pensioners' cars ending up in the side of someone's house due to careless mistakes.

Somehow, she got through, mainly because everyone squeezed along the side of the passageway so she couldn't run them over. As her rear bumper receded into the distance, I came to the centre of the upper town, an attractive square called Piazza Vecchia.

5

People were crisscrossing the burgundy-tiled square en masse. Some had gathered around a white marble fountain in the middle to stroke the stone lion heads that guarded it. Opposite the fountain was a staircase lined with a series of pink and purple flower arrangements. Each one looked like an oversized pompom. Six or seven people were standing on the stairs, striking poses for cameras below.

I moved to the centre to take it all in. Bergamo's central square was one of the best I'd seen in a long time. Tall palaces with shuttered windows took up two sides of the square and, in one corner, a tall rectangular stone tower looked out over everything. I noticed a troop of blue robed nuns wandering around, snapping away on tiny digital cameras. One was finding the sightseeing so strenuous that she had to stop and wipe her brow with a flannel. I walked over to the steps with the pompom flowers and decided to climb them. At the half way stage, I stared down at the paparazzi, gratified to see a dozen cameras pointed my way. I smiled for them, wondering what they would think when they looked back at their photos and saw the strange man grinning next to their wife, husband or lover.

I looked for a good deed to do. I considered buying someone an ice cream, but quickly discounted this. If a strange man bought me an ice cream, I'd assume him a psychopath. I climbed back down the steps to find an opportunity. A young man was taking a photo of his girlfriend on the steps and I offered to take one of them both. After deeming me un-thief like, he passed his camera and they bolted up the steps. I took three photos, two normal ones, and a third framed at a wacky angle that they'd probably delete. I nodded to myself. These good deeds felt good.

At the far end of the square was a large stone atrium. A middle-aged man and woman were playing a flute and violin respectively: a fitting soundtrack to the classically themed buildings all around me. I walked past them, finding the Basilica di Santa Maria Maggiore and its small chapel through the other side. The basilica was almost pink in colour, adorned with statues, decorative arches and a fabulous circular window in the middle that looked like a porthole. I decided to give it nine out of ten for its looks. In fact, it reminded me of some buildings I'd once seen in Venice, and well it might, because the Venetian Republic had ruled Bergamo from 1428 until 1797. I went inside, finding the nuns already there. We all gazed up at the high vaulted ceiling, then at the vibrant tapestries, the vivid frescos and the abundance of sculptures. One of the nuns whipped out her camera and took a photo. I did too. When they wandered over to light some candles, I headed back outside.

I decided to climb the stone tower in the corner. After negotiating a set of steps, I emerged onto a draughty viewing platform. Above me dangled a set of massive bells. Two teenage girls were at the other end of the platform looking down. I looked down too. Virtually the whole of the old town was below me: gorgeous stone buildings, spiky towers and tall chimney pots. I stared at a gold man sitting on top of a bulbous dark green dome. He looked a dandy with his feathered hat and cloak. Just then, the bells tolled. They produced the loudest sound I'd heard in years, and a split second later, screams accompanied the clangs. Both teenagers were shrieking in terror, one crouching on the stone floor in shock. With hands covering her ears, her friend joined her, where they both cracked out laughing. I wasn't laughing, though, because my fillings were shaking loose. The noise was horrendous. ACDC had got it exactly right with *Hell's Bells*; I was staring right at them.

Back at ground level, I watched some men placing rows of chairs in the shaded stone atrium. The musicians had moved on. At the front was a wide curtained box, large enough to fit a person, perhaps a man armed with a set of puppets. As soon as the chairs were down, people began sitting down, all facing the front with expectant faces. When nothing happened, I left the square to find other sights of Bergamo. I'd have a look later if time permitted.

6

Higher in the town, I found a second funicular railway. According to the sign near it, there was a castle further up the hill. Even better was that it was about to set off and so I jumped aboard. I was delighted to find the carriage mostly empty and so I stood behind the driver. As we set off, I watched him, wondering how hard it was to control a funicular carriage. Not very, I concluded; the man simply sat there and did nothing. Not once did he touch any of the dials, knobs or buttons on his dashboard. His only job, as far as I could tell, was pressing a button that opened the door when it stopped.

I left the carriage, rounded a bend and found myself face to face with a tall stone wall and round tower. It looked satisfyingly castle-like, even if it was undergoing some restoration work. I managed to find my way to the top of the tower, where the view was great, offering an unbroken panorama of the old town, the surrounding countryside and the newer part of Bergamo below. For a moment, I felt a twang of sadness that I was experiencing this by myself. Angela should be with me to savour the view, to enjoy the old-worldliness of the old town. Instead, I was alone.

Half an hour later, I was back at the funicular station, waiting for the return journey. Suddenly, I felt something slip down my leg. A coin had fallen through a hole in my pocket. I picked it up, placed it in the other pocket and investigated. The hole wasn't actually in the pocket as such, but in the lining. My camera must have ripped it. As I pondered this, the man in charge of the funicular declared it was open for business. Since I hadn't bought a ticket for the return journey, and did not know how much one cost anyway, I waited for everyone else to board and then held out a handful of change for the man to sift through. He looked at the coins but decided he couldn't be bothered with the hassle and so waved me through for free. I pocketed the cash, pulled my stomach in and squeezed aboard the packed-to-capacity carriage, taking up position behind the driver's compartment again.

Two little girls, sitting just inches away, studied me. That was when I felt all the coins in my pocket slip down my leg. I tensed, waiting for the resulting clatter, but there was none. They were either precariously balanced on my shoe or had somehow collected inside my socks. I stood stock-still.

I spied the driver walking towards the train. He stepped aboard but because I was pressing against his driver's compartment door, he couldn't get to his seat. He waited for me to move but there was no room for me to do so. He gestured that I should step outside the carriage.

Without a good reason not to, I gingerly raised my right foot a millimetre, waiting for the tell-tale sound of escaping money. I probably had about twelve euros in change dangling in my leg. None rattled and so – ever so carefully – I manoeuvred myself away from the driver's door as sweat began to bubble on my forehead. This is what bomb disposal experts experienced, I thought. The wire cutters were dangling over the red wire. With the little girls watching me intently, I backed out of the carriage like a man with wooden legs, unable to comprehend why the money had not cascaded out of the bottom of my trousers yet. I stood on the thin platform with my limbs tensed and my feet anchored to the spot. The driver squeezed past me and then tapped my shoulder. This action was all it took to upset my fragile equilibrium and all the coins tumbled out onto the platform, some rolling down onto the tracks. All eyes were now upon me for I was a human slot machine paying out good money. With nothing to lose now, I scrambled about on the floor picking up the highest denominations before reclaiming my place at the front. Job done, I wiped my brow, formed a stiff upper lip and waited for the embarrassment to die down to manageable levels.

7

Back in Piazza Vecchia, the puppet show had still not started but the audience had grown immensely. There were no empty chairs left, which forced about fifty people to stand behind and around them. Altogether, I judged over two hundred people were waiting for the entertainment to begin. Glancing at my watch, I noticed it was a quarter to five and so decided to wait fifteen minutes to see what all the fuss was about. If it hadn't begun by then, I would call it a day.

I found a vantage spot near one of the atrium columns. Behind me, the sky was darkening but the ice cream vendors were still doing a roaring trade. I quite fancied one myself but, just as I was about to buy one, the show finally started. Punch appeared from behind the top of the curtains, receiving a rapturous round of applause. The puppet scurried about, jabbering in Italian, stopping at either end of his podium to squeak and holler. The kids in the audience loved it, especially when a second puppet appeared carrying a bomb. It had a sparkler in the end. I decided enough was enough, bought myself an ice cream and set off down the hill.

A hundred yards from the hotel, the sky unleashed its torrent, followed by an ear-splitting clap of thunder. I'd not heard thunder so loud since visiting the tropics. And now I had two options: run or walk. I tried the former but my feet would not allow such abuse and so I admitted defeat and got soaked. By the time I got to the hotel, I was dripping from head to toe.

8

That evening, the storm continued unabated. Flashes of lighting lit the upper town of Bergamo, making it look like a village in a Frankenstein film. I donned my cap and, running between the cover of shop awnings, found a small cafe close to my hotel. I ordered a pizza.

Mealtimes are always the worst thing about travelling alone. And it didn't help that I was feeling so weary and my feet were throbbing. In fact, I felt *fatigued*. When my pizza arrived, I began chewing away on the rubbery dough as the rain threw itself down outside. I began to feel fed up. There were still ten countries to go: a daunting number that made me sigh and want to give up there and then. At the rate I was going, I'd be exhausted in four days' time. I finished my meal and headed back into the storm.

Later, I rang Angela and told her of my feelings. She tried to buoy me with talk of all the exciting things I'd see in places such as Carcassonne and Athens, adding that most people would give their right arm to visit some of the cities I was getting to.

"I know all of that," I said, "but my mistake is doing this all so quickly. A country a day is insane."

"Well I did warn you about that. But look, it'll be finished before you know it. Ten days is just over a week. And then you can relax and show me the photos."

Later, I slept fitfully as rain pounded the window. When sleep did overcome me, my imagination saw me battling gigantic puppets wearing Ryanair uniforms as they giggled and popped up from behind yellow chairs. Flying low-cost airlines every day was clearly affecting my mind.

Top row: View of Citta Alta – Bergamo's old city; Nuns on the run
Middle row: Wandering the old city; Detail on Bergamo Cathedral
Bottom row: The prettiness of Piazza Vecchio; Golden statue on the top of Bergamo Cathedral

Day 7. Bratislava, Slovak Republic

Milan Bergamo – Bratislava: Ryanair: £21

I woke up feeling like a rock star.

I'd read somewhere that when on long world tours, band members often wake up not knowing which city they are in. To help them remember, tour managers slip pieces of paper under hotel room doors so that, when the rock stars wake up, they will know where they are. When my eyes fluttered open, I didn't know where I was. And then it came to me. I was in northern Italy and I had another flight to catch.

My watch told me it was almost 10.30am. I'd slept for ten hours and so I tentatively curled my toes, feeling a hot slice of pain shoot to my shins. I felt my calf muscles tense and I wondered whether to bother getting up, because my flight wasn't until four in the afternoon. After ten minutes of dozing, I got up and looked outside. It was overcast and drizzly, but at least the storm had moved on. I pottered around for another hour, allowing my feet to become accustomed to my roused state, then decided I needed some food – in particular, some fruit. The last time I'd had a piece of fruit was back in England. I squeezed into my shoes and winced at the pain from around the toes. When I walked, stabbing pains flared up to my hip.

I managed to hobble to a small supermarket around the corner from the hotel and traipsed the aisles filling my basket with bread, ham, a couple of chocolate bars and two bananas. And that was when I did my good deed of the day. An elderly woman in front of me couldn't reach some olive oil and so I did it for her. She thanked me in Italian, gushing praise my way as if I had saved her son from drowning. Deed done, I returned to the hotel with my bounty, feasting on a breakfast costing a fraction of what the hotel would have charged.

The airport bus stop was opposite my hotel. A few people were waiting with me. One was a young woman in a Ryanair uniform. She was deftly rolling herself a cigarette. There was an older couple and a few men of mixed ages too. Just then, another young woman arrived pulling a small suitcase behind her. She immediately became the centre of attention for all male eyes because she was wearing the tightest pink dress available in Italy. One man, wearing a Mona Lisa T-shirt with a difference (she had her boobs out), almost dribbled. Miss Ryanair caught sight of the newcomer and, after looking her up and down, breathed out a lungful of smoke in dismissal.

The bus rolled up five minutes later, which was a good job because it was starting to rain. I didn't have a ticket, so planned to buy one from the driver. Miss Pink boarded first, then the Ryanair girl. Both simply walked past the driver and sat some distance apart. A man with a backpack was next. He didn't have a ticket either, and asked the driver whether he could buy one.

The driver shook his head. "I no sell the ticket."

"Where I can buy one from, then?" the backpacker asked with a Germanic accent. "Because there is no machine at this stop."

The driver pointed up the road, towards the train station.

The backpacker sighed. "So you will not let me get on the bus? Even if I pay you the money?"

The driver shook his head. "Not without ticket."

The young man muttered something under his breath and then barged his way off the bus, looking about as pissed off as anyone could. I didn't blame him. What a farcical situation it was. But I had the same problem. Instead of asking the driver for a ticket, I confidently walked past him and simply found a seat. The driver didn't say anything and, if a ticket inspector came on board, I would smile and plead foreigner ignorance. But none did, and the bus pulled up outside the airport terminal twenty minutes later.

3

Bergamo Airport was home to quite a few low-cost airlines. Ryanair had flights to Krakow, Rhodes and Mallorca, as well as my destination: Bratislava. Wizz Air flew to Prague while Meridian (an Italian low cost airline) had planes flying to Sharm el Sheik. With so many flights at the same time, the departure lounge was heaving. Mine was leaving first, so I decided to get something to eat before I boarded.

At a McDonald's counter, I ordered a Big Mac without mayonnaise. As usual, this garnered a look of confusion from the teenager working behind the counter.

"No mayonnaise," I repeated, swishing my hands apart in a gesture that hopefully conveyed I did not want any white condiment.

"Err, the berger come with the mayonnaise already, prego!"

I smiled and sighed, wishing I knew the word for 'no' in Italian. His supervisor came over, and I repeated the message to her. I added that I had an allergy to eggs, which, though not entirely true, brought about some discussion between the teenager and the boss. Eventually the woman turned back to me. "You have the allergic to the chicken, yes?"

I nodded. "The egg that comes from the chicken, yes."

"Okay. So a Big Mac without the sauce, yes?"

I thanked her, pleased that everything had gone so well.

After eating my food, I stood up. I knew which gate my flight was leaving from without even looking. The stupidly long queue gave the game away. I recalled an article I'd read in a UK tabloid that quoted something a Ryanair captain had posted on his own Facebook page. The pilot had taken a photo of a Ryanair queue and written: 'You now have seat assignments, so why are you still queuing up like morons? Please locate your brains.' When the newspaper printed this, a furore erupted, calling for the man's resignation. In the end, though, the pilot kept his job because he was entirely right.

Ten minutes later, before the departing passengers had even left the plane, the line started to move. This action brought a raft of stragglers who had been waiting in the wings. One man in the queue was wearing a Panama hat. He carried it off well, mainly due to his age – early sixties, I guessed. Panama hats ought to come with an age restriction. No one under fifty should ever attempt to wear a Panama hat – not even in Panama City, as I had. In a moment of pure folly, I'd bought one there a few years previously, believing it would give me the air of a seasoned traveller. The photos my wife took proved otherwise and I hadn't worn it since. I was going to give it a second try on my sixtieth birthday.

I ignored the queue and found a seat instead. I was on a mission today. I wanted to be the very last passenger to board. When the final announcement came over the speaker system, a few more people joined the fray, which was now down to the final stragglers. Two minutes later, I stood and wheeled my luggage towards the gate. I was the last passenger. A woman in Ryanair uniform scanned my boarding card and checked my passport. Then I felt a presence behind me. I turned to see a large-bellied man wearing a blue cap, green T-shirt and white Adidas trainers. He looked about fifty and, though I may have imagined it, I saw him smile at me: a sneer of victory. I turned away, but worse was to come. I was about to experience my most miserable boarding experience ever.

4

The monsoon outside was partly to blame. Because of it, Ryanair had provided a bus so that we would not have to walk to the plane. However, because only around fifty or so passengers at a time could use the bus, a second queue was now in operation. What a cruel twist of fate it was to escape the gate queue to find myself at the rear of the bus queue. When it was almost my turn to board, I saw that the bus was parked some distance away from the terminal exit. To reach it, a mad dash through the rain would be necessary. I watched the people at the front hunch their shoulders as they ran for it. A couple behind them utilised hand luggage as shields. One passenger had brought a raincoat with him, complete with hood, which I thought showed great forward thinking. When it was my turn, I simply walked. The fat-bellied man in the Adidas shoes ran past me at top speed, his cap shielding him from most of the deluge. So I was the last man to board, after all.

The bus was crammed to capacity. When the doors closed, it caused an immediate rush of condensation that coated the windows. Even so, I could see enough outside to tell that the bus was taking a long-winded journey to the aircraft. First, we circled a Wizz Air plane, then a Ryanair one before finally stopping by a third airliner. As everyone tensed in preparation for the doors opening (and the resulting mad rush that would ensue), the bus moved off again. It was all very strange.

Then I realised what was happening. Due to the horrendous weather, the cabin crew had abandoned the standard open-air steps in favour of some heavy-duty covered ones. We were waiting for someone to fit them into place. By the time our bus finished a few more circuits, they were ready for action and we stopped near them. Everyone prepared for battle.

It was like waiting for the starter gun. We all knew that those who delayed or were too tardy in their exit would suffer two things: they would get drenched and would lose vital cabin bag space – an unbearable combination. People began crowding the doors in anticipation. When the hydraulic systems lowered the bus, we knew the time was imminent.

And then the doors whooshed open.

A human tidal wave was unleashed, surging towards the steps, wanting to reach the sanctuary of the protective shield before anyone else. Stupidly, I dawdled, worried I might be caught in the no-man's land between the bus and the steps. The mob of people behind me pushed me out anyway. I ran for my life.

All around me, veterans of rugby scrums and January sales leapt forward, landing on the steps like panthers, forcing me to stop in the open air. As I'd predicted, I was exposed to the wind, the cold and, worst of all, the rain. I couldn't return to the bus because of the people behind, and I couldn't move forward because there was no room. I tried to move forward an inch but couldn't. Water was dripping down my head, splashing into my ears and sluicing down my neck. I was a broken man, and that's when I noticed my nemesis. He was standing inside the dry entrance of the bus, his large Adidas trainers poised for action. I felt like kicking a puddle in his direction.

By now, I was two people behind the start of the steps, waiting to jump in the first chance I got. Next to me, in third place, was a woman carrying a baby. Like me, she was soaked, her hair dripping like a mop, but her baby was toasty dry inside its wrappings. When the queue moved forward, I offered her my place, doing my third good deed in Bergamo. She took it with thanks and slipped in front and, while she did so, a nudge on my left shoulder meant someone was trying to slip in on my unguarded flank. I barged the shoulder back in retaliation and was gratified to feel the presence behind recede. The respite didn't last long, though: a white Adidas shoe appeared in front of my feet, not to trip me up, but to stake their claim on the first step. I was having none of it and so, in an unprecedented move, I dropped my luggage on the foot. It retreated and I stepped forward into the protection of the stair-cover and onto the first step. A few minutes later, I entered the aircraft in jubilation and took my aisle seat. Three or four people later, my nemesis trudged down the aisle. He was saturated.

5

"Good afternoon from the flight deck," said an Irish voice. "This is your captain speaking. Sorry for the delay with getting you aboard – but as you know, the rain was holding things up a little. But with a flight time today of one hour and five minutes, we should get you to Bratislava on time. And you'll be pleased to hear there is no rain there. Just to let you know, though, the initial departure may get a little bumpy, but nothing to worry about. So sit back, relax and enjoy the flight."

The take-off wasn't as bad as I'd feared, and soon we were climbing over the cloud layer to enjoy bright blue sky. While the cabin crew busied themselves with their tasks, I saw the man in the Adidas shoes rush down the aisle. At first, I thought he was coming to find me, but he was running for the toilet. When he returned, he looked ashen, and I felt a little bit sorry for him. The worst time to have a dicky stomach had to be when cooped up inside a plane. He sat down just as the scratch cards came out. A member of the cabin crew wandered the aisle with an array of them spread out like a Japanese fan. Unbelievably, someone bought one. The cabin crew member looked as astonished as me.

Whoever had bought the card would probably not win anything. If they did, they might decide to eat the card instead, which is what happened in 2010 when a man flying from Poland to the UK ate his. He had just bought a Ryanair scratch card telling him he'd won €10,000. When he handed it to the cabin crew, they told him he couldn't have the money because they did not carry such a large amount of cash in the air with them. He would have to claim his prize from the scratch card company instead. The man did not accept this news graciously. In front of his fellow bemused passengers, he stood in the aisle and scoffed the card in protest.

Drastic action, I'm sure, and one the man probably ended up regretting, but the scratch cards have caused other controversy too. For a start, no one has ever won the grand prize of €1 million in the eight years of the cards' existence. And that is despite over two million cards being sold. This is *bad* odds. But it is not surprising. To win the million euros, first the buyer has to scratch a YES on the card. The chances of this are minuscule. But if someone is lucky enough to reveal a YES, then Ryanair makes them attend an event where 125 envelopes await them. Inside one of these envelopes is the big cheque. The other 124 contain cheques for €10,000. Of course, ten grand isn't bad, but if I bought a scratch card and it said *Win €Million*, and then I scratched a big fat YES, I'd assume I had hit the jackpot. To be then told I had to go to some trumped-up event to pick out the right envelope didn't seem right or fair. Critics of Ryanair's scratch cards agree and have called for an investigation.

Thirty minutes later, we landed in Bratislava, a city I'd visited many years previously with a bunch of mates. The old town had impressed me back then, with its dollhouse buildings and friendly bars. I was looking forward to seeing it all again.

I waited for the clapping to start as we turned onto the taxiway, but there was only polite conversation. I looked at my watch: we were dead on time, and I wondered why the cabin crew hadn't played the trumpets. Then, as if a switch had been flipped, the brass resounded in its full glory, followed by the longest round of cabin applause I had heard so far.

"Welcome to Bratislava," said a woman's voice, "where the local time is ten minutes to six in the evening..."

I zoned out the voice and prepared myself for another country.

6

I exited arrivals and found the tourist information desk. I wanted to know the best way to get into the centre of the city. The woman explained there was a bus that left in a few minutes' time, and it would drop me off at the train station. "From there," she added, "you will need to get another bus to your hotel."

Two buses sounded like too much effort. I asked her about a taxi.

"Taxis go from outside, but they are very expensive, I would advise you to get the bus, it is only a few euros."

I thanked her and wandered to the taxi stand. A driver looked at the name of my hotel and quoted the ridiculous price of thirty euros.

"Thirty euros? But it's only a ten minute drive."

"More like fifteen to twenty. But that is the price and it is fixed – look."

A nearby sign backed up his claim. I decided to try the bus, which was parked over on my right. Virtually all of my fellow Ryanair passengers were already on board. I grabbed a seat, stuffed the luggage between my knees and waited to set off. When we did, I found out that the journey to downtown Bratislava involved a zigzag that paused at every stop between the airport and the railway station.

A few passengers alighted at a graffiti-splattered bus stop, the fifth one we had stopped at in five minutes. I stared outside. Away from the central core, Bratislava was a grimy industrial city full of ugly apartment blocks and tram wires. But at least the sun was shining. I sat back waiting for the journey to begin again and wondering what would happen when we reached the train station.

Half an hour later, we finally got there. All the remaining passengers left the bus and fanned out in different directions. I noticed a couple of taxis parked nearby, but leaving them, I powered up my Sat Nav app to see where I was. It said my hotel was 1.4km away, which didn't sound too bad, even with my aching feet. I decided to walk.

At first, the hike wasn't too bad. The incline was gentle and the path of good quality: exactly the sort of surface I liked when dragging luggage. When my app told me I'd walked 0.3km, I felt I was in control of things. Yes, it was a bit humid and, yes, the luggage seemed to be getting heavier, but, all told, I was in good spirits.

Five minutes later, the first beads of sweat made an appearance. And, since I was the only person lugging luggage along the street, quite a few citizens of Bratislava were noticing me. Most people seemed amused, probably wondering why I hadn't caught a taxi, and while I pondered this myself, my luggage decided to act up. It was almost imperceptible at first, and I hardly noticed, but half a kilometre later, I couldn't ignore it. Instead of rolling freely, the wheels seemed jammed. I stopped to kick them, hoping to dislodge a stone or something, but it made no difference and so, to punish the bag, I dragged its sorry ass through a puddle. Maybe one of the wheels was loose, I considered. The last thing I needed was to buy some new luggage mid-trip. That thought made me slow down, and when I came to the next kerb, instead of roughly hoisting it up without pause, I lifted it.

With half a kilometre still to go, and my feet aching like mad, the luggage was really starting to annoy me. I might as well be dragging a large bag of potatoes along with me, and when the incline of the road shifted upwards, the potatoes morphed into heavy rocks. With sweat now freely pouring down my face, I lumbered through a concrete underpass, finding an uphill cobbled path on the other side. It was so rough and uneven that I ended up carrying the luggage despite the pain in my feet, legs, back and arms. With salt stinging my eyes and my T-shirt sodden from the exertion, I hated the luggage and its despicable wheels. By the time I reached the steps of the hotel, I was in the foulest of foul moods. This was not what I signed up for when I'd planned this trip. I'd planned on sitting in a bar in the old town, sipping on cooling Zlaty Bazants, not staggering into a hotel looking like I'd run a marathon.

Thinking of the beer suddenly made me dizzy with thirst and the only thing I wanted now was to get to my room so I could crack open a bottle of water hidden in the depths of my luggage. I entered the hotel, where more hell awaited.

7

Three large men wearing motorcycle leathers and carrying helmets stood by the counter. One had skull tattoos around his neck. When he spoke to the young man behind the desk, he sounded Russian or Ukrainian. From what I could gather, the trio were checking into three separate rooms, which they thought they had already paid for.

"You have only paid for two," said the young man, "Which is okay if two of you share. But if you want the third room, you will have to pay. I'm sorry."

I sighed and shuffled my aching feet. I was sweating like someone who ought to be in hospital. I needed water desperately but had to wait while the men conferred. They took a good while doing this before agreeing to pay for the room. This involved a protracted scrabble about in their belongings until one produced a credit card. It did not work and so they had to search for another.

By this point, I was ready to burst a blood vessel. I had just walked a mile in the heat of an August summer with Satan's luggage along for the ride, and the last thing I needed was this infernal delay. I must have huffed and puffed a bit too loud, because one of the men turned around. I looked at my feet. Finally, they walked to the lift.

It was my turn to check in. The young man didn't say anything about my appearance and quickly processed me, passing me the key. Finally, I could get a drink of water and end the rabies-like madness.

"All I need is the city tax, sir," he said, stopping me in my tracks. "One euro, seventy-five cents."

"Okay. I'll pay later." My voice cracked with dryness.

The man shook his head. "I'm sorry, sir, but you must pay now."

I looked at him wildly. "I have no change." Sweat was dribbling into my eyes, anger flowing into my brain.

"We accept credit card payments, sir." He was a jobsworth of the highest order.

I glared at him. "Really? You can't wait until tomorrow?"

He shook his annoying head. "Sorry."

I slammed the key on his desk and grabbed my wallet. I took bitter satisfaction in passing him a 100-euro note even though I had a five in my wallet. He looked surprised, but elected to say nothing. He then had to open a safe to give me my €98.85 change. I snatched it from his grasp and hurried to the lift. When I pressed the button, the door opened straightaway, revealing the Russians. Why they had taken so long was a mystery, but they moved over to allow me in. It was another ride in silence, except for the dripping of sweat landing on my luggage.

8

Bratislava's old town was beautiful, like a fairy-tale land of *olden day* Europe. It was also exceedingly compact. Every side street (each as picture-postcard pretty as the next) led towards the heart of the city: the stunning central square.

I'd calmed down since my arrival. To reach this nirvana, I had lain down on the bed for a full fifteen minutes and then had a shower to cool off the last vestiges of fire. Afterwards, I'd checked the luggage for damage, discovering one of the four wheels was loose. It had wedged itself into the side of its bracket. I pulled it back into position but knew it would not last long; a portion of the metal screw had sheared off. And it had seven more countries to go. I laid it flat to ease its pain.

The main square was busy with tourists, tour groups and people sitting in bars, waffle shops or cafes. A trio of elderly women had elected to sit on a bench overlooked by a bronze, life-size representation of a Napoleonic soldier, a reminder of a time when French troops had besieged Bratislava. The pensioners were staring at the Old Town Hall, one of Slovakia's oldest stone buildings. Its tall yellow tower adjoined a larger white section. A dramatically sloping orange roof topped it off. In front was a stage. As in Bergamo, a sizeable audience was already waiting even though no one was playing or performing. Bratislava's central square reminded me of a TV program I watched as a child: *Trumpton*. All it needed was the fire brigade brass band to walk onto the stage.

A waft of hot waffles and coffee washed over me and I could not believe how much my mood had altered in just forty-five minutes. But the aromas reminded me I'd not eaten in a while. I grabbed a large slice of pizza from a little store just off the square, eating it near a strange statue depicting a bronze man called Cumil climbing out of a manhole. While I ate, I watched the people of Bratislava pass me by: young lovers, families with children, groups of men, elderly couples and long-haired girls dancing the cobbles in their heels, lipstick and perfume.

A skinny dog slunk past. It glanced at the pizza shop but then lowered its head in resignation that it wasn't going to get any. Instead, it sat by the kerb and scratched itself. This was my chance to do a good deed. Nothing in the rulebook said good deeds had to be performed on people, and so I went back into the pizza joint and bought a second slice. The dog was still outside; when it saw me approach, it looked fearful, but then its hunger took over, and it looked alert. I put the slice of pizza down on the ground and it immediately stood up and grabbed it, scoffing it down in two seconds.

Back in the square, an acoustic band were in full swing. The lead vocalist was singing in Slovakian, but the melody was easy to follow. I watched them awhile as the sun went down, clapping with everyone else after each song. Then I decided to find somewhere to get a drink. As the light faded over central Europe, Bratislava's bars were getting busy. Many patrons were young men, but none looked like stag parties, or, if they were, then they were all well behaved. I bypassed an Irish Pub, and then the Loch Ness Scottish Pub before settling on a quieter bar around the corner. I found an empty table and ordered a Zlaty Bazant, pleased to find that the cost of alcohol had plummeted since leaving Italy. When the drink came, I toasted myself at having survived another day in Europe.

9

"You sit alone," the man said in accented English. "I sit alone, and I think, this is not right, so I come over to talk with you." He introduced himself as Jozef, a Slovak businessman. He looked about my age.

Jozef told me he was a citizen of Košice, in Eastern Slovakia close to the Hungarian border. He was in Bratislava on business, which involved some aspect of steel manufacturing. When he found out I was in Bratislava for just one night, he looked incredulous. This changed to outright disbelief when I told him of the ridiculous trip I was on.

"You are a monster!" he guffawed. "A travelling monster!"

Jozef was a little bit drunk. He sat down and then started eyeing most of the girls wandering past, giving a commentary about each, despite the wedding band on his finger. *Big breasts and big nose. Nice legs but too small in the arse. Thick lips and tiny waist – just right for me.* He was the Goldilocks of sleaze.

When he ceased staring at Bratislava's female folk, I mentioned that I'd been to Slovakia before. I said, "One thing I remember is how cheap the taxi was from the airport. Not like now."

Jozef nodded. "When we changed to the Euro, prices went up by twenty percent. But our wages dropped by the same amount. But things are okay now." He told me that his job paid him well, meaning his children could go to university and his wife could buy 'stupid stuff for the house'.

"Bratislava is a rich city," he told me, swishing his bottle around. "People who work here can earn much money. Everything is so close, you see. Budapest is two hours away by car, Vienna an hour. If the government can sort out unemployment, especially in the east of the country, then the Slovak Republic will be a powerhouse of central Europe."

Jozef had referred to his country as the *Slovak Republic*, and so I asked him whether Slovakia was also an acceptable term.

"Slovak Republic is better," answered Jozef.

"Most people in the UK would say Slovakia."

My new friend considered this. "Slovakia is okay, but I think Slovak Republic is better. It's what the politicians use."

A drop of rain landed on my face, and then another. Jozef felt some too because he lifted his palm and nodded knowingly. "This is the first rain we have had in a long time. It has been too hot, maybe 37 degrees on some days, so it is good that it rains; it will cool the city down. But here's something you may not know. When it rains in the Slovak Republic, we call it *happiness day.*" In the distance was a crack of thunder.

"Happiness day? Because of the crops?"

"That's right." Jozef picked up his bottle and took a large glug. "In England, it would be happiness day every second day, I think."

I laughed. But how nice that a nation thought rain was something joyful. In the UK, rain was depressing, a constant scourge on the landscape. With the drizzle getting heavier, I looked at my watch and realised it was time to go. I finished my drink and shook Jozef's hand. He'd been a fine companion for my short time in Bratislava.

On the way back to the hotel, I passed a large, neon-lit sign for an establishment called the Carat Club. The scantily clad girl on the poster left little to the imagination, and neither did the red lights and laser show illuminating from an upstairs window. The stag groups (and perhaps even Jozef) would be there later.

I wandered past the tramlines towards my hotel. Ahead of me, up on a dark craggy hill, was Bratislava Castle. There had been no time to visit it on this trip. Suddenly, a flash of lightning lit the sky, turning it from black to blue and white, all in the space of a second. The storm was getting closer. I rushed to reach the steps of the hotel. Another night, another hotel, another country.

Top row: Bratislava's magnificent Old Town Hall; Night falls over downtown Slovakia
Middle row: Cumil climbing out of his manhole; Bratislava coat of arms
Bottom row: Peaceful cafes are plentiful in the Slovak capital; Saint Michael's Gate – the start of the old town

Day 8. Charleroi, Belgium

Bratislava – Brussels Charleroi: Ryanair £21

I woke up feeling fed up again. The reason was self-evident: it was my birthday and I was going to be spending it alone in a foreign city. And not just any foreign city, but Charleroi, one I knew next to nothing about apart from that it was in Belgium. I opened my laptop to find out more.

Charleroi, it turned out, was the fourth largest city in Belgium. It was, by most accounts, a dump, long past its heyday, with some of the highest unemployment rates in Belgium. The city was wallowing in its faded industrial past and only had one tourist site of note – a photography museum. In 2010, a Dutch newspaper described Charleroi as the *'ugliest city in the world'*. More recently, a reviewer of the city said that the train station was the best thing to visit because it meant you were leaving. A travel piece in The Guardian offered the starkest advice for anyone visiting: 'An overnight stay in Charleroi is only recommended for the hardiest of travellers.' And yet, despite all this, an enterprising local man had set up a tour company. His tour offered an urban safari of Charleroi, which promised to show visitors the 'most depressing street in Belgium', the chance to climb 'a waste coal pile' and a trip to an 'abandoned metal factory' as the grand finale. I was tempted to email him, but by the time he opened the message, I would already be there. I rubbed my temples and closed my laptop. It was going to be a depressing day.

My phone rang. It was my wife, Angela. After wishing me a happy birthday and asking me to try on the T-shirt she'd bought (which had been lying inside my suitcase for this very occasion), she asked how things were going.

"Not so good, actually," I answered. "I'm tired and I don't want to go to Belgium."

"Look, I've been thinking: if you manage to last until Budapest, I can meet you there. I've looked at some flights and found a cheap one. Besides, I quite fancy a bit of European shopping. And then I'll fly to Dublin with you. We can have some Guinness to celebrate you reaching the finish line."

I took this in. To have my wife with me for the final two countries would be great, better than great: amazing. All I had to do was get through the next six days and she would meet me in Hungary.

"Really?" I said.

"Yes really. But I'm only going to book it if you promise not to give up before Budapest."

I was almost giddy with joy, but now I needed to change my single hotel rooms in Budapest and Dublin to doubles. When Angela put the phone down, I busied myself with my new task. And then it was time to head to the airport.

2

As soon as I entered the terminal, I switched to autopilot until I cleared security. On the other side, I bought a coffee, found a table and rested. If there had been a bed at the gate, I would have been on it, snoring within seconds.

My wife complained about my snoring and I'd tried all sorts of remedies. I'd tried nasal strips, nasal sprays and a peculiar mouth guard (which made my lower jaw jut out like a Neanderthal), but all had failed miserably. But the worst snore remedy was the gimp mask. Its black Velcro strap, sturdy fabric chin guard and disturbing head straps made it look like the apparel of a deviant. I wore the device three nights in a row and then threw it in the wardrobe. The only time I said I'd take it out was when Angela and I went on a camping trip with some friends and I threatened to wear it on the campsite when walking about at night.

An airport announcement pulled me from my stupor. A tinny voice was telling me that the gate for the Ryanair flight to Brussels

Charleroi was now open. I finished my coffee and wandered over to have a gander. Once there, I discovered that Bratislava Airport had a novel approach to controlling large masses of people waiting for a flight. There was still the same queue, of course, but instead of it leading to a dim corridor, it fed into to an open air holding pen. The pen had seats, but nowhere near enough to cater for all the passengers. I estimated about eighty people had bagged a seat, with another fifty left standing, all looking thoroughly miserable. I watched them from a small cafe opposite.

Boarding was on time. Instead of a Ryanair plane, it said Air Explore on the side. Gone was the yellow, blue and white design, replaced by an almost white paint job with a globe on the tail. Later, I found out that Air Explore was a small Slovakian charter company who leased their aircraft to boost other airlines' schedules in busy periods.

In the cabin, a gaunt man with long, tied-back hair was causing a blockage. He was trying to stuff his massive cabin bag into a space designed for something half the size. He pushed, heaved and then turned the thing sideways, stopping everyone behind him from taking their seats. While we waited, he tried again, this time shoving with primeval brute force. It was like shoving a square peg into a circular hole, and I wondered how the gate staff had missed his bag. If ever a piece of luggage deserved to go in the hold, then this was it. Aware, but unconcerned that we were caught in his bottleneck, he turned the bag upside down, hoping that would help. It didn't; it resolutely refused to fit into the compartment. Finally, a male member of the cabin crew took the bag and put it somewhere else.

When I took my seat, I noticed that all the cabin crew were male. When the engines started, they played the same Ryanair safety announcement I'd heard every day for the past week or so. And when we took off, they served the same choice of food, perfumes and scratchcards. The only difference was more legroom. I settled back in my seat and dozed.

3

The flight was uneventful. I was soon in Belgium, standing at the bus top. Charleroi Airport was only eight kilometres away from Charleroi, and the bus stop had one other person waiting: a bespectacled old man eating a sausage roll. When I first turned up, he was already there, finishing one. This was his second. A minute later, he finished it and pulled out a third (and these were full-length sausage rolls and not the weedy party variety) from his luggage. I began to wonder if the portly gent was some sort of baker or else puff pastry fetishist. Maybe he could use my snore gimp mask.

He noticed me watching, so I turned away to look at a Ryanair aircraft taking off. Within seconds, the cloud layer enveloped it as it climbed to whatever destination awaited. The flight was one of around 1,600 that Ryanair would be operating that day, each one making approximately one thousand euros of profit for the airline. I looked back at the old man, who had stopped eating. He was watching a third man approaching the bus stop. The newcomer looked a soldier type: shaven head and hard features. The three of us waited for the bus to Charleroi.

It came fifteen minutes later. When we climbed aboard, we all sat equally spaced from one another; we were the only passengers aboard. When we set off, I stared outside at the warehouses we were passing. They looked like any other warehouses, except in worse shape. Then we turned onto a motorway where I caught my first sighting of Charleroi between copses of lush green. It looked okay, nothing special, but certainly not depressing. Then the vision was gone, replaced by concrete.

We were in an underpass. After a brief period of dark, Charleroi reappeared and I reassessed my initial perception. It might not be the world's ugliest city, but it was damned close. The city was stuck in a bleak 1970s time warp of crumbing grey concrete and graffiti. The exceptions were the huge piles of coal by a railway track and sets of ugly redbrick apartment blocks that looked abandoned but probably weren't. A huge factory loomed. Behind it, industrial chimneys churned out acrid black smoke. L.S. Lowry might have painted the scene I was seeing. When we passed a derelict factory covered in barbed wire and graffiti scrawls, I wished myself a happy birthday and then wished I were somewhere else. Charleroi *was* the ugliest place I'd been to.

4

Once upon a time, Charleroi thrived with its double industries of coal and steel. People from all over Europe flocked to the city with its promise of work and prosperity. The city's population soared. To cope with the newfound demand for Charleroi's high-quality steel, canals were constructed and railways expanded. Many factory owners grew rich from their spoils, and their workers had money in their pockets too. Charleroi, for a brief period in the nineteenth century, was the place to be in Western Europe.

Then it all went wrong.

Suddenly, other countries began manufacturing steel, and at cheaper prices than Charleroi could. Then the First World War started, with heavy fighting in and around the city. Charleroi never recovered, and by the 1950s, most of the factories had closed down, sending unemployment rocketing. In 1984, the last coal mine closed its doors: the final nail in the coffin for the city. An even steeper decline in fortune followed, so much so that, during the latter part of the 1980s and 1990s, Charleroi became renowned across Belgium for its frightening crime statistics, high unemployment and poverty rates. Though things have improved for the city in recent times, these three issues still blight Charleroi.

The bus stopped by a dour bus station. All three of us clattered out with our luggage. The military gent walked towards the station entrance while Mr Sausage Roll headed to a nearby bus stop. I took in my surroundings.

Opposite the station didn't look too bad. A row of tall town houses, one adorned with a large blue and red sign saying La Gazette, which I assumed was the local newspaper, offered respite from the concrete surrounding them. But then I turned to face the station: it was an ugly grey structure of concrete slabs and towers. It had to be one of the most depressing bus stations in Europe. Adding to the sad vista were browbeaten locals standing at the bus stops, balefully eying the sky for rain. A minute later, a nasty wave of drizzle rewarded them.

I crossed a thin pedestrian bridge that passed over La Sambre, a grey strip of water that masqueraded as a river. On the opposite side, crossing towards me, were a trio of gangly youths. Instead of moving over to allow me passage, they swaggered onward, making me move to the very edge of the bridge. They passed with a sneer and flick of cigarette ash.

At the other side, I turned right, walking along the river, finding myself alone on the cobbles. Even the buildings overlooking the river seemed abandoned. The drizzle was making the cobbles slippery, and as I passed another bridge, which offered myriad shaded spaces for assailants to wait and skulk, I began to think that I should've caught a taxi to the hotel.

I turned left, heading away from the river. More loitering youths waited at the end of a narrow street that my Sat Nav app suggested I use. They looked like extras from *The Wire*, so I decided to take an alternative route, passing a tall building with every window missing or broken. A car rumbled past, its occupants gazing at my small suitcase and then at me. Maybe they thought I was a drug dealer. From a doorway, a wiry black man leaned, one knee bent in a pose of relaxation. When I passed, he studied me but said nothing. In the air was the unmistakable aroma of marijuana.

I found my hotel at the end of that street. I wasn't expecting much and I wasn't disappointed. When I asked the man behind the desk for a tourist map of Charleroi, he told me he didn't have one. I took the key and headed to the lift. When the doors closed, I fixed my eyes on the electronic display. It stayed on zero all the way to the top floor, where the lift shook like an earth tremor before opening.

The fifth floor smelled of urine mixed with leaking drains. My room was only slightly better. When I tried the toilet, I had to keep the seat up with my knee. In the main room, I noticed the clock on the wall. The hands were frozen at nine thirty. Half past nine, 1973, I thought miserably. I wandered over to the windows, parting the curtains so I could see outside. The view revealed a set of grey office blocks and a roundabout. I sat on the edge of the bed and sighed. It was perhaps the most miserable birthday I'd experienced in my life on the planet.

5

I was the only tourist in town. Of that, there was no doubt. Why would anyone want to come to Charleroi? At least Nowy Dwor Mazowiecki had a fortress and some nature trails. Moss had a harbour and a good statue. What did Charleroi have? A bloody photography museum (which was closed) and some spoil heaps.

With drizzle falling, I walked along a shopping parade full of stores catering for the lower end of the market. *Tout A 1€* was the name of one shop, *Everything one euro*.

A hijab-wearing woman with a pushchair went in. When I saw her struggling with the pushchair, I helped her. While she held open the door, I lifted the carriage in. It felt good to do another good deed of the day, and she thanked me profusely.

Further along the street were some familiar names – Footlocker and C & A, but then I spied something new – a café-takeaway called Mr Cod, which as well as selling 'fine fish', also peddled chicken, chips and hamburgers. It was closed.

I stumbled upon the central square, *Place Charles II*, which was more of a roundabout. Even so, it was home to the nicest buildings in Charleroi. One was the City Hall, a proud and stately building of arches and limp flags. Towering above it was a tall brown belfry.

The other notable building was Saint-Christophe Church. I took a photo of it, though I didn't know why. It was hardly inspiring. Only the copper-green dome (stained brown in places) offered any respite from the glumness. When a couple of youths passed, they turned to see where I was pointing my camera. They laughed and shook their heads when they saw. I heard a screech of wheels. A police van was tearing around the roundabout, its sirens blazing as it turned off near the church.

I found a fairground, exactly the type of thing found in fading British seaside towns. Because of the rain, punters were thin on the ground, but a harried mother and her two kids were wandering through, the kids haranguing her to go on the bumper cars.

From somewhere, tinny music played from crackly speakers. The woman shook her head, and when one of the youngsters said something, she yelled at him, silencing the boy in an instant. I passed them and found a dripping-wet shoot-the-duck stand and then a set of mini waltzers. A middle-aged woman was sitting reading a newspaper in a little booth between them. When she looked up, she eyed me suspiciously. Not surprising really, since I was a single man wandering around a place frequented by children. With the sickly sweet aroma of candyfloss and warm toffee coming from somewhere hidden further in, I decided to leave.

Beyond the fairground was something interesting. It was a monument, cast in bronze, showing three giant and freakishly spindly hands reaching into the air.

Designed by Charleroi-based sculptor, Martin Guyaux, it was the most interesting thing I'd seen so far. The hands were close to a concave yellow building that declared itself the Palais des Beaux-Arts. And that was when I spotted Mr Sausage Roll again. He was standing across the street from me with another equally portly man. He had noticed me too. A look of recognition flicked across his face and then he nodded. I nodded back and wandered towards another drab street of Charleroi.

6

I entered a grocery store. As well as selling an array of fruit and vegetables, it sold ladies' wigs. They were arranged on mannequin heads on the counter. I ignored them and headed straight for the bananas. The young Turkish man behind the counter watched me.

"Bonjour," I said. "Can I buy two bananas?" I was the only customer in the shop. I didn't want to have to buy a whole bunch.

The man nodded. "Of course."

I snapped a couple off and took them to the counter. The man tapped on his till and told me the price. "Where are you from, monsieur?" he asked as he wrapped my fruit in a clear plastic bag.

"England."

The man considered this. "You are here for work?"

I told him I was a tourist.

"Tourist? Why did you not go to Brussels? Or even Liege? Tourists do not come to this city; there is nothing here."

I nodded at his accurate summing up of Charleroi.

He offered me some advice. "Please, monsieur, if you are drinking in the bars tonight, be careful. Many people will want to pick fights. They have no job and no money. They will wait for people who have drunk too much so they can rob them."

I told him I didn't intend to drink in any bars that evening. In fact, I'd already decided to hole up in the hotel for the night. But to celebrate my birthday, I would crack open a can of cheap Belgian larger. But I had a question for the man. "Tell me," I said, "is Charleroi famous for anything?"

The man thought for a moment. "Apart from the murders, no."

"Murders?"

The man appraised me. "I thought everyone knew about Marc Dutroux. He killed those girls twenty years ago. I was only a small boy, but my parents still talk about it. But apart from him, there is nothing famous here ... no, wait! There might be one thing. It is something called a Mayonnaise Bracelet. I have seen it on the internet. I think they might have them in fast food places."

"Mayonnaise Bracelet?" It sounded like something concocted in Hell.

"Yes, I think so."

I paid for my bananas and left the shop with horrible visions. The bracelets sounded truly hideous. I decided to try to find one.

7

Mr Cod was open now but did not sell mayonnaise bracelets, and neither did a pizza joint further on. I looked for somewhere else, but found myself walking along a street full of decrepit, broken-down buildings. Even though the drizzle had stopped, it had left dirty puddles on the pavements and road. Due to my surroundings, I felt slightly uncomfortable and quickened my pace. And then I saw a group of four youths loitering up ahead.

"Bonjour, monsieur," shouted a twenty-something man sitting in the doorway. I was about fifteen feet away from the group. "Ou vas-tu?"

He was asking me where I was going. He stood up, took a drag from a cigarette and watched me. His pals watched me too. I was now only a few feet away.

I ignored him and carried on walking. The man laughed and sat back down. I turned left, and saw another group of teenagers hanging around a small convenience store. In all my travels, in so-called danger zones such as Iraq, Iran and Nairobi in Kenya, I had never felt my hackles on edge as much as they were right now. The perceived danger was no doubt all in my head, but walking along a crumbling street, with only the depressed youth of Charleroi for company, was putting me on high alert. I suddenly disliked Charleroi. I hated the fact it was making me feel this way. I wanted to stroll, not hurry, but the hard stares I was receiving from the teenagers made me rush even more.

They didn't say anything as I hurried past. And then I turned a corner and found the relative safety of the central square again. In the distance, another police siren sounded.

In 1996, there had been plenty more police sirens in Charleroi. The city had made world headlines that year. A man called Mark Dutroux had built himself a few dungeons in the vacant homes he owned.

After abducting young girls (sometimes with the help of his wife), Dutroux sexually abused and tortured them, often filming himself while he did so. When he tired of the girls, he murdered them.

When he was finally arrested, a media storm erupted around the globe, especially when people discovered that the Belgian police had arrested him the previous year on suspicion of car racketeering. During the arrest, a pair of eight-year-old girls had been alive inside his dungeon. A locksmith, accompanying the arresting police officers, heard their cries for help, but the both officers thought the sounds had come from children playing outside. No search was made for the girls. Whilst Dutroux was incarcerated, both girls died of starvation.

I arrived back near the town hall and walked along the main shopping street I'd come up earlier. After a cursory look in another fast food restaurant for evidence of the mayonnaise bracelet, I gave up. In the end, I simply wasn't that bothered.

Later, however, I went online and discovered that Mayonnaise Bracelets did indeed exist, but not in fast food restaurants, but in the mind of some internet joker. For some unfathomable reason, a man called Nicolas Buissart had 'invented' a homemade wristband with a small cup attached. He decided to make a film with him wearing the bracelet and picked Charleroi as the location. Wearing his invention, Buissart entered a fast food joint and ordered some fries. The proprietor obliged and then squeezed some mayonnaise into the little wrist cup. The Mayonnaise Bracelet was born and Buissart dipped a chip into it and went on his way.

8

I decided I had one more thing to see in Charleroi, and that was Rue de Mons. I wanted to see if it really was the most depressing street in Belgium. After a ten-minute walk through town, I arrived at a large concrete underpass. Its underside was stained and pockmarked, supported by graffiti-covered pillars. On the other side was the famed street.

A tall glass and concrete building, topped with an advertisement for a twenty-four hour casino, was the first thing of note. It wasn't particularly eye-catching, but nor was it particularly ugly. Then I passed a row of town houses, which, had they been cared for a little more, would have looked okay. But up ahead was grim. A trio of tall chimneys took up position on the horizon: abandoned outlets for the blast furnace they had once serviced. Bathed in sunshine, they would have looked bleak, but in the dreary overcast conditions, they were apocalyptic: totems of the industry that eventually choked Charleroi. Across from them were some hills covered in what looked like thorny and overgrown vegetation. But instead of being elements of nature, they were abandoned slag heaps.

My goal was to reach the rusting old blast furnace, but when my feet started aching, and I passed a motorcycle store with its windows shuttered and protected with sturdy steel bars, I decided to turn back. I couldn't take any more of Charleroi. It was sapping me of my strength.

Back in the hotel, I rang Angela to tell her about my day.

"Never mind," she said. "Tomorrow will be better. Carcassonne will be amazing. The castle looks like something out of a film. You should have gone there for your birthday, not Belgium."

I absently gazed out of the window. A police car had stopped a motorist on the roundabout. Flashing blue light was refracting against the raindrops on the window. But my wife was right: tomorrow would be better; it could hardly be any worse. After saying goodbye, I packed my luggage, inspected the broken wheel (it was still hanging on), and decided to brave the mean streets of Charleroi before it got too dark. It was a brief foray, though, with only one stop: a small Carrefour supermarket not far from the hotel. After purchasing the staples of my diet: bread, ham and cheese (plus a can of lager), I returned to my room on the dank fifth floor to celebrate an unhappy birthday. As I chomped into my sandwich and took a swig of my beer, I grimly nodded to myself. Country number eight was almost finished. I was over half way through my silly plan to conquer Europe by low-cost airlines.

Top row: Charleroi's Place Charles II (City Hall on the left, Saint Christopher's Church on the right)
Middle row: Reaching hand monument 'Passation'; Palace des Beaux-Arts
Bottom row: Everything for one euro; faded town houses of Charleroi

Day 9. Carcassonne, France

Brussels Charleroi – Carcassonne: Ryanair £19

"Please remove your belt, sir," said the female security official at Brussels South Charleroi Airport. She had red hair and a neatly-pressed uniform. The former made her look outlandish but the latter put her firmly in charge.

I told her my belt was made of fabric. She repeated the instruction.

"But it does not contain any metal."

"Last time I will ask, sir."

So I removed my fabric belt, the first time any airport had asked me to do so, and placed it in the tray. Then I made a show of removing some spare socks from my luggage. I placed them in a separate tray too. The woman watched with interest but said nothing. Next, I rooted around in my pocket until I found a sheet of paper printed with my hotel's address. That went in the tray as well. I was making a point in the most ridiculous of ways.

The airport rigmarole was clearly getting to me: my actions were wholly out of proportion to what the security official had requested. But I was tired and irritable and the only reason I'd worn the belt was so I wouldn't have to remove it in airports. The woman accepted my belt, socks and paper without comment and pushed it under the scanner. Then I walked through the metal detector without a murmur. At the other side, I waited for my things, and everything came except my belt. I wondered whether the woman had done something to it, but discounted this as paranoia. I waited for a few minutes but when it did not appear, I complained to another security official.

"What does it look like?" he asked.

"It's black and made of fabric."

"Why did you put it through the scanner, then?"

"Because she made me." I pointed at the red-haired woman.

The man nodded and went to look for it, returning a minute later with it in his hand. "It got trapped," he told me. I thanked the man and threaded the belt through the annoying loops in my trousers.

2

The display monitor told me my flight was boarding. By the time I arrived at the gate, everyone was already queuing up. One person still sitting, though, was a pilot. She was a young first officer in full uniform, a company policy for pilots travelling as passengers with the Irish airline. I guessed she was heading to Carcassonne to fly a later Ryanair flight.

Ryanair had an interesting policy for employees. According to their *Terms and Conditions for Staff Travel*, Ryanair staff could not jump the queue because 'fare paying passengers always come first'. Neither could they sit in any of the emergency exit rows unless they paid the premium price out of their own pockets. To me, this was idiotic. Who better to have sitting by an emergency exit but a qualified airline pilot? Another rule for pilots flying as passengers was that they had to give their undivided attention to the safety briefing, even though they had heard it a million times before. But one rule seemed to be more important above all others. It stated that Ryanair pilots (and cabin crew) could not behave in a way that could bring their airline 'into disrepute'.

Not like the crew of a Latvian airline the week before. The crew had been about to perform a routine flight from Oslo to Crete, when, following an anonymous tip off, Norwegian police raided the cockpit and breathalysed the pilots before they could start the engines. Both were well over the limit, as were two members of the cabin crew. Police arrested all four.

In court, the 38-year old first officer (who was seven times over the limit) admitted that their Oslo drinking session had been a bit wild, stating: "We lost control." He claimed that between the four of them, they had drunk two bottles of whisky and numerous pints of beer. With a planned take off time of 6am the next day, the boozy crew hadn't stopped drinking until two in the morning. They had clearly disregarded the long-held pilot rule of 'eight hours from bottle to throttle'. The judge sentenced him to six months in a Norwegian jail. The two cabin crew members received a month each. The captain, a 50-year old Latvian man, rejected the claims that he was drunk. At the time of writing, his case is yet to be heard. Nevertheless, the airline suspended all four crew members.

Another famous drunken pilot story involved a Russian Aeroflot 767 captain due to fly from Moscow to New York in 2009. The first indication that things were not right was when he wobbled into the cockpit. Some passengers were so spooked that they refused to fly and left the aircraft there and then. Things did not improve when the captain spoke over the intercom. His message was slurred, meandering and often repeated. When he appeared from the cockpit a short while later (while the plane was still at the stand), he was ruddy-faced and had unfocussed, bloodshot eyes. Even more passengers protested and started to leave. When the captain returned to the flight deck, a forward-thinking member of the cabin crew picked up the microphone. He told the mutinous passengers to stop making trouble, adding that it was 'not such a big deal if a pilot is drunk. The worst that can happen is he'll trip over something in the cockpit'. The passengers disagreed and refused to fly unless the airline brought another pilot in, which is what they did, three hours later.

Another story did not end so well. In 2012, a Kamchatsky Air turboprop was attempting to land at a domestic airport in the far eastern part of Russia, a region noted for its mountainous terrain. The plane ended up severely off course and, while the pilots argued back and forth, it descended through a cloud layer and struck a forested mountain slope. All but four passengers and crew died. In the resulting investigation, both pilots were found to be over the alcohol limit, backed up by witnesses who claimed they had seen the two men drinking the night before.

In 2008, another crash involving a Russian airline killed all 88 passengers and crew. Before the aircraft had even taken off, a passenger had texted a friend saying that the captain sounded drunk. The cockpit voice recorder seemed to back this up, playing back a scene of chaos in the flight deck. As the crew descended to land in the city of Perm, they correctly disengaged the autopilot, but then one of the pilots tried to steer the plane left, while the other tried right. The Boeing 737 crashed into a railway line on the outskirts of the city.

I looked at the waiting Ryanair pilot and deduced she was neither drunk nor acting in any way that would put her airline into disrepute. I joined the line just before she did and we walked towards the now-empty gate. From somewhere came the sound of a piano. I turned and saw a couple of kids banging on a keyboard near a cafe. The discordant tune sounded like the accompaniment to a horror film score: an appropriate soundtrack to my last minutes in Charleroi.

3

It was another almost full flight. So I was surprised to find my entire row empty, apart from one man on the opposite side sitting by the window. He had the most ridiculous haircut I'd seen in a long while. For a start, it looked like someone had draped a yellow mop on his head and then trimmed it with garden shears. He also had a stupidly bushy moustache. If he was attending a fancy dress party for the Carcassonne Yodelling with Lederhosen Society then I might have understood, but I knew he wasn't and so shook my head at how silly he looked.

After hauling the luggage into the overhead compartment, I took my seat by the window and plugged in my earphones. Ryanair, like many European airlines, allowed uninterrupted use of electronic equipment as soon as you boarded. It was infinitely better than Air China's rules for electronics. Four months previously, I had been flying from Beijing to Hong Kong and the cabin crew had resolutely banned everything – for the entire flight. When one member of the crew caught me reading a book on my phone, I thought she was going to slap me.

A few more passengers arrived. A man and a boy took up the seats opposite, filling the spaces next to the mop-haired man. A minute later, a woman and her pre-school son walked down the aisle and stopped next to my row. I was by the window, but could tell the boy was eager to look out of it and so, in a moment of pure impulsiveness, I decided to do my good deed of the day. Through a mixture of pidgin French, a smattering of English and some wild gesturing, I offered my seat to the little boy. The woman smiled and spoke to her son, who nodded gleefully. I allowed them in, with the woman sitting in the middle beside me.

The man and boy across the aisle were part of the same family. As I put my earphones back in place, the woman next to me reached across to her husband and passed him a bottle of water. A few seconds later, he passed it back. Then a sandwich changed hands and then a packet of crisps and then a biscuit. Then the water again. I mentally gnashed my teeth.

I flicked open my Kindle app and began to read, just as I felt a tapping on my shoulder. I looked to see Dad staring at me. I removed one earpiece and looked at him.

"François, Deutsch or Anglais?" he asked.

"Anglais."

"Ah, okay. I was just wondering whether you would like to sit with more room?"

I looked at him blankly. Was he asking me to sit on his knee? I was tempted because it looked more comfortable than the Ryanair standard issue blue leather seats. He pointed to the row behind. Apart from one person, two seats were free and up for grabs. I considered them. Even though it would be a pain in the arse moving seats for a second time, I would have more room and there would be no one passing food across my chest. I looked up and down the cabin to check that everyone had boarded and then nodded. I unbuckled my seatbelt and moved to the row behind. Everything was good again.

And then some new passengers arrived.

As they made their way up the aisle, I was already unbuckling my belt. I had taken one of their seats and so I stood up and shuffled forward. I had to wait to sit back down, though: there was a picnic on my vacant seat. As I took my seat for the fourth time, I gave the husband a withering look. He pretended not to notice.

4

Landing at Carcassonne was like taking part in a Dambuster bombing run. The pilots flew down and then sharply up again. After dropping one wing, they did a scud run under the clouds, which, for once, caused a cessation to the endless food and beverage swap going on in my midst. The little boy by the window looked stricken and, for the first time on over two hundred flights, I wondered whether something was genuinely wrong. A town appeared briefly in the window and then sky replaced it. The engines flared as we gained more altitude, and then powered back as we skimmed the rooftops of Carcassonne. Instead of hitting a line of trees, we landed firmly on the airport's runway, which meant the trumpet could sound. Clapping soon followed and, for the only time, I joined in.

Carcassonne Airport was tiny; our Ryanair flight was the only aircraft there. Maybe I was wrong about the pilot flying as a passenger: perhaps she lived in Carcassonne. As for me, I was through arrivals in record time, revelling in the sunny and pleasant weather conditions of southern France after the grey of Belgium. The airport bus was already waiting and twenty or so Ryanair passengers and I climbed aboard. As I bought a ticket from the driver, he asked where I was staying. When I told him, he nodded and told me to sit down.

Outside the airport perimeter, the landscape turned rural. Rustic cottages with slanted orange roofs dotted the land as we threaded our way downhill. With the slopes and vineyards, Carcassonne's outskirts looked like a painting.

Over on the left, perched upon a slight hill, the town's famous twelfth-century castle appeared: a fairy-tale fortress of towering walls, pointed turrets and endless battlements. It conjured up images of jousting, maidens and moats. It looked like the best castle in the world. But then it was gone: hidden behind trees. Shortly afterwards, we arrived in the centre of Carcassonne, opposite a little river. The bus stopped and everyone got off. I was about to follow them but the driver motioned that I should stay on board. "I take you to hotel."

Two minutes later, we set off again, with me as the only passenger, twisting and turning our way through a distinctly medieval town full of taverns, bakeries and cafes, all of which spilled out into the streets before them. "Monsieur," said the driver, "your hotel is coming soon. Come up here and wait. There is no stopping allowed but if you are quick, I think it will be okay."

I dragged the luggage forward, thanking the driver. I could not imagine many UK bus drivers going out of their way to help someone like this. The bus turned along a shaded street that formed one edge of Square Gambetta and then it stopped. "Go!" urged the driver. "Your hotel is on the left."

I jumped out and waved goodbye.

With a hiss of the doors, and a quick blast of his accelerator, he was off, trundling around the far edge of the square. I turned tail and entered my ninth hotel of the trip.

5

Fifty-two watchtowers, three kilometres of walls, one sturdy drawbridge and a (now dry) moat make Carcassonne's fortified city a schoolboy's dream castle. In 1991, Hollywood filmmakers sent a film crew to shoot scenes for *Robin Hood: Prince of Thieves* there.

I was staring at it from a vantage point on a stone bridge. Plenty of other tourists were doing the same thing, all of us vying for the best photo location. I stood and balanced on a raised platform, risking death should a gust topple me, but got a great photo. When I stepped down, someone replaced me and soon there was a queue. I carried on across the bridge, passing through a medieval street of cafes, patisseries and boutique hotels, the buildings tall enough to obscure the castle behind them. I was following a family of four; mum and dad were forging up the incline towards the castle while their teenagers trailed behind looking bored out of their skulls. At the top of a bend, the castle came into view and dad stopped to take a picture. Mum pointed out something to the kids, but they were not bothered in the slightest. One of them, a surly-looking girl of about fifteen, glanced at the castle and yawned. Her brother was staring into a mobile phone.

I passed them, walking in the shadow of the gigantic walls. I could imagine archers and swordsmen parading on the battlements while, inside the walls, peasant traders shouted for trade. It was a fanciful image, and one based entirely on what I'd seen in films and TV. Up close and personal, however, Carcassonne Castle was a high-end tourist trap.

At the other side of the reclined drawbridge was a horse-drawn carriage together with a line of willing tourists. To the left of them was a long walkway lined with conical-roofed towers. I headed straight forward, passing the stone bust of Lady Carcas, a fictional princess and saviour of the walled city. According to an eighth century legend, Carcassonne had been under siege for five years and was running dangerously low on food. Lady Carcas demanded an inventory of what remained. When her advisors told her there was only one pig and a bag of wheat left, she ordered them to give the wheat to the pig. Scratching their heads, they carried out her order, and when the pig was fat enough, the princess told the soldiers to take it to the highest tower and fling it towards the siege army. Everyone thought she was mad, especially the pig, but the troops did as they were told, and launched the porcine projectile over the battlements.

What happened next amazed everybody. The siege army packed up and departed. Lady Carcas smiled knowingly; her guile had saved the castle. She explained that when the siege leaders had received a fat pig into their camp, they had mistakenly surmised that the town had so much food to spare that they could afford to use it as ammunition. If this was the case, then the castle could last out the siege for many months, even years. They has simply given up and left.

Lady Carcas's statue depicted her with a wry grin, an expression of someone who has played a risky game and won. I walked past her and made my way to the arched entrance of the old town.

6

Beyond the horse and carriage was a crowd of people trying to gain access to the main parts of the walled city. Many were day trippers and would be gone later that evening but, for now, time was forcing me to join them in the crush to get inside.

Through the stone archway, a whole street of shops awaited me: many of them selling panoramic postcards, T-shirts, bags, pillow covers and plastic knights. One busy shop peddled Carcassonne cups, key rings and flags, but its stock of plastic knight armour and swords seemed the biggest seller. Mind you, as long as something had a picture of a castle, it was fair game for the shops of Carcassonne.

From somewhere, I could hear loud cheers and hollering. I rounded a corner and the sound grew louder. By peering through a crack in a large wooden fence, I saw some men dressed as knights. They were jousting. Each time they passed one another the crowd roared its approval. I could hardly see, though, only the occasional bobbing head or swish of a horsetail. I left the wall and found a stand selling tickets for the show. If I wanted to watch the knights unobstructed, then it would cost twelve euros. I looked at my watch and decided to pass. Instead, I walked towards a street performer.

The man's act was a mixture of acrobatics and magic, an apt choice for Carcassonne. He balanced deftly on his arms, then flipped over and placed some small sticks on a large piece of cloth. All the while, eerie music played from his portable stereo. Then – quick as a flash – he made one of the sticks disappear. The gasps from his sizeable audience were real, but I was already moving to pastures new. I'd seen something called the *Musee de l'inquisition* on a tourist map I'd picked up.

7

The thin, pasty man in charge of the Museum of the Inquisition sold me a nine-euro entrance ticket. He then said, "You have forty-five minutes in the museum. Please don't overstay. Oh, yeah, good luck." With that, he swept the curtains aside and pointed into darkness.

Hidden speakers piped in spooky noises. The sound effects consisted of weeping, creaking and snoring. I couldn't see a thing and so shuffled forward with my hands outstretched. The weeping became louder, and then I saw something: a dimly lit exhibit of a man writing something down. The mannequin had its back to me. When my eyes adjusted, I began to realise how amateurish the whole thing was. The mannequin seemed of very poor quality, with a cheap wig plopped on its head. No wonder it was so dark. Bathed in light, the whole display would have been laughable.

The Inquisition was no laughing matter, though. In an attempt to keep their orthodox branch of Christianity pure, Roman Catholic Inquisition officers tortured any unbelievers they came across and then executed them as heretics. In medieval Carcassonne, church bells would frequently ring out in celebration whenever the Inquisition killed another godless soul.

Deep inside Carcassonne castle was an Inquisition prison called The Wall, which had once resounded with the screams of the unfortunates. Tiny cells, in perpetual darkness (so that prisoners could not tell whether it was day or night) filled the terrible dungeon.

Inside each cell, officials shackled and bound their victims, who included women and children. When they were fed (which was rarely), guards offered them delights such as the 'bread of adversity' and 'water of affliction'. The bread would have been stale and mouldy, the water impure. To eat and drink it would almost certainly guarantee serious stomach problems.

After a period of solitary confinement, many Inquisition victims embraced death. When interrogation officers finally came to them, they heartily confessed their heresy, implicating their friends and family too in the hope of ending the torment. Once confessed, they were executed. Those who failed to confess went to the torture chambers.

The *rack* was a favoured torture device. Inquisition officers used it to dislocate limbs by mechanical stretching of wrists and ankles. *Torture of the Pulley* was another method they liked, where a pulley system slowly hoisted prisoners off the ground and then dropped them from a great height. Other tortures involved pulling fingernails, flogging and submersion in boiling water. Usually they worked, but if they didn't, then eye gouging and having thumbscrews attached did the trick.

When interrogators tired of these traditional methods of extracting a confession, they took their charges to the hot room. There, branding irons and red-hot pincers hung ominously. If a prisoner was being particularly headstrong, officers would force them to sit on a spiked chair so they could roast their feet over an open fire until their 'bones fell out'. Worse was something called the *boot*. This hellish device was a box that tightly enclosed a person's feet. When in place, the torturer would hammer in wooden wedges until it crushed bones, making the boot gush with 'blood and marrow'.

I peered at the 'scribe' hidden in the gloom. The mannequin's shoulders seemed hunched as he pored over a document that would seal another unfortunate's fate at the hands of the Inquisition. Maybe he was asleep, which would explain the snoring. I moved away, finding daylight at the end of a corridor.

In a tiny outdoor courtyard, a dummy with what looked like tomato sauce splashed across his face was swinging from a noose. The museum's fancy dress department had stuck a joke shop beard on his plastic face. Crouching below the figure was a weeping plastic woman. While a constant loop of sobbing sounded, the deceased swung limply in the breeze. I noticed he had a missing leg, but whether this was because of his 'torture' or because it had simply dropped off, I didn't know.

I followed a route back inside the museum. More snoring came from a supposed torturer. The information sign claimed he was resting between his activities. I nodded miserably. What a cop out. Instead of posing the mannequin mid-torture, they had placed him in a seat with a few implements around him. It was a poor show and, when a family of five stood next to me, peering into the lacklustre display, I felt sorry for them. They had paid almost forty euros for the privilege of seeing crap like this. That must have been torture for dad. I left them and shuffled off to see a woman dangling from some chains, her bare breasts annoyingly indistinct in the woefully poor lighting. And then I was at the end of the exhibits. I checked my watch and saw I'd been inside for ten minutes.

"Do you know if it's possible to see the castle's dungeons anywhere?" I asked the pasty man who had sold me the ticket. "I'd like to see the real thing."

He looked nonplussed.

"This museum shows things that happened inside Carcassonne's castle's dungeons, yes?"

The man looked uncertain but nodded.

"So do you know if I can see the actual place it happened?"

The man shook his head. "Non."

I didn't have time for this, and so left the Museum of Torment and headed back outside.

8

With my visit to the castle finished for the time being, I wandered towards the lower town. Place Carnot, named after a French Revolutionary hero, was the central square. It had a huge fountain of Neptune in the middle and flowers, cafes and tourists around the sides. A beggar noticed me taking a photo of Neptune and wandered over. I didn't give him any money but I did offer him one of the peaches I'd just bought from a small grocery store. He waved it away with a sneer.

I spied an establishment called the Bastid' Cafe at the far side of Place Carnot. It was around the corner from the excellently named Hotel de la Bastide. I left the beggar and walked towards the cafe, managing to bag an outside table with a view of the whole square. I ordered a beer and a cassoulet, a Carcassonne speciality of duck, white beans and vegetables. It turned out to be delicious, even though it looked a little burnt on top: a proper meaty taste mixed with a few choice herbs for added flavour. And while I scooped it from the bowl, I smiled to myself. What a difference a day makes, I thought. The saying really was correct: from depressing Charleroi to lively Carcassonne. Doom and gloom to sunshine and castles.

"How is your food?" asked the waitress, catching me, as they always do, with my mouth full to bursting. I swallowed a hot gulp and nodded. "Very good, très bien!"

She smiled and was about to walk away when I stopped her. "The name," I said. "Bastid' Cafe. What does it mean?"

She looked at me quizzically. "I'm sorry?"

I pointed at the large brown sign spelling the name of the establishment.

"Ah, I see..." she smiled. "A bastid is a ... ah ... a ..." She was searching for the right words. "It is ... a town inside a wall. That is the only way to describe it."

That made sense.

When she was gone, I continued with my meal, noticing that the beggar was now hanging around outside a tiny Carrefour store. He soon grew bored and shuffled off along a side street. As for me, I was about as content as I could be.

9

As evening rolled in over Southern France, I crossed the same bridge I'd traversed earlier, but this time, instead of heading along the medieval street, I turned right. There I found a small church and, beyond that, a trail that led upwards towards the ramparts and castle walls. Now that the day-trippers had departed, I had the castle to myself, apart from a few pigeons roosting inside gaps in the stonework. I carried on around the perimeter until I found an entranceway and went inside.

Carcassonne's walled town was now almost serene – with only the sounds of polite conversation and cutlery tap dancing on plates in the cafes. Many of the tourist shops were closing for the night, their proprietors sweeping around the entrances or bringing signs in from outside. The street performers had all left, leaving the sun to soak the towers and walls in a gorgeous sheen of gold. The only problem was my feet. In Charleroi, they hadn't been too bad because I'd not walked that much, but today they were bad again. Every step brought a piercing pain underneath my big toes.

To rest them, I found a bar and ordered a beer. While I waited for it to arrive, I found an app on my phone that kept count of my daily steps. It told me I'd walked 12.5 miles that day. When I pressed another button, it told me I'd walked almost seventy miles the previous week, which was about the same distance from Sheffield to Leicester. No wonder my feet hurt so much; I'd walked the equivalent of three marathons.

My drink came and I thought about my next destination: Eindhoven. It was a place I'd heard of but knew next to nothing about. It was close to the Belgium border and was famous for one of its sons – Gerald Philips, who founded an electronics company there in the late nineteenth century – but that was all I knew. But Eindhoven was tomorrow and so, for now, I drank my beer, basking in the warm sun of a French evening. Carcassonne had been just what the doctor ordered.

Top row: The fairy-tale Carcassonne Castle; A street performer setting up for his act
Middle row: Bastid' Cafe in Place Carnot; Monument and flag in Square Gambetta; One of the turrets of the castle
Bottom row: Place Carnot; Exhibit in the torture museum (note the missing leg); Lady Carcas

Day 10. Eindhoven, the Netherlands

Carcassonne – Eindhoven: Ryanair £26

Today I came close to missing my flight, but it wasn't my fault. I apportion half the blame to the Carcassonne Airport Bus company and the other half to Carcassonne Airport.

The bus company was to blame due to its published timetable. Whoever had designed it had done so around the six flights taking off from Carcassonne over the day. This was a sensible idea. Instead of buses going every hour, and then possibly missing flight departures, buses worked their schedule around individual flight times. For my Ryanair flight to Eindhoven, the timetable said the bus would pick me up at 8.50am, and would arrive at the airport ten minutes later. This would leave me one hour and fifteen minutes to get on the flight. Perfect.

It was far from perfect. The bus trundled up at the appointed time of 8.50 and then waited. A few passengers climbed aboard and I did too. I was pleased to see the friendly driver from the previous day in the hot seat. He recognised me. "Leaving Carcassonne already?"

I nodded. "Very short stay."

He didn't comment on that and so I sat down. Two minute later, we set off, but instead of going straight to the airport, the driver did a tour of Carcassonne, driving along narrow roads, through pleasant vineyards, picking up more passengers as he did so. I glanced at my watch and felt the first stirrings of alarm. When we eventually rolled up outside the airport fifteen minutes later, I was about to find things a whole lot worse.

Carcassonne Airport's minuscule departure terminal was too small to handle anything but a single flight. With three Ryanair flights leaving within twenty minutes of each other, there were over five hundred passengers crammed into the terminal; it was a scene of bedlam and disorder.

I stood in the entrance to Hell surveying the chaos. The queue for the two check-in desks was about a mile long, almost filling the entire room. The people in it looked angry, and quite rightly so; there was a good chance they would miss their flights. Perhaps because of this, a harried airport worker was fluttering around, trying to put out fires, but there was an inferno coming from a group of passengers on the Glasgow flight. Their flight was due to leave ten minutes before mine, in about forty-five minutes.

One Glaswegian lady looked particularly scary. She had dreadlocks, tattoos and a stomach that could squash people to death. Her teenage daughter was just as nasty, only without the dreadlocks. Both had suitcases to check in. "Look, love," mother shouted at the airport worker, a young woman in her early twenties, "this is effin' insane. Are we ganna make the flight or wah?"

The airport official looked in the scary woman's direction, but another passenger prodded her shoulder and she turned towards him instead. Mrs Glasgow was not to be ignored. "Hey, love! I said are we ganna make the flight?"

The young woman looked like she was about to cry. She managed to say something to the Glaswegian, which caused a huff of pure disgust. I left them to it and walked towards the queue at security. I still had time for my flight, but only just, and that was if the hundred or so people in front of me didn't mess about with their luggage. But then the dynamics of the queue changed. A man appeared, telling anyone on the Glasgow flight to go straight to the front, and this they did en masse. It was like the Battle of Bannockburn. This lot would have stormed Carcassonne Castle no problem, pig or nor pig.

"Let me through!" belched a Scottish voice. "I'm on the Glasgow flight!" With flying dreadlocks and quivering arm tattoos, she and her daughter barged their way to the front until some passengers stopped them in their tracks. For a moment, I thought she was going to punch an old man, but when she discovered they were on the Glasgow flight too, she nodded and joined the back.

"Anyone for Eindhoven?" said the same airport official ten minutes later. A whole bunch of us raised our hands and we were shepherded to the front too. And by the time I was through security, the plane had already half boarded.

2

"Thank you so much!" said the girl sitting next along from me. She was about seventeen and I'd just allowed her to have my window seat. Her companion, a slightly older girl, had shuffled up to the middle seat, leaving me on the aisle. To be honest, I wasn't bothered about sitting by the window and felt it easier to ask them to shuffle along rather than have them crowd the aisle to allow me in. When all three of us had buckled up, the girls seemed giddy with excitement.

After they had taken a selfie of themselves, one of them offered me some chewing gum. I politely declined but smiled at their generosity. The girls introduced themselves as Elise and Tess, sisters from Brussels.

Elise said, "We are visiting our aunt in Eindhoven and we have never been on a plane before."

"Wow." I was astonished. I thought everyone of a certain age must have flown on an aeroplane at some point in their lives.

"We are so excited," added her sister, revealing a smile of genuine delight. "I can't believe we're sitting in a jet plane. I've been looking forward to this for months."

"Me too," added her gum-snapping sister.

I tried to recall my first ever flight. I had been ten and on the way to Australia with my family. The years since then had dulled the pleasure of flying, especially when flying Ryanair every day. As the girls took another selfie and then studied what was going on outside, I envied their enjoyment of travel.

The captain came over the intercom. He sounded Dutch. He told us that the flight would take one hour and forty minutes, and that the flying conditions would be calm. This news pleased me for the sake of the girls and, during take-off, they squealed with delight and took a third selfie.

When the trolley made an appearance fifteen minutes later, I bought a Ryanair coffee. The old man opposite got one too, and I waited for him to try his first. His grimace was the answer I needed and so I took a tentative peek inside the cup. It looked like tar and it tasted like tar with bits of gravel in it. Lavazza Coffee, it boasted on the side of the cup, supposedly Italy's favourite.

I waited for the fun of the scratch cards to begin. By now, I knew the routine by heart and wondered whether anyone would bite. First, two members of the cabin crew arranged the packs in their hands, one standing at the front of the cabin, the other in the middle. Then the announcement began; a soft Irish brogue that informed us that seven scratch cards – instead of the usual five – were for sale today. All for the special price of five euros. No one bought any except for one person: me. I handed over the money and stuffed the cards in my pocket for later.

3

The landing at Eindhoven was smooth. The trumpets sounded and most people clapped, including the girls next to me. Half an hour later, I was inside an airport bus on my way to the city centre. I was standing with my luggage, keeping it under guard with my knee. Another woman was doing the same thing. She had a large coat folded over her arm. Everyone else was sitting with their luggage.

My fellow passengers were a mixed bunch. There was a young woman sitting in a seat in front of me, with a couple of middle aged Brits opposite her. A young family of four were sitting further back. Almost everyone was staring outside. The forest around the airport was thinning, and agricultural fields were replacing it. Then the outskirts of Eindhoven, the Netherlands' fifth largest city, pulled into view. Rows of spotlessly clean semi-detached homes with perfectly manicured gardens formed a long vista along the side of the pristine road. Some had bicycles parked outside. There was not a whiff of litter anywhere. Eindhoven was squeaky clean.

We reached the city centre where a smattering of glass-covered skyscrapers appeared. These, together with some modern offices and tree-lined streets, made central Eindhoven seem even more clinically clean and ordered that its outskirts. Not a bad thing, of course, but after the grime of Charleroi and the historical buildings of Carcassonne, this contemporary look seemed strange.

Just then, the driver did an emergency stop to avoid an errant cyclist. Two things happened in quick succession: first, I lost my balance, then I flew forward toward the young woman sitting ahead of me. I managed to catch a glimpse of her stunned expression as I hit the bulkhead before everything went black. I hadn't passed out – something was covering my head. It was a coat. I righted myself, passed it back to the shocked woman next to me and resumed a nonchalant stance as if nothing had happened.

4

My hotel was interesting, and I'd picked it by pure chance. The Inntel Hotel Art Eindhoven, like its name suggested, was part art gallery and part accommodation. Strange sculptures dangled in the lobby and eye-catching paintings hung in a large atrium near the lifts. I stopped to stare up at a wooden rowing boat before heading upstairs.

My room was massive. Its sheer size dwarfed the double bed. I walked into the cavernous bathroom, which was so big that my footsteps echoed like a giant in a cave. I stared at myself in the mirror; I looked drawn and fatigued, but I didn't have time to feel sorry for myself, and so grabbed my camera and left the room. Before I went to the lifts, though, I walked towards a large window at the end of my corridor. It looked like it might offer a good view of the city below. I had to be quick, though; I didn't have much time in Eindhoven.

Smack!

My nose, then my forehead smashed into a thick sheet of invisible glass. The pain was immediate and excruciating and, like a cartoon character, stars spun around my vision. With my eyes watering and head reeling, I staggered back to the room, wondering how in hell I'd not seen the pane of glass. The cleaners needed sacking; they had cleaned it too well. Back inside my room, I headed straight for the bed, groaning and holding my nose in my hands. Five minutes later, when the pain had subsided enough to let me think clearly, I shuffled to the bathroom to inspect the damage.

A smear of blood covered my nose and right cheek. I wondered whether I'd broken the bridge of my nose and hesitantly touched it but backed off immediately when a flare of hot pain rushed to my head. I decided to lie down again.

I woke up an hour later. My body had simply shut down after so much abuse over the past week or so. My nose was throbbing, my feet were aching and my stomach was rumbling. I went into the bathroom to wash off the blood. My nose looked bruised and had a small cut in it. I looked like I'd been fighting. A small part of me liked this fact.

I noticed the pack of Ryanair scratch cards on the hotel desk. Maybe some luck was coming my way and so I opened them. After scratching all seven cards, I threw them all in the bin, then picked up my sunglasses and donned them like a battered wife. On the way out, I stared at the hateful glass panel along the corridor. There was a greasy stain on it where my nose had made contact. There was a bit of blood too. I jumped in the lift, bypassed the art and headed out to see Eindhoven.

5

The Blob was just down the road from my hotel, and I wasn't taking about the Scottish woman from the airport. Instead, the Blob was a large, curved dome of steel, coated in blue and white glass, which sat in the centre of the city near a shopping centre and a McDonald's.

I stared up at the strange construction. It didn't have a roof, or any discernible walls; so the name *Blob* seemed apt. Instead of containing a museum or upscale restaurant, there was a clothes shop called Sissy Boy inside, exactly the type of establishment I tried to avoid.

Behind the Blob was the iconic Philips Light Tower, a tall white building that used to be a light bulb factory. The letters on the top spelled out Philips even though it now housed offices unrelated to Philips. My phone rang; it was Angela. She wanted to know if everything was still on for our rendezvous in Budapest.

"Rendezvous in Budapest?" I said. "It sounds like something from a spy film. But yes, everything's fine." I told her about crashing into the glass panel.

She laughed. "You're like Mr Bean."

"Thanks for the sympathy."

"So what's Eindhoven like?"

"Clean, well-ordered and full of shops. The weather's nice. I'm about to see what else there is."

Twenty minutes later, I was ambling along a busy shopping arcade with recognisable names such as C&A, Foot Locker and Mango. It was almost as if I were in England, except for two noticeable differences: the lack of litter and the absence of obese people. I'd already noticed the lack of litter on the way into the city, but my second observation was more baffling. Why was an affluent city in Western Europe (and one not that far from the UK) not full of overweight citizens? They were eating the same pastries, licking the same ice creams and munching on the same pizzas as their counterparts across the water, and yet they were slim and healthy. What was the reason? Did they eat junk food in moderation, or did Dutch genes burn fat quicker than their English counterparts? Or was it because the Dutch rode bicycles so much?

Bikes were everywhere in Eindhoven. And though they kept to their own special lanes and stopped at their own traffic lights, they made crossing a road a hazardous affair. The only warning you would get was the tinkling of a bell before you were on the ground with tyre marks across your temple.

As well as the cyclists, there were huge numbers of young adults in Eindhoven. Many were wandering around in large groups wearing T-shirts of a certain colour or theme. A group of yellow T-shirt wearing young woman had gathered around a city waterfall. They were clapping and giggling, taking photos and making lots of noise. Quite a few young people were riding around on bikes, some wearing silly hats. One young man was wearing a tall conical red hat, while his pals sported rabbit ears. Another group donned sombreros. Later I discovered they were all university students enrolling on their technical degrees. For the next two weeks, it was party time in Eindhoven before the real work set in.

6

I walked back along the main shopping street and heard a raised voice. An old man, with a thick white beard, was riding a mobility scooter, bellowing at the top of his voice. He was carrying a large sign written in Dutch, and was parading up and down the arcade. I had no idea what the sign said or what he saying, but later found out the man's name was Arnol Kox, a self-professed street preacher. As he manoeuvred outside C&A, bellowing good naturedly, the locals of Eindhoven either moved out of his way or dismissed his presence entirely.

I ignored him too, studying an unusual couple walking towards me. He was sour-faced and middle aged, she was much younger with long blonde hair and high heels; they sauntered along arm-in-arm with their collection of expensive shopping bags. As they passed, I caught a snippet of a sultry Russian accent from the young woman and a whiff of perfume, and then they were gone, him strutting like a peacock.

Behind the shopping street was a large square full of cafes, shops and a noisy carousel. A small boy was sitting in a cream-coloured tank while his sister sat aboard a leaping pig.

I stopped next to a tall bronze statue of a slender, dapper looking man. He resembled Prince Philip but turned out to be Frits Philips, son of the famous electrical company's founder and a popular son of the city in his own right. During the war, he had saved the lives of almost four hundred Jews from concentration camps. He told the Nazis that they were irreplaceable in his company's factories. They left them alone.

I walked away from his statue, past an Irish Pub called O'Shea's, until I arrived at the start of a quiet side street. A man sitting in a shop alcove was busking with a scratched and chipped wooden guitar. Instead of strumming a chart hit, he was running his fingers over his faded fretboard to play an intricate classical piece. I watched his nimble dexterity for a few moments; his fingers were jumping around complex scales and arpeggios. He noticed me watching and so I walked over, dropping a couple of euros on his blanket to complete my good deed of the day. He thanked me, not missing a note.

I found myself on a long street filled with bars. Almost all of them were closed, with staff clearing up the previous evening's mess: streamers, knocked-over chairs and the like. Later that evening the bars would be full of students, I guessed, enjoying themselves in places called the Crazy Kangaroo, The Jack and the Tipsy Duck Pub, a name that would prove hard to pronounce after a few jars of Grolsch. I stopped by the window of The Jack. A poster advertised an upcoming concert by Sacred Reich, a US thrash metal band. Tickets were limited to the first thousand people who paid the fifteen-euro fee. I wondered what the Americans would make of Eindhoven. Maybe after their performance, they would visit a museum, just as I was about to do.

Eindhoven is famous for three things: PSV Eindhoven football club, DAF trucks, but most of all, the Philips electrical company. The latter two both had museums in the city, but because the Philips one was closer, that's where I decided to go.

The museum was smack bang in the centre of the city. Glass panels covered the entrance, and when I walked in, the old gent behind the desk sold me a ticket for eight euros, which I thought was steep. Nevertheless, I took my stub and walked around the corner where a large timeline of Philips' company information awaited my gaze.

I found out that Frederik Philips, a serious-looking individual with a thick bushy moustache, started the company in 1891. Seven years later, the fledgling Philips Corporation had their first big breakthrough when the Czar of Russia ordered 50,000 of their light bulbs. The business never looked back, and soon established themselves as one the biggest electronics companies in the world. Their headquarters remained in Eindhoven until 1997 when it moved to Amsterdam during a corporate restructuring.

The main part of the museum was full of old TVs (some of which reminded me of my 1970s childhood), radios, light bulbs and movie cameras. One section had an authentic-looking 1960s living room, with a black and white football match showing on a tiny square-shaped television. Next to it was an old reel-to-reel tape player.

I found a display of newer electronic equipment, including a 1980s personal stereo. Then I saw something I never knew existed: a record player for a car. Somehow, the device fitted underneath a driver's dashboard, where 7-inch singles could be fed through a small slot. It looked like an oversized CD player. It could even cope with the bumps and shakes of a 1960s convertible. I wandered upstairs, ambling by some Philips medical equipment until I reached the end of the museum. I looked at my watch: it was time to search out some old bones.

Beneath the modern concrete and glass veneer of Eindhoven lies evidence from its long lost medieval past. Under the imposing Gothic spires of Saint Catherine's Cathedral, archaeologists recently discovered the skeleton of a fourteenth century boy, his bones and DNA left almost intact despite the presence of underground water. When they dug deeper, they found more skeletons and then even more. In the end, they had 750 of them.

A few of the skeletons were found inside lime-coated wooden coffins, the lime an indication that they had died of the plague. Around this period, the Black Death was all over Western Europe, killing forty percent of the population, and mass graveyards such as Eindhoven's would have been common, especially around churches.

I removed my sunglasses and entered the tall brown cathedral, finding the inside tranquil and calm, as all places of worship are. Vivid stained glass windows allowed light to caress the vaulted archways and high ceilings, but I wasn't interested in them, I was on my way to a tucked-away section of the cathedral, far from the altar and pews. It featured a small display dedicated to the archaeological find. Inside glass cabinets was a collection of artefacts that had been found with the bones: coins, pottery fragments, necklaces and what looked like random bits of rock. A sign told me that most of the things had been found in the square outside. I decided to investigate further.

Back in the sunshine, set back from the entrance, a long glass panel caught my eye. I peered down through the cloudy glass, trying to make out what was there. My eyes focussed on some bones set amid loose rock and stone. It looked like a skeleton. The bones were not real, of course, but were indicative of how close to the surface archaeologists had found the real ones.

By now, afternoon was making way for evening, and so I went in search of food. Instead of sitting by myself in a restaurant, I elected to go for some junk food and bought myself a large slice of pizza from a shop along the high street. The Street Jesus had departed, I noted, as had most of the students. They had all relocated to the newly-opened bars further up the street. None was rowdy or raucous. Dutch technical students were evidently a conservative lot.

As the light faded, I found a quiet outdoor table in a bar underneath the Philips Light Tower. When my beer came I realised I was now down to the last five countries. Only Serbia, Greece, Cyprus, Hungary and Ireland remained. I had been on the go for ten days solid and I was dog-tired. My shins ached, my nose ached, my thighs ached and my feet ached most of all. But there was still something quite nice about sitting in a bar in a foreign city, watching the world pass by, thinking that tomorrow would bring a new adventure.

Top row: The Blob with the Philips Light Tower on the right;
Statue of Frits Philips, son of the co-founder of Philips Electronics
Middle row: Sombrero-wearing students; Downtown Eindhoven
Bottom row: Gothic spires of Saint Catherine's Cathedral; 1960s
room in the Philips Museum; A thoroughly modern apartment block
in the centre of Eindhoven

Day 11. Belgrade, Serbia

Eindhoven – Belgrade: Wizz Air £23

Today was the earliest start of any of my flights across Europe. The taxi picked me up at 8am for my 9.25am flight to Serbia. No Ryanair today; instead I was flying with Wizz Air, a Hungarian low-cost airline that had made great inroads into budget travel across Eastern Europe. I was looking forward to seeing how they compared to the Irish airline.

The taxi driver was an affable fellow in his late fifties who spoke excellent English, as most Dutch people did. He told me I was his first fare of the day. He also glanced at my bruised nose but elected not to comment. I said, "Do many tourists visit Eindhoven?" We were driving along a pristine highway, largely free of traffic.

"No. I do not think so. Well, I haven't met any, put it that way."

I nodded and kept quiet. I had decided that from now on, if anyone asked me whether I was a tourist, I was going to lie. My cover story was that I was on business. That would explain my short stays.

He continued. "Most people who come to Eindhoven are experts in electronics or high-tech industries. Like you, I expect?"

I nodded noncommittally.

He continued. "We get many visitors from India and China. Many of them live here and work."

We passed a massive football stadium – home of PSV Eindhoven. The taxi driver was clearly a fan, telling me about a local player called Memphis Depay. Manchester United had just signed him. But instead of being annoyed that the English club had purloined Eindhoven's home-grown talent, the taxi driver was pleased. "Dutch clubs cannot compete with English teams; they don't have TV rights to generate massive incomes. So when Manchester United agreed to pay 35 million euros for Depay, I was delighted. This means PSV has money in the bank to buy some world-class players."

We turned onto a stretch of motorway and the driver pressed down on the accelerator, causing the meter display to quicken worryingly. I suddenly thought of something. "If I asked you to drive me to Belgrade right now, what would you say?"

"Belgrade? As in Serbia?"

I nodded again.

"Then, I would turn the car towards the east and drive you there. Why? Do you want to go to Belgrade?"

"I'm flying there, but I was just wondering whether you would actually do it."

"Of course I would. Remember the massive Icelandic ash cloud of 2010 that grounded flights across Europe? Well, I was working that day. Two French businessmen were in my taxi. I was driving them to the airport but someone rang and told them their private jet would not be taking off. They made me pull over while they rang people about trains and buses, but everything was booked up. They looked worried because they had an important meeting to get to in Normandy. In the end, they asked whether I would drive them there. So that's what I did. It took six and a half hours and when we got to their destination, the meter said 1400 euros. It was my highest-ever fare. They just paid it in cash and said goodbye."

I whistled. "Wow."

"When I got back to Eindhoven, a friend of mine told me about other stranded passengers. With all the taxis and hire cars fully booked, some people ended up buying second hand cars just so they could get home. Madness. Utter madness."

Five minutes later, he dropped me off outside the terminal. I paid the fare, said goodbye and began the madness of my own again.

2

For the first time since Norway, I had to pass through passport control. Because I was leaving the Schengen Area, the 26-country travel-free zone of Europe, I was required to show my passport. In front of me were two queues: a short one for EU passports holders; a long one for everyone else. My EU passport holders' queue had only three people in it. Most of the Wizz Air passengers were in the other line: Serbian nationals returning home, I guessed.

Boarding was a painless process, and my randomly allocated seat placed me in the front of the cabin next to the window. The people next to me were a young couple who fell asleep as soon as their seatbelts were on. The legroom seemed similar to Ryanair's, but there was a distinct lack of advertisements plastered across the overhead bins. Exactly on time, the Airbus pushed back from the gate and we were in the air heading east towards the Balkans.

Wizz Air's coffee was much nicer than Ryanair's, but apart from that, their cabin service was much the same, only without the scratch cards. When we landed at Belgrade's Nikola Tesla Airport one hour and fifty minutes later, I was gratified that no trumpet sounded. And nobody clapped, either.

As we rolled towards the gate, I absently gazed at some ancient Russian turboprops parked at distant stands. They looked barely able to fly and I wondered whether they were permanent fixtures of the airport. Quite abruptly, we turned right and trundled to a stop next to a modern Air Serbia jet. Even before the unfasten seatbelt chime had sounded, half the passengers were out of their seats. No order came from the cabin to sit down. When the chime sounded, I stood up and headed into the terminal, which was awash with casinos and slot machine advertisements. I found an ATM and withdrew ten thousand Serb dinar, about £60, then prepared myself for the onslaught of Balkan taxi drivers.

The last time I'd been to Belgrade they had pounced within ten seconds, but this time I was better prepared. Instead of looking starry-eyed and clueless, I fixed my gaze forward, as if I knew exactly where I was going, and kept on walking. At the far end of the terminal were some car hire desks. I stood near them and, after scanning the terminal for a few moments, I found what I was looking for and walked straight to it.

"A taxi to central Belgrade, please," I said to the young woman behind the official airport taxi desk.

"Which hotel?"

I told her and she gave me the price. 1800 dinar, about eleven quid. I nodded and she led me outside to a waiting car. "Pay him when you arrive."

Simple, straightforward and painless. I threw my luggage in the back and jumped into the front seat.

"Hi," I said to the driver, an old man of about sixty with a stubbly chin of white.

He nodded but said nothing. I took this as my cue to shut up. Outside, the weather was overcast. Drizzle was splashing against the windscreen. When we picked up speed, water coated the glass and everything became blurred. Even so, the taxi driver seemed loath to switch on his wipers. Only when he couldn't see a thing did he turn them on, and only then for one single swish across the windscreen.

In that instant of clarity, I spotted a road sign for Beograd, the alternative spelling for Belgrade. It said the Serbian capital was six kilometres ahead. Then the rain got even heavier and I heard the first rumblings of thunder. Finally, in the face of such liquid onslaught, the driver turned his wipers on, shaking his head as if he had somehow lost the game. I noticed we were passing a series of Communist-era apartment blocks. They were ugly things: concrete monstrosities with no other function except to provide accommodation for the masses. As far as I could tell, none had been decorated with flower pots, or anything of any colour whatsoever. In the face of such concrete overkill, what would be the point?

The worst offender was the extraordinarily ugly Western City Gate. Its architectural style was called *Brutalism*, a movement popular in the 1950-70s. It was an apt term for the tower block. Like all examples of Brutalism, it was massive, bleak and made of copious amounts of concrete. Half of its mass was residential apartments, the rest set aside as offices. Think of a 1970s-era UK shopping centre and you will know what Brutalism is. But the Western City Gate took Brutalism to a new level.

It was 35-storeys high (making it the third tallest tower in Eastern Europe) and consisted of two grey towers connected by a bridge. In the centre was a circular protrusion (that was actually a restaurant) with a large antenna on the top. Built in 1977, it supposedly represented a gate – thus the name – but to me, it looked hideous and depressing, a repulsive blot on the landscape of Belgrade. Perhaps to cover up portions of the concrete abomination, a full-length advertising hoarding covered one tower. Instead of dull grey, it offered gigantic images of a chocolate drink.

We crossed the Danube, which sounded better than the reality, since it was an angry and swirling mass of gunmetal grey, and then entered the old part of Belgrade, the location of my hotel. When we stopped, I grabbed my luggage, paid the driver and regarded the park opposite my place of stay. It was an asylum seeker camp.

3

Reviews of my hotel stated that the camp had scared many guests. Some people had refused to leave the hotel due to the number of 'foreign looking people' hanging around. It didn't look especially dangerous to me, though it was busy with people loitering. I decided to investigate it further but first I needed something to eat. Just along from the hotel was a small convenience store. I went in with my luggage and bought some beef jerky type meat and a bread roll. Then I went to my room, dumped all my stuff and ate my cheap lunch. I headed back outside.

I estimated that there were three to four hundred people in the park, most of them young men between the ages of twenty and thirty-five. It was a small park and it adjoined a busy bus station. A few tents were dotted around on the grass, and washing dangled from nearby trees. A threadbare teddy bear lay outside the entrance to one tent. A hijab-wearing woman's head poked out of the tent, assessing the weather. Everywhere else, people were simply sitting around on stone walls or strolling aimlessly with their belongings. Almost everyone had a small battered suitcase – their only possessions reduced to hand luggage. Parents cradled or cuddled bewildered children. At one end of the park, a news crew filmed the scene.

I headed across the puddle-filled road and entered the camp. A few people stared, but most carried on with whatever they were doing, which was mostly nothing. Someone had glued a laminated white sheet of paper to a tree in the middle of the camp. *'Accommodation in the Centers for Asylum'* it stated at the top. Underneath, it told asylum seekers that they were in the Republic of Serbia and that they were entitled to ask for asylum if they had good reason. If so, then Serbia would offer them protection. *'You should express intention to an authorized police officer. The police will refer you to the Asylum Centre where you need to register within 72 hours.'* Once they reached the centre, health care would be provided, as would three meals a day. Those with children would be top of the list.

I looked around for a police officer. I couldn't see one. The Serb authorities had not completely abandoned these people, though, because a row of portable toilets stood at the far end of the park. Litter was everywhere, though: food wrappers, discarded chicken bones, empty water bottles. Every bin was overflowing with the detritus of people on the move.

I saw a man of about thirty sitting by himself with a holdall-type bag. I went over and said hello, sticking my hand out. He stood up and shook it. He looked nervous, his face drawn and his eyes flickering. He clearly felt I was someone in authority, or perhaps some Belgrade hard nut who wanted to cause trouble. I tried to calm him down with a smile but it didn't work, and when I asked if he could speak English, he vigorously shook his head. I nodded and left him alone.

Next I tried an older man sitting with a small boy aged about five. They looked Middle Eastern, like everyone else. When I smiled and stuck my hand out, he looked stricken and shook his head immediately, lowering his eyes. He looked scared of me, something I was not used to. No doubt the cut and bruising around my nose didn't help. His eyes flicked up at me for a moment, willing me to leave, and so I did, the boy staring at me wide-eyed while I backed away. At one end of the park, near the bus station, I tried a third man. He was standing by himself with a small flea-bitten suitcase. When I tried to engage with him, he cowered and looked so fearful that I felt I had actually struck him. When he shuffled away, I felt like a cad.

A slim white woman in her thirties was handing out toys to some of the migrants. People were accepting them with thanks. Some even spoke to her. I walked over and introduced myself. Her name was Jana, one of the twenty volunteers who helped in the park most days.

"Sometimes I give them shoes," she told me. "Sometimes shampoo and things like that. Mostly I give out food."

I asked her where the things came from.

"Donations. We have a Facebook page."

I followed her towards a thin blue tent where a toddler's face poked from the entrance. Jana reached into her plastic bag and offered the girl a small teddy bear. She reached out and took it, disappearing inside. Jana turned to me. "Even though some of these people don't look it, most of them are happy to be here. After all, they have escaped the wars and torture zones of Syria and Afghanistan. They are in Europe now. But they only stay in this park for a couple of days."

I asked, "Then do they go to the asylum centres?"

"No, they go to the border to cross into Hungary. They will set off when it gets dark. Once they reach the EU, they have freedom of movement. Most of these people want to get to Germany. But every day more people come, and so it seems like they never leave. The problem is that Serbia is not a rich country. We don't have enough money to look after our own people, let alone from other countries. For most people in Serbia, these migrants are unwelcome. That's why we help them."

I told her about my attempt at speaking to a few men earlier. We were now heading towards the eastern end of the camp, where a whole set of domed tents lay.

She nodded. "They think you are a Serbian official or maybe someone who wants to harm them. People sometimes come here to attack the migrants."

I thanked Jana for her time and watched as she handed out more things to the people in the tents. Without people like her, the migrants would have an even harder time. For them, the journey to Europe had been long and arduous, and not one they had undertaken lightly. I could only imagine the anguish of what they had gone through to get here: grabbing as much as would fit into their small suitcases, perhaps family photos, jewellery, some warm clothes for the kids, before leaving everything behind. I recalled news stories in the UK press before I'd left on my trip around Europe. They were having a field day about asylum seekers breaching security at Calais, trying to invade Dover so they could get their hands on British benefits. Sections of the British tabloid press had demonised these asylum seekers, likening them to leeches sucking the money from our already outstretched economy. The people I was looking at were not leeches. They were desperate.

I crossed a road and came to a large concrete underpass. Family after family were hunkered beneath tarpaulin, fear in their eyes, straining to live amid the stained concrete of downtown Belgrade. Who in their right mind would uproot their family, leave their home and country behind, and then walk thousands of miles across unfriendly territory to end up in a country where much of the population didn't want them there? Desperate people, that's who.

The European Union was worried about this mass movement of people, especially the country at the front line of the EU: Hungary. The day following my visit to Belgrade, the Hungarian authorities began building a barbed-wire fence along its border to stop the flow of migrants. In neighbouring Macedonia (another of the major transit routes), police began spraying water cannons at arriving immigrants. The problem persists and appears never ending, especially with countries closing their borders to quench the onward march of thousands of migrants.

As for me, I went into the shop near my hotel and filled my basket with bananas, apples and oranges. I took them outside and handed them to another of the volunteer workers – a man this time. It was a good deed, but only a small one. He thanked me anyway and I left him to it. Overhead, the clouds darkened and lumbered northwards, much like these people would be doing later that evening.

4

It started raining. It was not normal rain, either, but a storm-condition, torrential downpour that caused people to wear plastic shopping bags on their heads as they ran for cover under shop awnings. I was lucky that it had commenced only a short distance away from my hotel; I managed to run back. Even so, in the ten seconds it took, I ended up drenched, dripping and cold. When a thunderous cacophony accompanied by a flash of lighting shook the lobby windows and door, I knew I was in for the long haul and so returned to my room. If nothing else, it would give me a chance to rest my feet.

Forty minutes later, the storm had eased off enough to attempt a second outing. The people in the park opposite looked like they were emerging from their tents to resume their vigil of the park and bus station beyond. I watched a bus trundle past the park, sending an arc of spray towards the pavement. The streets of Belgrade were like rivers. I set off towards Republic Square, negotiating the puddles and potholes. Ten minutes later, at a point too distant from the hotel to run back, the Second Great Deluge stated.

It was even worse that the first. Within seconds, I was drenched like a rat. And so was everyone else. I tried to find cover in a produce market, but found its stalls were open to the elements. One vegetable vendor was wearing a T-shirt so sodden that it looked like it had gelled to his considerable stomach. A woman at the next stall, with a cigarette dangling from her lip, tried to lower some clear plastic to protect her ancient scales but ended up drenching herself when a torrent cascaded on her head. It might have been funny had it not been for the water running down my spine.

I found a concrete column and waited near it, shielding myself from the worst of the rain. But I couldn't wait in a market forever. What if the rain lasted another hour, or the rest of the day? I would see nothing of Belgrade. I decided to get on with my sightseeing and to hell with the weather. I stepped back into the onslaught, pressing my lips together and hunching my shoulders tightly. Hurrying forward, I passed a cafe with a large Nutella sign outside. Nutella was highly popular in Belgrade, featuring on numerous billboards across the city. The photo I was staring at showed someone pouring a dollop of Nutella into a coffee. I didn't linger, though, and up another hill, I walked by the Erotic Shop then crossed through a damp and grey underpass. Through the other side was the Hotel Moskva, a tall cream-and-green-coloured building that stood on one side of a busy shopping street. Because of the rain, most people had given up any semblance of keeping dry – in particular two teenage girls. They were embracing the rain, taking selfies that showed their lank hair and laughing faces. Another man looked less amused. He was aged about twenty and because of his long hair, beard and sandals, he bore an uncanny resemblance to Jesus. He passed me and glared at the sky, seemingly damning his God.

I trudged along the shopping street, passing shoe stalls, mobile phone shops and what seemed like endless clothes stores. Then I realised I'd been premature with my earlier underpass journey because I now had to cross the road again. Republic Square was on the other side. I waited at the kerb for a gap in the traffic.

Joining me was a young man, who, like me, was wearing a hat to keep the worst of the rain at bay. I glanced down at his feet and saw they were just as soaked as mine were. Just then, a car turned the corner, its wheels sluicing through the ankle-deep water. Both of us stepped back, but the driver hit a deep puddle. Before we had time to react, a wave of cold water hit our thighs, drenching us as if we'd fallen into a pond. The car sped off around a corner. I looked at the teenager and he looked at me. We both stared at each other's legs and then burst out laughing. It was absurd to find our predicament so amusing, but we guffawed nonetheless. Then the little man changed to green and we crossed the road. The teenager walked into a large department store whereas I sloshed toward Republic Square.

5

Even though I'd been to Belgrade before, I hardy recognised Republic Square. Prince Michael, sitting on his horse in the middle of the square, looked vaguely recognisable, as did some of the surrounding buildings, but the massive Transformer-type robot statues were new. One was Megatron, a twelve-metre high monster man weighing ten tons, designed by Montenegrin sculptor Danilo Baletić. He was also responsible for the other robots in the square, all made from recycled car parts. I stared upwards at Megatron, flinching when a nasty splatter of rain hit my face. Baletić had fashioned the monster's shoulders from two halves of a Ford Explorer's front grille. Its arms were exhaust parts, its fingers spark plugs. It looked amazing.

Despite the rain and modern sculptures, it was easy to see the glory of Belgrade's past. Tall and grand buildings, a well-kept palace and the stout National Theatre were throwbacks from an imperial age when Belgrade had been in the hands of the mighty Austro-Hungarian Empire. Harder to find was evidence from the Ottoman period prior to that. Back then, Republic Square had been an area of execution, with the impaled heads of unbelievers making the cobbles run red. Nowadays, paving blocks and waterlogged flowerbeds covered the cobbles and, instead of blood, it was rainwater sloshing around my feet.

I walked north from the square along a wide pedestrian-only shopping street that could have been anywhere in Europe. When the skies cracked and reverberated, sending down a vertical sheet of rain, I sought refuge under the entrance of a massive Zara store to wait it out. Opposite was an H&M store, its red neon lettering reflecting in the pools of water below.

A man wearing a clear plastic coat and hood walked towards me. As he neared, he proffered something in my direction: an umbrella. He had a whole batch of them in a large bag. I was tempted, but when he told me they were the equivalent of fifteen quid, I waved him away. Besides, the rain was easing. Five minutes later, I was on my way again.

At the end of the shopping street was a small park. A thin pathway led to it, flanked by an array of tiny craft stalls. Some offered paintings and T-shirts, others sold plates, scarves and fridge magnets. I stopped at a stall selling small wooden carvings of traditional Serbian houses. About fifty of them hung on a metal frame like a colourful village of pointy-roofed buildings. I asked the man in charge whether he had made them himself.

"No," he said. "A friend."

I nodded and picked one out, a maroon house with a pink and yellow roof. Angela would hopefully like it. I handed over three hundred dinar, about two pounds, and the man wrapped it in a sheet of brown paper. He then returned to his seat to read his book.

Beyond the stalls was a large statue of a valiantly posed woman, now the roost for a flock of sorry-looking city pigeons. Their feathers were ruffled and puffed up, and the birds looked thoroughly soaked. I left them, spying a path leading to a high wall. It overlooked the Danube. The great river looked cold and uninviting. A smoke-belching cargo ship was powering along the middle. In the distance was the concrete majesty of the City Gate Tower.

Jesus appeared again. He had a follower with him now – a man of a similar age but with much shorter hair. I nodded as they walked past me. Both nodded back. They climbed down some stone steps at the other end of the path.

I regarded the sky; it was still grey but with a large spot of blue. I removed my sodden hat and wrung it out before stuffing it in my sodden knee pocket. I headed for the steps.

6

At the bottom of the steps was another section of wall that overlooked the river. Jesus and his pal were nowhere in sight, but ahead of me I could see some battlements and fortifications and realised I had somehow found the grounds of Belgrade Citadel. On my last visit, I had climbed a steep hill to get to it, but this way had been much easier.

I walked away from the river, deeper inside the citadel, where I spotted Jesus and his friend. They were standing underneath a huge stone pedestal built in 1928 to commemorate Serbian victories in the Balkan and First World Wars. At the top was a bronze statue of a naked man holding an eagle in one hand and a sword in the other. The pair were trying to take a photo of themselves with it in the background. Because of the angle, they were struggling, so I stepped in and offered to take it for them. I took the photo and passed the camera back.

Jesus turned out to be from Brazil. His name was Ruben and he hailed from Sao Paulo, as did his friend Pablo.

"Brazil?" I said. "That's a long way to come."

"We are travelling around Europe," said Ruben. He told me they had just finished their university degrees in Sao Paulo and wanted to see a bit of the world before starting their careers in computing. "We started in Portugal and have reached Serbia after three weeks. This is the worst weather we have seen. Just rain and more rain."

I left them and passed various towers and gates until I ended up at the statue of Despot Stefan. I thought I'd misread his Cyrillic name plaque, but when I read it again, I realised I hadn't. His name really was Despot Stefan.

Despot Stefan had ruled Serbia between 1402 and 1427. His title 'Despot' was rather misleading, though, especially to modern ears. Back in the fifteenth century, the term 'despot' was simply another name for a lord or leader, similar to the ancient Greek word 'Tyrant' and the Latin title 'Dictator', both of which had morphed into something totally different. In fact, Stefan had been a brave warrior, a champion of arts and literature, and, for refugees fleeing Ottoman oppression, a saviour. Even though he had been responsible for much of the citadel buildings, the only section remaining from his spell in power was the appropriately named Despot's Gate, a round fortification of stone that was now an observatory.

I left the park, making my way back along the shopping street I'd walked along earlier. With the sun now shining over the Serbian capital, the city looked infinitely better. Instead of scurrying under umbrellas, the people of Belgrade now had a spring in their step. The dark puddles now reflected bright buildings, many rippling with colourful Serbian flags and city emblems.

7

On my last visit to Belgrade, I had visited Saint Sava's Cathedral. Back then, it had looked spectacular from the outside but dismal from the inside, building work spoiling any semblance of peace and beauty. I wondered whether anything had changed, and so typed its name in my Sat Nav app. It told me that Saint Sava's was two kilometres away, a walk of about thirty minutes. The question was, could my feet take it?

The answer was hardly. By a third of the way there, I felt on the verge of collapse. The pain in my left foot was excruciating, as if someone was stabbing behind my big toe with a fork and then battering it with a rolling pin. But I had to carry on and so hobbled a few more metres. Looming ahead at the end of the long boulevard called Kralja Milana was the spectral mirage of the giant blue and green cathedral. It shimmered elusively in the haze.

Somehow, though, I made it.

Like before, the cathedral looked truly spectacular: a panorama of green domes, golden crosses, extensive white marble and granite rendering. More impressive was its size: Saint Sava's was huge, one of the biggest churches in the world, forty percent larger in volume than Westminster Abbey. It took up almost the whole view in front of me.

I noticed a few people entering through the wide doorway and followed them in, hoping things had changed since my last visit. But it looked almost the same: bare concrete walls, grey floor and lines of scaffolding everywhere. The only additions were two stalls selling religious paraphernalia. It was a shame, I thought. The interior should reflect the magnificence of the exterior, but it didn't and, at the rate the Serbian authorities were going about things, it never would. For six years now, nothing much had changed.

On my way back to the hotel, I came across the former Yugoslav Ministry of Defence building. It looked like an earthquake had hit it. It was a hideous eyesore of gaping holes, twisted girders and crumbling concrete. But the damage had nothing to do with an earthquake: NATO cruise missiles had smashed into it in the early hours of 30 April 1999 as part of their efforts to stop the conflict in Kosovo.

From what I could see, the jagged red brick exterior of the Ministry of Defence building would have made it unremarkable, even in its prime. Nowadays it was unmissable. If anything in Belgrade deserved to be called *Brutalism*, then this was it. What made it stand out more was its location on a street that otherwise looked perfectly normal. I'd read somewhere that Donald Trump was thinking of pulling it down to build a hotel. I couldn't make up my mind as to whether that was a good idea or not.

8

My feet were in bad shape. Maybe it was my shoes, maybe it was my lack of general fitness, or maybe it was just bad luck, but whatever the reason, I needed to take drastic action. I was lying on the thin bed in my hotel trying to examine the sole of my left foot. The twisting action was agony, but at least I could see the problem.

Just behind my big toe was a large patch of white that looked like a large blister. I prodded it and squealed in pain, my head spinning at the sudden agony. I removed the needle from the complimentary sewing kit.

Gritting my teeth, I tentatively poked at the blister, hoping it would rupture without too much effort. It didn't and so I had to jab harder, wincing with the acute pain. But the blister was refusing to pop and the needle was slipping from my grasp because my thumb and forefinger were starting to sweat. I paused and took stock, resting my foot on the wooden floor. There was pain even in doing that, which made me more determined than ever to complete my nasty task. I twisted my foot back into position and then – before I could back out – thrust the needle in like a dagger. Jab! Jab! Jab! When nothing happened, apart from me screaming, I jabbed a fourth time, this time twisting the needle as I did so. With my eyes watering, my vision swimming and my mouth whimpering, I felt something give, and peered down to see a wave of clear liquid spurt out of the wound and splash on the bed linen. I dropped the needle and immediately squeezed my finger around the puncture mark, pressing with all my might while the iron was hot. In fact, if the room had contained an iron, I may have cauterised my newly opened blister into submission. As stood, with the thing drained of its sickly serum, I mopped up the mess with a tissue, covered the wound with a plaster and laid back to rest. Grim work always made me tired.

Later, I stood up and discovered that my homemade surgery had paid dividends. I could walk without limping and so decided to repeat the process on my right foot. While I did so, I prayed no one was walking past my room. Sniffles, screams and then sounds of pleasure would make anyone think the room housed a deviant.

At eleven o' clock that night, I put my shoes on and walked to the elevator. My feet still hurt, but nowhere near as badly as they had done. After exiting the elevator at the ground level, I walked outside to see what was going on in the park opposite. Jana was correct: the park was now a hive of activity and movement. Though it was dark, I could see bags slung across shoulders and infants cradled in arms. For those leaving, it would be a long night to the Hungarian border and, for those newly arrived, a period of relative rest until the following night when they would make their own journey.

I went back inside. I had my own journey to think about. Instead of heading north like the refugees of war, I was flying south to a city I'd never been to before: Athens. I was on the final few furlongs of my trip.

Top row:: Wizz Air – not much different from Ryanair; the Brutalism of the Western City Gate building; Statue of Despot Stefan Middle row: Me with my back to the Danube; Strange sculpture in Republic Square; Bombed former Ministry of Defence building Bottom Row: Republic Square; Saint Sava's Cathedral – bigger than you think;

Day 12. Athens, Greece

Belgrade – Athens: Aegean Airlines £26

From Belgrade, I could have flown to Geneva with Aegean Airlines for £44, which sounded appealing. Even better was the price to Malmo in Sweden, coming in at just over thirty quid. If I'd been particularly adventurous, I could've flown to a place I'd never heard of for £29: Mulhouse in France. Both of these bargains were with Wizz Air. But beating all these offers into submission was another Aegean Airlines flight to Athens for £26. And, unlike Ryanair or Wizz Air, Aegean Airlines was a full service carrier, meaning free luggage and free food.

I had been looking forward to visiting Athens for a long time. Even though I'd been to Greece twice previously, I'd never managed to get to the historical mainland. Instead, I'd holidayed on a couple of islands where the youth of Britain woke up at midday, and then enjoyed a Full English breakfast with HP Sauce and 'Real British Sausages'. By 3pm, after attaining their much sought after All-Over-Red-Body-Tan, they would spend the rest of the day drinking copious amounts of Mythos before being arrested or vomiting in a cocktail bar. In my twenties, this would have been the best holiday in the world.

Not now.

Everything about Union Jack filled beaches made me shudder. And I especially detested the hell known as *Coach Drop,* a feature of almost all package tours to the Med. As part of the Coach Drop, people were deposited outside a never-ending parade of hotels, while those still on board looked and judged, hoping their hotel would be better and more exclusive. And then there were the reps, offering welcoming words of wisdom about how hot it was and how important it was to drink plenty of fluids. "We've got a welcome speech tomorrow at half-past nine," they would utter as you traipsed off the coach. "We'll see you then." No you won't, thank you very much.

That said, Athens was hardly the ideal holiday destination. For a start, not many people went there on holiday, mainly because the Greek capital was supposedly filthy and falling to bits. Then there were the riots. Just before setting off on my trip around Europe, Greece had been facing an exit from the Eurozone, with bailouts and austerity measures not going down well for the citizens of the country. News reports showed protesters hurling petrol bombs at police in central Athens. A few weeks on, things were still tense in the Greek capital.

I woke up early in Belgrade for my journey back to the airport. While I waited outside the hotel for the taxi, I had another look at the camp opposite. It was quiet, with only a few people slipping around the edges. A couple of blue tents sat in the middle of the park, but whether anyone was inside them, I couldn't tell. A truck pulled up and a squadron of men in overalls piled out. Each had a powerful suction machine that gathered all the detritus from the previous day. While I watched them at work, my taxi pulled up. It was time to say goodbye to Serbia and hello to Greece.

2

Belgrade's Nikola Tesla Airport catered mainly for destinations in the Balkan region. Flights to the Montenegrin capital, Podgorica, were popular, as were flights to Sarajevo in Bosnia. Zagreb in Croatia, and Skopje in Macedonia also had a couple of flights, as did Vienna. The strangest destination was to a place called Twat.

That couldn't be a city, I thought. Even in a foreign language it sounded *wrong*. I got out of my seat and walked up to the monitor. Then I smiled to myself. The place was Tivat, a coastal town in Montenegro popular with Serbian holidaymakers.

I sat down again, recalling an incident from years ago when a ten-year-old boy in my class had come up to my desk with an atlas. He opened it at the index and pointed at a city he'd found. He wanted to know how to pronounce it. When I looked, I saw that it was the Japanese city of Fukui. The boy was staring at me, hoping for a reaction, and so I mouthed my response carefully. Foo-kay-oo, I said nonchalantly, even though I had no idea whether this was correct or not. The boy nodded and sat back down, disappointed at my level-headed answer. But secretly, I wondered what the correction pronunciation of the city was. I could just imagine a police officer stopping a Japanese tourist in London and asking where he was from.

"Fuk-yu."

"Right son, you're coming down to the station with us."

"But Fuk-yu, officer! You ask and I say, Fuk-yu!"

Back in Belgrade Airport's departure lounge, I bought a cheap coffee, which was the most expensive thing on the menu, and then sat down to count how much Serbian dinar I had left. I found almost four thousand in my wallet, which was about twenty-five quid. That meant I'd spent about sixteen pounds in Belgrade, not including taxis. The Serb capital had definitely been the cheapest place so far.

When boarding was announced, I walked to the gate with my luggage. When I joined the line, a woman in uniform stopped me. "Sir," she said, "your bag is too big for the cabin. I'm afraid it will have to go in the hold, free of charge, of course. Please collect it when you arrive in Athens."

"Really?" I said. "I've taken it aboard every other flight recently."

"This plane is small, sir."

Damn, I thought. This would mean an infernal wait at the carrousel, but I could hardly refuse. Outside, I waved goodbye to my two-wheeled companion for the time being and placed it on a luggage trolley. Then I regarded the aircraft. As the gate agent had told me, it was smaller than the planes Ryanair and Wizz Air used, and was powered by propellers. The cabin was narrower too. Instead of the usual three-by-three seat arrangement, it was two-by-two. I found my seat by the window and a heavily made-up young Greek woman with dyed blonde hair was in the seat next to me. For some reason, she seemed flustered.

As I put my belt on, she turned to me. "Excuse me," she said in a heavy accent. "Do you understand English?"

I nodded.

She looked embarrassed, as if she was afraid to speak. Then she started to say something but stopped, searching for the right words. Finally, she spoke. "Erm ... my boyfriend is ... erm back there somewhere. I am wondering if you might move into his seat so he can sit with me. He is in 19B."

I glanced back. Row 19 was about four seats behind; on the aisle, which would be no skin off my nose. I turned back to the young woman. "No problem."

She gushed a lipstick smile. "Thank you so much!" She turned around, gesturing to her boyfriend to get up, but he seemed reluctant to move. I caught a slight shake of his head. He seemed embarrassed.

I unbuckled my belt anyway, waiting for the switch, but the man wasn't going anywhere. His girlfriend turned back to me and gave an uncomfortable smile. "I think he is nervous." She stood up and moved into the aisle, jabbering away to her boyfriend, who now looked mortified to be the centre of attention. But after a few seconds, he stood up and began walking towards us. As he tucked himself into my seat, he turned in my direction, thanking me profusely. "You are so kind."

I smiled and walked down to my new seat, discovering that my new seat companion was the most beautiful woman on the aircraft. She was in her late twenties, with long dark hair and supermodel features. No wonder the boyfriend had been reluctant to move. The raven-haired beauty smiled as I took my seat but then stared out of the window, fluffing her hair at the reflection. Then she started flicking through a magazine full of clothes. In her lap was a Serbian passport.

I did my usual routine of working out where the emergency exits were and then powered up my music. Within a minute of the stated departure time, the engines spooled up and we trundled for take-off. Athens here we come.

3

Twenty minutes after take-off, the cabin crew handed everyone a plastic-wrapped sandwich. I read the ingredients with care, looking for tell-tale signs of egg or mayonnaise. All it said was that it contained Roast Chicken and Farmer's Sauce.

Farmer's Sauce? That didn't sound very nice. Which part of the farmer had it come from? I imagined a slack-jawed farm hand being 'milked' in a dirty grey potting shed. I stopped myself; the resulting image too disturbing to linger on. When I peered into the bread roll, I saw that Farmer's Sauce was white and creamy. It looked *mayonnaise* based. I couldn't risk it, and neither could the young woman next to me. She pushed it away unopened and resumed reading her fashion magazine.

Half an hour later, she fell asleep. And then something happened to me that had never happened before. One minute, the girl's head was upright, the next it was slipping towards my shoulder, where it soon came to rest. Her black hair was flickering against my cheek. Feeling the first stirrings of alarm, I didn't know what to do, and so kept as still as possible.

She really was beautiful, though, and I almost took a selfie, but the thought of her reaction if she woke up stopped me. So I moved my shoulder a fraction, hoping the transfer of weight would nudge the woman awake. It didn't. She was fast asleep, mouth open. Then the fasten seatbelt chimed and she awoke with a jolt. One second she was on my shoulder and the next she was sitting upright, fluffing her hair as if nothing had happened. We were beginning our descent into Athens International.

4

The Greek security official barely glanced at my passport before allowing me through to collect my bag. Miraculously, the first bags from the Belgrade flight emerged from the rubbery plastic strips after just five minutes of waiting. So much for Greek baggage handlers being a slovenly bunch; they had been working like demons. Like a contestant from *The Generation Game*, I scanned the bags as they went past, hoping that mine would be one of the first. It wasn't, and then I realised why. The suitcases, pushchairs and assorted bags parading past were all from an earlier British Airways flight from Heathrow. Sighing at the bother of it all, I found a chair to flop myself upon. The supermodel girl appeared from security and wandered over to the carrousel, attracting glances from most men in the vicinity. And then the couple I'd swapped seats with saw me. Both walked over.

"We want to thank you again," said the man. He was about twenty-five, with a layer of thin black stubble on his chin. "You are very kind man."

I stood up to shake his proffered hand. It was my turn to feel a little embarrassed. "Don't worry about it. It was nothing."

He shook his head. "It was more than nothing. It was everything. You made that flight special for us." His girlfriend was smiling and nodding. "And so we are wondering if we can help you? If you have not arranged your airport transportation, we would like to offer you a ride. My brother is waiting outside in his car. I've already spoken to him. He will drive you anywhere in Athens."

I was astounded. Me moving seats really had been no big deal for me and now these people were prepared to go massively out of their way in return. I thanked them, but declined, saying I already had a taxi booked, which was true. The previous night, with my feet in repair, I'd gone online and booked a taxi. We all shook hands, and they thanked me once more.

Forty minutes after landing, my luggage appeared. Thankfully, my taxi driver was still waiting. The journey into central Athens took half an hour, and by the time I got to my hotel, it was almost 2pm. Luckily, I had only one sight to see during my time in the Greek capital, and it was just a twelve-minute walk away: the mighty Acropolis.

Athens was hot and sticky. Even the cats seemed annoyed by the humidity. One tabby was perched on a window ledge near my hotel and, when I made suitable cat-friendly noises in its direction, it hissed and flashed a paw. If I had a jar of Farmer's Sauce with me, I would have flung a dollop in its direction.

At the bottom of the street was a main road full of speeding yellow taxis with madmen behind the wheels. All of them seemed intent on racing, screaming past and then hammering their brakes a couple of seconds later when they came to traffic lights. On the other side of the road was Hadrian's Arch. Almost two thousand years old, the gateway looked at odds with its surroundings because it was perched between a collection of modern buildings and the busy road. A bunch of tourists was taking photos of it, and so I crossed the road to do the same thing, hearing the sounds of chirping insects all around. Wherever they were, they were making a racket.

The arch was two storeys high, made of white marble and, as well as the large arc, featured classical columns, pediments and fancy brickwork. Just beyond it was a tall fence. I walked up to the railings to gaze at a series of tall columns belonging to the ancient Temple of Olympian Zeus. In the second century, the temple had been gargantuan, consisting of 104 columns topped with a limestone slab the size of a UK football pitch, all of it dedicated to the king of the Greek gods. It looked nothing like that now. Only sixteen columns remained (most of them clumped together), with one lying flat on the ground like a fallen pin in a game of ten-pin bowling. Later I learned that thieves had pilfered most of the marble to use as building material for other structures in the city. A terrible storm in 1852 was responsible for the one that had fallen.

"Hello," said a man's voice.

An elderly man with a sun-weathered face was smiling at me. Tufts of white hair sprouted from the side of his head.

"Hi," I said.

He asked me where I was from, and when I told him, he informed me he was from Santorini. "You know Santorini?" he asked.

I nodded. "I've not been there, but I've seen pictures. It's beautiful."

The man considered this, then stuck out his hand. "I'm George. Pleased to meet you."

I shook his hand and told him I was called Jason.

"That's a nice name. Why don't we go for a drink? I know a quiet place around the corner. You can tell me about yourself."

Was the man trying to pick me up? It seemed unlikely. I looked at the man's hand, searching for a wedding ring. There was none. Maybe he was some sort of travel guide, trying to sell a tour to Santorini. Either way, I didn't know what to say, and so I told him I didn't have time, which was true. "I'm going to the Acropolis," I said. I could see it on the other side of the archway, perched on a high rocky outcrop. "But after that, if you're still here, I'll go for a drink with you," I lied.

The man nodded. "I will look out for you, my friend."

I walked under the arch, crossed the road and headed towards the Acropolis.

6

I was following a route towards the entrance of the Acropolis. Busy taverns and tourist souvenir stalls, interspersed with an assortment of street musicians and beggars, vied for my attention as I made my way along it. One old man, sporting a fisherman's white beard, was lying on the ground. In front of him was a sign written in both Greek and English, which claimed he was suffering from brain damage. Further along was a man dressed as an ancient Greek warrior, complete with shield, spear and bronze helmet. A couple of elderly tourists were having their photo taken with him,

I passed a pair of tourist trains waiting for passengers. One was called the Athens Happy Train. The driver was a young man staring glumly into his mobile phone. It reminded me of a shopping mall in Doha, Qatar. Just inside of its many entrances was an area set aside for children's trolleys – the type that could house a small child in a racing car themed-shopping cart. Every time we went there, the same dour-faced man sat behind the counter. Above him was a large sign that read Cuddle Corner. No one ever cuddled him.

Along from the train, I noticed a few small children playing tuneless flute-type instruments. Most were wandering freely among the crowds, playing with one hand and begging with the other. One young girl of about eight was sitting down. A metre in front of her outstretched legs was a clear plastic cup with a few coins in the bottom. As two Scandinavian-looking young men walked past her, one accidently knocked over her cup.

"Hey!" the girl yelled, suddenly ceasing her playing.

Both men looked around and stopped. The blonde man who had kicked the cup retraced his steps and righted it, replacing the coins he had spilled. Then he added a few more of his own. The girl nodded and carried on with her recital.

Further up the hill, a trio of teenage boys were crouching beside something. One of them was taking a photo of whatever they had found. When they moved on, I saw it was a tortoise minding its own business in the undergrowth. Then I spotted another and, while I watched, the first one dashed over to the second and head butted it. The victim squeaked and retreated into its shell. I waited to see if anything else was going to happen but, when nothing did, I left them to it and found a woodland trail that led me up around a series of bends and steps. With the sounds of chirping insects coming from all directions, I arrived at the Acropolis ticket booth. Opposite it was a stand selling drinks and snacks. I went there first, asking the man in charge how much a small lemon-flavoured slushy was.

He told me.

"How much?" I said, sure I'd misheard him.

"Four euro fifty," he repeated.

It was daylight robbery. He knew it and I knew it, and so I toyed with the idea of walking around the Acropolis without a drink, but realised how foolhardy this would be on such a hot day. Belligerently, I handed over the money, which could have bought a meal and a beer in Belgrade. I walked away in disgust at the blatant rip off, and then paid another twelve euros to climb into the ancient site.

7

I'd been looking forward to seeing the Acropolis since the start of my low-cost European adventure. I was hoping for the same wow factor, the same gaping amazement I had experienced when I'd first set eyes upon the Great Pyramids of Giza and the Taj Mahal in Agra. But all I felt was keen disappointment: the Acropolis was a building site. The Parthenon was the worst offender. Scaffolding covered most of it, with a parked crane at one end and a whole load of building materials and equipment filling the middle. None of this stopped me and everyone else from taking photos, of course, but I couldn't help but feel a little bit cheated.

I was irrational to feel cheated, of course; I knew restoration work was needed in order to preserve the site for future generations. And I knew that the only way the Greek authorities could do this was by having JCBs and cement mixers dotted around the Acropolis. I got all that. But what irked me was this work had been going on since 1975! Surely it ought to be finished by now.

The view of Athens was unparalleled, though, especially from a high point near a gigantic blue and white flag of Greece. Beneath me, the relatively low-level city spread in all directions until it disappeared in the haze or else hit the distant mountains. Nearer in, a few hills coated in luxurious layers of green rose up from the city, their gradients too steep to support any construction. In the haze, I could just make out the Port of Athens, its ghost-like ships anchored in the bay.

I spent the next hour wandering the Acropolis ruins: the Old Temple of Athena, the Sanctuary of Pandion, the intriguingly named Erechtheum (the columned remains of a temple dedicated to Athena and Poseidon) and the Theatre of Dionysus, the latter a dramatic open-air theatre that could still seat 17,000 people. Everywhere I went the crowds were with me. Perhaps the restoration work schedule was justified, I thought. With so many people traipsing over every inch of the ancient site, day after day, year after year, it wasn't surprising that some sections were working loose or rattling in their foundations. When I walked past another bag of cement, I decided to return to ground level. I fancied visiting a Greek market I'd read about. As I retraced my steps back down the hill, I made sure that I avoided any route that would take me anywhere near George from Santorini.

8

Monastiraki Square was a hotbed of souvenir stalls, corn-on-the-cob stands, street cafes and tourists wanting to try everything. Stray cats lazed in the sun, waiting for evening to arrive so they could beg for food from the tables. Pigeons preferred the limelight in the central section, searching for titbits as they pecked in the dust. Behind a stall selling an array of dangling bananas and bunches of green grapes was a large sign saying Athens Flea Market.

Cheap designer T-shirts were popular in the market, as were sunglasses and shoes. *I Love Athens* bags hung from many stores, the same design I'd seen in countless other cities across the world, all manufactured in the same cheap Asian sweatshops. Suitcases, military costumes, postcards and jewellery made up the bulk of the other stalls, each one watched over by keen-eyed salespeople.

One of the great things about travelling solo was that none of the touts bothered me. Without a wife, girlfriend or daughter, I was on the lowest rung of the shopping ladder, lower even than a child. Even though many stallholders looked at me, they dismissed me within a second as being a non-shopper. And they were correct; I had no interest in any of their wares. I was through the other side in less than five minutes. Had I been with Angela, it would have taken an hour.

Later that evening, I decided to do my good deed of the day and bought a tin of cat food from a shop near my hotel. I tried to find the unfriendly cat from earlier, but it wasn't there. Instead, I found a trio of kittens hanging around a street bin, all skin and bones. They scurried for cover when I approached, but after I'd emptied the contents underneath the bin, and then backed off, all three began devouring the chunks of meat like there was no tomorrow.

I wandered back up the hill, past the taverns and tourist trains. The trains were gone but the eateries were doing good business due to the onset of evening. As for me, I was heading back to the Acropolis to watch the sunset from a good vantage point.

9

The woman at the entrance to the Acropolis would not let me in. She said the ticket I'd bought earlier was only valid for one go, and, since I'd already used it, I would have to pay another twelve euros for a second go.

I tried to disarm her with a smile. "But I only want to go up and take a few photos of the sunset."

She shrugged. It was none of her concern.

"You're not going to let me in, even though I've already paid for a ticket today – and not that long ago?"

"No."

"Thanks." Seething, I walked away and found some steps that led up a white marble outcrop. There was no entrance price to climb them. On the way up, the sound of chirping insects was the loudest I'd ever heard. It deafened my footsteps and the conversations of the other people who had already climbed up. The outcrop was known as Areopagus Hill, the supposed place where Ares, God of War, was once tried for the murder of Poseidon's son. It looked nothing like a court of law; it was merely a rough piece of rock full of jagged cracks and stunted trees. But the view was amazing, offering not only a commanding view of Athens, but also the full-on spectacle of the Acropolis. I mentally stuck up two fingers at the woman who had just denied me entry: this view was much better.

I found a rock to sit on, well away from the crowds. Below me, the setting sun was reflecting off the stucco walls and terracotta tiles of modern Athens, making the city appear warm and inviting. Even the scaffold-covered Acropolis was looking better with a splash of orange coating its marble surfaces. With a short while before the actual sunset, though, I decided to seek out the source of the infernal chirping. I arose from the rock and walked up to the loudest bush in the vicinity. It was a straggly thing, sprouting brittle green leaves attached to spindly branches. As I neared, the insects quietened, as if sensing my arrival. When I was up close to the bush, they turned silent, invisible to my eyes. I sought another bush, repeating the same process. The bugs spotted me well before my arrival.

And then I saw one. It was only because my eyes were staring right at it that I noticed the creature. The bug was almost hidden against the tree trunk, but there it was, a large camouflaged insect. It resembled an oversized moth mixed with a grasshopper and, if it hadn't been for the white tip of its abdomen, I might have missed it all together. It was sitting absolutely still, waiting for me to depart so it could resume its evensong. Later, I found out it was a cicada. It was the males doing the screeching, trying to attract the cicada females. The ancient Greeks had considered them a delicacy.

With sunset upon us, I relocated to my rock and gazed out across the city, as the colours turned from orange to deep red. Then, when the sky started to darken, I proverbially tipped my hat in the direction of the Acropolis and made my way down the hill. It was time to pack for the thirteenth country of my adventure, and the most southerly and easterly of them all: Cyprus.

Top row: The Parthenon – the best part of the Acropolis; Graffiti of downtown Athens
Middle row: Wandering along the stalls near Monastiraki Square; The view of Athens from Areopagus Hill
Bottom row: Monastiraki Square; One of the buildings at the edge of the square

Day 13. Larnaca, Cyprus

Athens - Larnaca: Blue Air £52

I was looking forward to some adult-themed entertainment aboard my flight to Cyprus. The airline was Blue Air; thus high-definition DVDs and saucy cabin crew sounded fair game. Yet, despite the promise of the name, the in-flight entertainment aboard the Romanian low cost airline was decidedly family friendly. I settled back in my aisle seat and then spotted something.

In the pouch in front of me was a *Hello* type magazine called *Beautiful People*. At first, I thought someone had left it behind but, when I saw that everyone had one, I realised it was part of the flight deal. I removed it and flicked through the first few pages. Paparazzi photos of women in skimpy bikinis were the main feature. I didn't recognise any of them, and I couldn't read the captions either, because they were in Romanian, but I still got the gist of what was going on. The editors had rated each woman out of ten for their style and sexiness.

A little girl, aged about five, sitting next to me in the middle seat, saw what I was looking at and then stared at me. I closed the magazine and got my phone out instead. She watched me switch it on and then craned her neck to see what I was doing. I twisted it towards me so she couldn't see, but she merely leaned over, making no bones about the intrusion.

Kids her age were utterly unabashed by social norms. Her father, over in the next seat, was unaware of his daughter's antics because he was staring out of the window. I smiled at the youngster but she didn't smile back. I flicked through some songs on my phone's playlist, just as a member of the cabin crew came past. The young woman stopped at my row, pointed at my electronic device and shook her head.

I put it in my pocket with the ever-watchful girl scrutinising my every move. She then decided it would be more fun to flap her arms like a chicken. Her father noticed this and, though I couldn't understand him, what he said made her stop. The girl looked at me again and I shook my head, as if to say, naughty girl. During take-off, she squealed with delight, which actually made me smile. Dad glanced at her, then picked up his Beautiful People magazine. He stopped at a page showing a woman with a 10/10 rating. When the aircraft levelled out for the cruise, his daughter began looking at a picture book about a princess and a lion. I read it over her shoulder. Or would have done had it been in English.

2

The flight was uneventful, and we landed at Larnaca International Airport slightly ahead of schedule. As I was walking towards arrivals, a male uniformed security official stepped in front of me. Other passengers looked at what was going on, and then gave us a wide berth. A female officer came over and joined us. *Yes, this is Mr Big,* her look suggested. *We have his sorry ass now.*

"Please come with us," said the first officer, a man in his forties. "We need to check your luggage."

He led me to a special place where a long metal table waited. It gleamed ominously. "Please," he said, gesturing to the table. "Put your luggage here."

I placed it on the table.

Both watched me, not saying anything, the female officer now hovering in the background. I had nothing to hide and so tried to appear nonchalant and sought some free Wi-Fi on my phone. This seemed to annoy the man and so he asked me where I was from.

"United Kingdom. Why?"

"Tell me why you are in Cyprus?" he asked.

I decided to tell the truth. "I'm on holiday."

"By yourself?"

I nodded.

"In a hotel?"

"No, I'm sleeping on the beach. Yes, in a hotel."

He ignored my flippancy. "Please open your suitcase."

I unzipped it, wondering what they thought it contained. If smelly socks were illegal in Cyprus, then I was done for. With his gloved hands, he started rummaging around, checking various pockets and lifting various items to see what was underneath. I left him to it and even rested on the edge of the table with my back to him; my phone had picked up some Wi-Fi and I was now checking my emails.

"Any alcohol in here, sir?" he said.

I shook my head.

"Please stand up and face me."

I did so. "Is there anything wrong?

Finally, the woman spoke. "Have you got anything in your luggage which we should know about?"

Yes. I have a stash of heroin and a box of amphetamines. I shook my head. "I don't think so."

This was the correct answer because she shrugged at her colleague and he told me I could zip it back up again.

"You may go," he said.

I did so and walked into arrivals. Welcome to Cyprus, a banner told me. Yes indeed.

3

Larnaca was exactly how I imagined it would be. Palm trees, bars, a stretch of sand crammed with overweight sunbathers and a long row of hotels mixed with fast-food restaurants. The sky was cloudless and the temperatures blazing.

I checked into my hotel and, after washing a whole pile of clothes in the sink and then draping them over the balcony, I was wandering along the palm-fringed beach promenade with all the other tourists. A group of middle-aged men were walking towards me, all of them tattooed and topless. Behind them were their wives, equally tattooed, but wearing flimsy sarongs to cover their modesty. The women stopped to browse one of the tourist shops while the men were on a mission to get to the nearest bar showing an English Premiership match.

I noticed a man on the beach wearing blue speedos. His tackle looked like a bag of bolts. He was watching a drunken game of volleyball. I walked on, passing a piercing parlour and a sign advertising Sunset Cruises for five euros. A long boardwalk led to the marina, home to the pleasure craft. I walked along it, hoping to find something interesting, but gangs of touts lurked and so I turned tail.

I decided to get something to eat and made my way back to the seafront. All the usual suspects were there: Pizza Hut, McDonald's and KFC, but I went into a restaurant called the Tuck Inn, which specialised in kebabs. I sat down and ordered one, asking for a bottle of Keo to wash it down with. When it all came, I found the kebabs delicious and the beer refreshing. I ate it while the tourist horde wandered up and down: people from the United Kingdom and Russia mainly. Wide Slavic features were almost as easy to pick out as the lobster-red paunches poking from beneath Manchester United T-shirts.

One thing they all had in common, though, was they seemed to love Larnaca. And fair play to them if that's what they wanted. But two weeks here would kill me. Larnaca was a facsimile of Tenerife, Kefalonia and the Spanish Costas.

Later that afternoon, I decided to head away from the sea. The crowds of tourists thinned as I moved inland into the town itself. As the sounds of waves and outboard motors faded, I found I had Larnaca to myself. Only a few cats peeking from beneath cars kept me company. Then I arrived at a small mosque. Its tall sand-coloured minaret poked above some mangy trees. In a house opposite, an old Cypriot woman was sitting on a veranda reading a small handwritten notebook. She didn't look up when I passed, and so I stopped and said hello.

She eyed me suspiciously, probably thinking I was a British lout. I smiled and said hello again, interested in what she was writing even though it was none of my business. Perhaps it was a novel, I mused, and the notebook was her character and plot jottings. Or maybe it was a diary, the beginnings of her memoirs. More likely it was a shopping list, but I didn't get a chance to find out because she mumbled something and disappeared inside her house. In the same situation, I'd have probably done the same thing.

Feeling guilty for bothering her, I walked towards the mosque, finding it quiet and secluded. I climbed some metal steps to the entrance where a darkened door stood. A handwritten note on it told me that prayers were in progress. I tried to peer in but could see only shadows. I left as quietly as I'd arrived, threading my way through the narrow streets of old Larnaca in search of sights anew.

I came upon a small church. It was called Saint Lazarus's, according to the information placard in front of it. Saint Lazarus was the man who Jesus once raised from the dead. Sometime after this momentous event, Lazarus moved to Cyprus and then didn't smile for the next thirty years. In fact, he died without smiling, and was buried for the second and final time. The church I was staring at was supposedly built on top of his grave.

The church featured a tall stone bell tower and an impressive archway running along one side. I walked under the arch, passing a shop selling a range of religious paraphernalia and tourist postcards. At a side entrance to the church, I stepped in, where an old woman tinkering with some candles glared at me. I removed my hat and she nodded.

The inside of the church was small but decoratively ornate, but I wasn't interested in the altar or the chandeliers, I wanted to see the sarcophagus of Lazarus down in the crypt. I descended some steps to find a ramshackle vault of stone walls, with incense burners dangling from thin chains. In the centre of the crypt was a marble coffin. I peered inside, finding it empty. Where his body was, nobody knew. Just then, I heard shuffling behind me and turned to see the old woman, who had followed me down. She said something in Greek that I didn't understand. She was shaking her head again, and I took this as my cue to leave. She watched me all the way out of the door.

4

The next morning, with quite a few hours before my next flight, I decided to visit Northern Cyprus.

In 1983, Cyprus split itself into two distinct sections. The southern part was full of beaches, hotels and holidaymakers; the northern part was a self-declared state that only Turkey recognised. The split arose partly due to the island's independence from the British in 1960. When this happened, a tense situation developed, mainly due to Greek Cypriots (the majority) wanting to unite with Greece, while Turkish Cypriots (the minority) couldn't think of anything worse.

In 1963, simmering resentment turned to violence between the two groups. Anger was so great that the Greek Cypriots expelled all Turkish political representation in the government. An uneasy truce followed, but things were not finished.

A decade later, a group of fierce Greek Nationalist staged a coup d'état. They claimed power and, fearing unification with Greece was close, Turkey responded by sending in troops. During a few weeks in the summer of 1974, while I enjoyed a caravan holiday in Northern England, thirty thousand Turkish troops arrived in Cyprus and took over forty percent of the island. Before a ceasefire could take effect, the Turkish army overthrew the coup leaders and ejected 200,000 Greek Cypriots from the North. In return, thousands of Turkish Cypriots left their homes in the south and moved into the Turkish-controlled north. Nine years later, this northern part declared itself the Republic of Northern Cyprus, a state recognised by no other country except Turkey. To separate both 'states,' the UN established a buffer zone called the Green Line. A portion of this line bisected the capital, Nicosia, with UN troops policing it. This buffer zone still exists today, making Nicosia the only divided capital in the world, rather reminiscent of Berlin during the Cold War.

After a quick search on the internet, I found out there were seven crossing points into Northern Cyprus. Five of them were for vehicles, but two were for pedestrians. Both were in the capital, an hour away by bus. Better still, one of these crossings was close to the Nicosia bus station. I grabbed my passport, camera and wallet, and went in search of the bus.

I found a stop opposite my hotel, near a large ice-cream stall. The bus was already there, but wasn't due to leave for a short while. I jumped aboard and sat down anyway. As I waited, the bus began to fill up, but the seat next to me remained empty. Then, with one minute to go, a trio of young women tottered aboard. They sounded Russian, and with the lack of seats, they had to spread themselves around the bus. One took the space next to me.

She was tall, blonde, long-haired and wore a tiny skirt. But she did not look like a Russian tennis player; instead, she was a babushka in the making and her girth pressed me into the side panel. As I considered this turn of events, a kafuffle started at the front. A middle-aged woman was screeching at the driver. He shouted back and she yelled even more. I strained to see but a crowd of heads blocked the view. Then something bad must have happened because there was a collective 'aah' from the front. More passengers stood to see what was going on, including the Russian girl next to me. And then I saw a dark-haired woman attacking the driver. Whether she was insane, drunk or both, I didn't know, but she was giving him a good few whacks. The driver was no slouch to combat, though, and sharply pushed the woman away. She almost fell down the steps. She managed to right herself in time to shout more abuse. The driver shouted back. The woman moved in place to attack him again.

An old man a few rows ahead of me got out of his seat and rushed along the aisle. The woman noticed and yelled at him too. He scurried back to his seat like a mouse. And then the police arrived outside. This brought a fresh wave of excitement along the bus, which was notched up further when they came up the steps and manhandled the woman out. I couldn't see anything else because everyone was blocking the view. From what I could gather, though, the police took her away, so we could begin our trip. This journey was turning out to be exciting.

5

The countryside north of Larnaca was mainly terraced hills dotted with Mediterranean shrub. A large sign caught my eye. It showed a colour-coded semicircle with a movable black arrow. *Danger of a Forest Fire*, it said above the arrow. It was pointing at the red section – high danger.

The driver, perhaps trying to make up lost time, was racing up the hills. Every time we rounded a bend, we swerved and the centrifugal force sent the Russian girl into me, squashing me half to death. Then things calmed down when we reached the plateau of the tallest hill and began a long straight journey downhill. The girl closed her eyes. Five minutes later, she was asleep and resting on my shoulder.

It was almost unbelievable: a strange woman resting her head on my shoulder on two consecutive days. What were the chances of that? Once more, I faced the dilemma of whether to move or to keep still. In the end, I had to move because her hair was tickling my arm and one of her headphones was digging into my skin. All it took was the slightest shrug of my shoulder and the Russian girl jolted upright, wiping her mouth. I pretended nothing had happened and stared outside as the fringes of Nicosia appeared.

Some of the houses on the outskirts of the capital looked magnificent. They were large and modern, standing in their own huge plot of land, well away from any of the neighbouring homes. Some were so big that they resembled mansions. I wondered whether they were retirement homes for wealthy Brits.

The centre of Nicosia looked less appealing, at least on the route the bus took. Generic office buildings, a few glass-panelled high-rises and plenty of faded shop fronts made the city seem almost down at heel. But then again, areas around bus stations were seldom the best a city had to offer. When the doors opened, almost everyone headed towards the city's main shopping areas; I walked in the opposite direction, following a walled street towards the Ledra Palace crossing. At a roundabout further along, I had three roads from which to choose. To make sure I picked the correct one, I powered up my Sat Nav app and waited for it to tell me the direction. The arrow pointed straight ahead, and so I found myself walking along a deserted street. Some tall buildings backed onto the road, but whether anyone lived in them, I could not tell.

Just as I was beginning to think I had somehow taken a wrong turn, I noticed a tall concrete wall topped with barbed wire. At the top of the wall were two flags: one from Turkey, the other from Northern Cyprus. Both featured the red star and crescent symbols of Islam. So the other side of the wall was Northern Cyprus, I realised, but the question was how to get to it.

I carried on walking, and five minutes later, saw two people: soldiers wearing blue berets. They were standing by a military checkpoint, guarding a couple of road barriers and lots of barbed wire. Behind them was a small white hut with the words UN written in large black letters. Beyond the checkpoint was a tree-lined road: the buffer zone. Even though it seemed utterly strange to do so, I headed towards the soldiers. And thus began my trip to the *de facto* republic of Northern Cyprus.

6

Both soldiers watched me approach and, when it clear I was not going to turn around, one of them stepped forward. He was a young man still in the throes of acne. "What do you want?" he asked in broken English.

"Is this the way to Northern Nicosia?" I said. I was well aware of his automatic weapon and serious expression.

Through narrow eyes, the young soldier studied me, and then shook his head. "That way." He pointed to somewhere around the corner. "You need the Ledra Palace crossing."

"This way is for cars only?"

"Yes. Cars only."

I thanked him and retraced my steps past the barbed wire and signs telling me not to drop any litter or take any photos. Around the corner, past a line of trees, was another official building: a low-rise portacabin with two uniformed people sitting inside. The man and woman were Greek Cypriot security officers. When I approached their little window, they both looked up. I showed my passport, and when they saw it was from the UK, they waved me on. I did so, entering the no man's land between the borders. I was the only person doing so.

A series of staggered concrete barriers lay in front of me. They were probably aimed at slowing vehicles down along the UN protected buffer zone but only succeeded in making me zigzag my way through. Once I'd negotiated them, I followed the road until I came across an abandoned building. It looked like the former residence of someone important. Old shutters hid smashed windows, but were so ruined themselves that they failed dismally. Peeling paintwork and cracked brickwork made the building a victim of its location: no one lived in the buffer zone and therefore nobody did any repairs. If the mansion had been just a hundred metres up the road, it would probably be the home of a wealthy family.

On the other side of the street was a large structure that looked like an upscale hotel, which it once had been. The former Ledra Palace (from where the border crossing received its name) was now UN barracks. Draped troop fatigues hung over balconies, the only evidence of anyone in the vicinity apart from the border personnel I'd seen earlier. In fact, as I carried on walking through no man's land, passing more deserted and broken down buildings, I felt as if I was passing through a ghost town, which I supposed I was. And then, after five minutes of traipsing along Markou Drakou Street, I saw the Turkish side of things.

The border was made up of a large white building. A yellow and red sign read: *Turkish Republic of Northern Cyprus FOREVER*, the upper case letters unmistakable in their meaning. A smaller sign next to it said, *Welcome to T.R.N.C. You are now entering the Sovereign Republic.* Above the signs fluttered the two flags of Turkey and Northern Cyprus.

To the left of the building was another portacabin where two uniformed officials from Northern Turkey waited. A man pushing a bicycle had just left the window of one. I passed him and went up to the first official. She was a young woman with long black hair. She asked for my passport. I passed it through the opening and she scanned it on her little machine without comment. Then she looked up. "First time here?" she asked.

I nodded. "I'm just visiting for a couple of hours."

She didn't comment and passed my passport back. I was free to enter the Republic of Northern Cyprus. I took a deep breath and did exactly that.

7

Markou Drakou Street looked almost the same across the border. The pavements were slightly more cracked, though, and the road surface looked a little rougher, as if it had not been cared for quite as well as the road on the other side. Smatterings of Turkish words scrawled on many storefronts were another clue that I had left the European Union.

The sound of children's laughter came from somewhere. A residential block was on my right and, in a garden, a group of women were chatting and preparing lunch. Some children were playing behind them. As I walked by, the women looked but paid me no heed. Suddenly, a tennis ball flew in my direction, bouncing just ahead of me before disappearing under a parked car. Seeing an opportunity to do my good deed of the day, I scrabbled beneath its bumper to retrieve it. A small boy was peering over the gate. I handed it to him and received a large toothy smile in return.

I carried on walking until I arrived at a main road busy with traffic and minibuses. A few people were waiting on the kerb sticking out their arms for a minibus to stop. The men were dressed in Western clothes, whereas the women wore headscarves. It really was as if I was in Turkey, and when I passed a large sign advertising Efes Beer, this notion was cemented further.

Away from the main road was a busy square. Near a line of parked taxis, a group of men sat smoking and playing backgammon. One laughed at something and smacked his pal on the back. A woman in a black headscarf was pulling a small boy across the square. He was holding a tiny plastic car. I took it all in, relishing the fact I'd left the tourist bars and sun loungers back in Larnaca. Nicosia, at least the Turkish part I was in, was a real, living place, not catering to the tourist horde in any way.

Next to the square was a large statue of Mustafa Kemal Ataturk, the first president of Turkey. His arms were folded, his expression stern, and the inscription below his likeness read: *Ne mutlu Turkum diyene, How happy is the one who says I am a Turk.* Judging by the people I could see, he was right.

At the end of a street that specialised in banks, fast-food joints and small cafes, I found the Old British Colonial Law Courts. It was a grand brown building, over one hundred years old, full of arches, expansive verandas and topped with a wide, two-tiered roof. Its surrounding gardens were well kept, full of blooms and potting plants. The courts formed one side of Ataturk Square. When the British were in charge of Cyprus, the area around the law courts formed the administrative centre of Nicosia. They built a post office, some governmental buildings and a police station. Back then, men in suits and top hats paraded around the law courts, and did so until the 1960s when British rule ended. The law courts passed into the hands of Turkish Cypriots, who have carried on using it for the same purpose to this day.

I couldn't see any lawyers but I could see a few outdoor bars. A few men were drinking Efes under shady parasols. They were sitting on white plastic chairs as they conducted deep conversations full of expressive hand gestures. As I walked past them, they all smiled and nodded. Beyond the bar was a strip of tired-looking shops, including the unfortunately-named, Anil Sport. In the centre of the square was a tall column that had arrived in Nicosia in 1550, plundered from the ancient city of Salamis, on the eastern coast of Cyprus. A trio of pigeons looked out from the top, one bobbing its head in the direction of some twin minarets over on my left.

The minarets belonged to the Selimiye Mosque, which, until 1570, had been the Cathedral of Sainte Sophie. In that year, the Ottomans stormed the cathedral, killed the bishop and smashed everything linked to Christianity. Then they painted over what was left and built some minarets.

I wandered the meandering and cobbled alleyways towards the mosque, finding covered markets, trinket shops and spice stalls, the pungent aroma of nutmeg, ginger and cumin clouding my senses as I passed them. A set of fearsome gargoyles guarded the entrance of the mosque. Once past them, I loitered inside the shaded courtyard, where an old man was folding white pieces of cloth into a pile. He wore a prayer cap and smiled when he noticed me. I smiled back, one again taken by the friendliness of the people in Northern Cyprus. When the man carried on with his task, I looked at my watch. If I wanted to catch the bus back to Larnaca, then I had to leave soon.

I retraced my steps past the law courts and the large statue of Ataturk. In my haste to return to the border, though, I somehow made a wrong turn and ended up near a tall wire fence topped with barbed wire. A sign said: TO TAKE PHOTOS AND MOVIE ARE FORBIDDEN. Next to it was a more ominous sign, featuring a scary graphic of a soldier wielding an automatic weapon. In six different languages, the sign said: FORBIDDEN ZONE. After a quick check that no one was watching, I walked up to the fence and peered through the wire. All I could see were rusty oil drums, a broken-down watch tower and masses of overgrowth. I turned around and found the road I was looking for – the one that led back to the border.

8

The return trip through both sets of borders, plus the bus journey to Larnaca, went without mishap. As I crossed the street towards my hotel, I realised that Angela would be setting off to Budapest soon. Her flight was with a UK-based budget carrier called Jet2, and she would be arriving a few hours before me.

When I got to my room, I collected the dry clothes from the balcony and packed them inside my luggage. Then I checked my flight details for later that night: Wizz Air to Budapest, arriving just before midnight. I rang Angela and verified that everything was still on, wanting to verify that I would meet her at the hotel in downtown Budapest. She told me she was having a coffee at Manchester Airport, waiting for the flight. "How is Cyprus?" she asked.

"Larnaca is what I expected – a beach, lots of bars and thousands of tourists. So today, I've been to Northern Cyprus – the Turkish side. It was much better. I'll tell you about it tomorrow."

I finished my packing and an hour later was inside a taxi back to the airport. It was dark and the neon was glaring along the front. Girls in tiny skirts and groups of young men were starting their evening's festivities in the bars.

The taxi driver asked me whether I'd enjoyed my holiday. I nodded, because I had – once I'd left the boozy beach bit behind and gone to Northern Cyprus. He asked me where I was from and I told him.

"Up until recently," he told me, "it was mainly British tourists who came to Cyprus. Now it's the Russians." I caught a scowl.

"You don't like them?"

The taxi driver shrugged. "They do not tip as well as British people. For them, if they return to Moscow with roubles in their pockets, then it has been a good holiday. British people spend every cent they have."

I asked the driver whether he had ever been to Northern Cyprus.

He scoffed. "Why would I go there? They hate us."

"Really? How do you know?"

The driver shot me a glance. "Why do you ask?" There was a tone in his voice that deterred me from saying anything else. We undertook the remainder of the journey in silence. Ten minutes later, I was outside the terminal where I paid him his fare. He took it without comment.

As he drove off, I entered my fourteenth airport in as many days. But after this, there would only be two more airports until I arrived back in Manchester. The end was in sight.

*Top row: Larnaca Marina and beach; Saint Lazarus' Church
Middle row: Me in the Northern Republic of Cyprus near a large
statue of Ataturk, the first president of Turkey; Approaching the
border with Northern Cyprus
Bottom row: The Old British Colonial Law Courts; Ataturk
Square*

Day 14. Budapest, Hungary

Larnaca – Athens: Wizz Air £55

We were taxiing towards the runway when the middle-aged woman with long black hair strode along the central aisle. She was walking unhindered because everybody else was sitting down, buckled in. As people strained their necks to see what was going on, the woman stopped an inch from a female member of the cabin crew and then, quite shockingly, let loose a tirade in a language I couldn't understand. The young Wizz Air girl took a step backwards as the older woman jabbed a finger in her direction. Just then, another member of the cabin crew rushed along the cabin, this one looking more experienced. The newcomer inserted herself between the angry woman and her younger colleague, saying something to them both. The female passenger threw up her hands in disgust and yelled. When the lead attendant said something else to her, the mad woman screamed.

"Go back to your seat," the older crewmember ordered.

This brought a seething froth of rage from the woman and I began to wonder what was wrong with her. Maybe she was drunk, but I didn't think so. Whatever the reason, she didn't follow the request and began ranting some more. In the meantime, a third member of the cabin crew was talking into a phone at the front, presumably letting the pilots know what was going on.

As we trundled towards the runway, a standoff ensued, but the woman had quietened slightly. Then the senior cabin crewmember said something to which the mad woman nodded. Next the two of them started moving back along the cabin. Everyone watched their passage with fascination. Her seat was about five rows behind mine, on the opposite side, and I felt sorry for whoever was sitting next to her. Finally she sat down and, just as we thought normal service had resumed, the woman screamed, shrieked and began sobbing, then another volley of high-volume yelling mixed with wild arm flailing erupted. The cabin crew woman battled with her, trying to keep her in her seat. The other two quickly joined her.

The young man next to me looked alarmed. So did most other people. Maybe the woman knew something the rest of us didn't. Perhaps she had a bomb under her seat. With the screaming getting louder, and with all three members of the cabin crew now physically holding her down in her seat, the aircraft stopped and then turned around. We were heading back to the gate. I wondered what would happen next.

At the gate, the engines spooled down. The woman was quiet again, sitting in her seat with a serene look on her face. The cabin crew were standing nearby, looking ready to jump on her should the need arise. Maybe she was one of those people who are so afraid of flying that they have to do everything in their power to get off a flight. If that was the reason, then it was a dramatic way to go about things, especially with the prospect of arrest and a fine. When the doors opened, a couple of hefty security officials boarded with walkie-talkies. Everyone waited for the woman to kick off again. But she didn't. Without any drama whatsoever, she allowed the men to lead her to the front, pausing only to retrieve her hand luggage from the overhead bin. When she exited the aircraft, the cabin crew crosschecked and secured the doors. Finally, we could get underway to Budapest.

2

The rest of the flight went without incident and we landed at Budapest Ferenc Liszt International Airport at 23.35. By the time I reached the hotel, it was approaching half past midnight, but Angela was still up. She noted my unkempt beard and bloodshot eyes but otherwise assessed me as healthy.

"I've already been shopping," she said. "But don't worry; it's all in the luggage." She pointed at her small suitcase. It looked slightly larger than mine did, but still small enough for budget airlines to allow as hand luggage.

"What have you bought?"

"Only a few Christmas presents and things for people's birthdays. Just bits."

I wondered why women were so obsessed with buying Christmas presents months before the event. If it were up to me, no one would get anything, especially not in August. But at least her mini shopping spree meant I wouldn't have to endure the torment of traipsing up and down endless shops the following morning. "That's good," I said.

I was awake now, and so was Angela. In a rare fit of unrestrained frivolousness, we raided the mini bar and opened a small bottle of red wine, toasting ourselves for arranging a midnight rendezvous in such an alluring city as Budapest. "Here's to Hungary," I said, raising my glass. "And surviving Charleroi."

Angela smiled. "It can't have been that bad."

"Oh it was. Belgium is officially the most dangerous country I've visited."

We finished our drinks and then, with my eyes turning heavy, retired for what remained of the night.

3

The next morning was sunny and warm, a perfect day for sightseeing in one of the most beautiful cities in Europe. Angela and I grabbed our sunglasses and left the hotel, map primed and ready. It was only 7.30am.

"Are you sure your feet are up to this?" Angela asked. We were making our way along a wide shopping street that led to the Danube, a river I'd last seen in Belgrade. Despite the early hour, it was already busy with tourists.

"I think so."

Angela had inspected my feet earlier, deeming them disgusting. She didn't dare touch either one of them, but claimed my left one looked 'pasty' and 'ragged'. When I'd removed the threadbare plaster covering my puncture wound, she almost gagged. But they felt okay, especially after the night's rest.

"Do you remember all this?" Angela asked a few minutes later. I nodded. The view in front was of Buda, the hilly part of the city that rose at the other side of the River Danube. The last time we had been in Budapest was on a cold February a few years previously. But the view looked the same, albeit warmer and greener. Perched on the high ground was the Royal Palace, the Fisherman's Bastion, and, further up, the citadel, home to the fantastic Liberation Monument. It was one of the most splendid pieces of Soviet metalwork still standing in Europe.

"I remember this statue." Angela walked towards the Little Princess; a life-sized bronze girl aged about six, dressed up as a pretend princess. She was sitting on some railings along the Danube Promenade, her back facing some tram tracks and the Royal Palace beyond. Her knees were shiny from all the rubbing she received from passers-by, including us.

"Right," I said, looking at my watch. A yellow and white Budapest tram clattered along the tracks just past the statue, its interior full with people going to work. "We've got eight hours before we head back to the airport. Let's get cracking. Time to see that church we missed on our last visit."

4

"It doesn't seem right," I whispered to my wife, "to be going inside a church with a bag full of beer."

Angela looked down at the plastic bag I was carrying. Inside was a bottle of Hungarian beer. "I can't believe you've bought alcohol before breakfast."

I nodded. "Needs must."

One of my follies when travelling was collecting beer stickers from around the world. My favourite was a beer sticker from Turkmenistan I'd picked up called *Berk*. My second favourite sticker was also from Turkmenistan. It was called *Zip*. Earlier, I'd bought the Hungarian bottle from a little tourist store near the Fisherman's Bastion on the other side of the river. The proprietor had looked at me oddly when I'd placed it on his counter at such an early hour, but didn't comment as he popped it into the bag.

Angela looked at the bag. "No one will know a beer bottle is inside."

Later I would remind my wife of these words, and how wrong she was about them but, for now, I followed her up the steps to the entrance of Saint Stephen's Basilica, Budapest's largest place of worship, named after the first king of Hungary, no less.

A crowd jostled us towards a room at the far side of the main entrance. Over the chatter of voices, we could hear the haunting melody of rich harmonies escaping the main part of the basilica. Ahead of us, people were depositing small change into a donation box. I scrabbled about in my pockets for some loose change, but found none. The lowest note in my wallet was 5000 forints, about £11.

"Have you got change?" I whispered to Angela.

Angela shook her head. The sound of the choir grew louder. I showed her the 5000 note and she agreed it was a little extravagant for a donation and so we walked past the box without putting anything in and entered the nave.

Friends who had been to Budapest had told us that the interior of the basilica was possibly the most stunning building in Europe. Perhaps that was an exaggeration, but it was an impressive view: a feast of columns, a shimmer of candelabras and an expanse of arches, iridescent in reds, blues and glittering golds. At the front, near a wide altar, was the choir.

"Wow," said Angela, looking at them.

"They're good," I whispered.

"Amazing, more like."

A matronly woman with a mop of brown frizzy hair was leading the choir. She was standing to one side, waving her hands and bobbing her head at timely intervals. But her leadership was paying dividends because the choir (mainly made up of young women) were pitch perfect, their tone melodious and rich, with exquisite harmonies weaving and merging with consummate skill and ease. Later we learned that they were part of the Basilica Choir who performed every Sunday. Their skill was so renowned that they were in demand all over Europe.

We moved further into the basilica, passing a series of mostly-empty pews. A few people were watching the singers, but mostly they were wandering around, looking at the icons, carvings and vaulted ceilings. Angela pointed to a set of wooden seats, around twenty in total, arranged to the right of the main pews. Seven or eight people were sitting in them, staring at the choir. We went over to join them.

I placed the plastic bag of beer by my side but the bottle was not falling right; I knew if I let go, it would clank onto the hard stone floor. I tried to rearrange it but, when I almost dropped the bag, I gave up and dangled it from my hand instead.

"You should video this," whispered Angela. "Their singing is so beautiful ... so moving."

I gestured to my bag of beer and shrugged. The sound of angelic singing filled the cathedral,

"Give it to me."

I passed my wife the bag and she gently placed it on her lap. With that sorted, I started filming the scene. I zoomed in on the woman leading the choir and then panned across to the singers.

And then the unspeakable happened.

As Angela reached into her handbag, she set a dreadful sequence of events into action. From the corner of my eye – as if in slow motion – I saw the plastic bag rearrange itself, settling into the contours of her knees. Then it opened itself up and the beer bottle emerged, imperceptibly at first, but still enough to notice its movement. All of this happened in a split second. Then it was rolling off the side of my wife's knee.

I tried to reach for it, just as Angela noticed the calamity. Both of us were powerless to do anything except watch it drop towards the hard stone floor. With the choir singing, the bottle smashed in a horrendous explosion of froth and glass. Because everything was happening in slow motion, the crash seemed silent. But then, a second later, the most horrendous, ear-piercing sound assaulted us. It was a crack of thunder, a deafening report, but instead of unleashing a torrent of rain, beer was its ungodly gift. It spewed in all directions, hissing like a demented beast. A second later, the people around us flung back their chairs to escape the torrent. In the aftermath, I eyed the alcoholic carnage in horror.

5

Angela sprang into action first and passed me the empty plastic bag. Then she dropped to her knees, scrabbling around to pick up the largest shards of glass. She handed me a few, and I placed them in the bag. One of them had the still intact sticker attached to it.

I joined her on the stone floor, scrunching my nose as the unmistakable aroma of beer hit my nostrils. Instead of doing a good deed of the day, we had done the worst kind of deed possible. Smashing a bottle of beer in a church during a recital was probably a cardinal sin. As I reached for some of the broken glass, I noticed some shards had come to rest underneath people's seats. It was at that point I noticed a woman rubbing her hair, trying to rid herself of the Hungarian lager dripping from it. When she caught my gaze, she regarded me with pure loathing. And who could blame her? She, along with everyone else nearby, had been enjoying a heavenly performance when suddenly, and contemptibly, a pair of heathens had invaded their serenity and smashed a beer bottle in their midst. *A bottle of beer!* At half past eight in the bloody morning! By now,

Angela had found a couple of tissues in her handbag and was attempting to mop up the puddle. It was like cleaning a monsoon flood with a household mop.

"Let's get out of here," I whispered.

"We can't leave it like this." Angela whispered back, staring at the ground. As far as I could tell, she'd not looked up once. "There's glass everywhere. And that smell. Oh my God...I'm so ashamed. This is a cathedral!" I thought she was about to start crying, but instead she carried on gathering the smaller bits of glass into a pile. As for me, I found the almost intact bottom section of the beer bottle and saw that it still had some liquid inside. I stood up and plopped it into the plastic bag of shame. Almost immediately, an arc of beer came out of the bottom. Evidently, it had pierced the bag, turning it into a beer-dispensing outlet. That was it, I decided. We had to go. I grabbed my wife's arm and led her away from the scene of disgrace. Without looking back, we exited the church, pausing only to deposit 10,000 forints in the donation box.

Outside, neither of us said anything until we were well away from the cathedral. Angela broke the silence. "I can't believe we did that. I'm so mortified. You and your bloody beer."

"Me! You were the one who smashed it. You were the one who wanted me to film the choir. I told you we shouldn't have gone in with a bag of beer. It was God's revenge for not leaving anything in the donation box." I suddenly remembered the sticker and stopped to look in the bag. It looked okay. I reached inside to remove it.

"What are you doing?" asked Angela.

"Nothing." The sticker was damp but was coming away easily from the glass. Then it ripped and I gave up. So the whole incident had been for nothing. The only thing left to do was dispose of the glass. I spied a shop selling newspapers and bought the thickest Hungarian language one I could find. Carefully, we wrapped the shards inside the pages and then placed the whole bag in a waste bin. As we walked away, Angela sighed deeply. "That is the most embarrassing thing I've done in my life. Those people hated us. *Hated.*"

6

Later, with the sting of embarrassment still keen in our minds, we ambled along the riverfront, watching another tram speed by filled with the people of Budapest. Later, they would probably be watching a news report about a dastardly deed that had taken place inside Saint Stephen's earlier that morning.

The Danube was busy with pleasure boats, some of which would be heading to Bratislava and Vienna as part of a grand European cruise. We watched one power along the river full of happy sightseers. "How long would it take to get to Bratislava?" asked Angela.

"By boat? I'm not sure, maybe three or four hours. Driving is quicker – about two hours, I think. Why? Do you fancy going there?"

"I've never been to Slovakia. Yeah, I'd like to go someday."

My brain flashed into overdrive. "Let's go right now. Not all the way to Bratislava, just to the first town across the border."

"The first town across the border?"

I could feel myself growing excited at the prospect. I opened my Sat Nav app and scrolled around the northern edges of Hungary until I came to Slovakia. "Here we go. There's a place called Sturovo. It's right on the border. It takes an hour by car, but there's a train station there. Let's go back to the hotel and get some Wi-Fi. We can Google the train times."

Angela looked at me as if I were mad. "Are you being serious? You've been travelling to all these countries, day after day, and now you want to visit another one – and one you've already been to. There's something definitely wrong with you."

I could hardly stand still; I was growing more energised by the second. We had seen most of Budapest on our last visit, and this morning, we'd visited the things we'd missed out. So jumping on a train to somewhere new sounded exciting, thrilling even. Angela remained unconvinced. "Look," I said, we'll check how long everything takes, and if it's not doable, then we can forget about the whole thing."

Angela was judging how serious I was about the proposal. Finally, she spoke. "If we can be back in time for our flight this evening, then I might be up for this."

Five minutes later, we were at the hotel. Google told me that a train left Budapest Keleti station at 9.25am and arrived in Sturovo an hour later. The return journey left at 1.15pm, which would get us back in Budapest by 2.35pm to catch our Ryanair flight to Dublin. So all in all, that would leave three hours to enjoy Slovakia.

"Is there anything to see there?" Angela asked, finally coming around to the idea that we were now going to another country.

I typed Sturovo into Google and searched for images. The results looked pleasing, showing what looked like a fetching central square, some pretty shops and a big green bridge that spanned the Danube. I showed the photos to my wife who nodded appreciatively.

The plan was a go. We jumped in a taxi and told the driver to take us to Keleti train station without delay.

7

The lady with purple hair working behind the ticket counter was most helpful, securing us a pair of return tickets to Sturovo for the equivalent of a fiver each. On the platform, a few people were milling around with luggage, most of them probably going to Bratislava or the ultimate stop, Prague. Ten minutes later, a blue-and-yellow diesel engine rumbled towards the station with a blast of its horn and screech of brakes. Everyone headed towards the rear carriages but we jumped aboard the nearest one at the front. We found the carriage empty, which was fine by us.

Soon after, a man blew a whistle and waved at someone. The time on the old analogue clock said it was 9.25, and then we set off, dead on time. Outside, the grime of inner Budapest was passing us by: a forgotten place of graffiti, crumbling brickwork and Cold War-era factories, a world away from the gorgeous and pristine tourist sites of the city centre. As the outskirts and suburbs eventually fell behind us, the scene changed to residential housing and woodland. We sat back and relaxed.

A uniformed ticket inspector came into our cabin. He was a middle-aged man with a friendly face and keen eyes. After studying our tickets, he told us we were in the wrong cabin. "You are sitting in first class," he said in excellent English. "Your tickets are for second class."

"Oh," I said.

He caught our crestfallen looks. "Let me see how much it will cost to upgrade you both." He tapped away on his ticket machine and told us it would be the equivalent of one pound fifty to stay in first class. I handed over the money before he could change his mind. When he was gone, I powered up the Sat Nav app on my phone. While it aligned itself with the unseen satellites above our heads, I stared outside at what appeared to be an outpost town of Budapest. When the app kicked into life, it told me it was a place called Dunakeszi, a small settlement with a gymnasium and a small airfield but little else. I zoomed out to see if anywhere else of interest was coming up. And that's when I had an epiphany.

I found Göd.

8

Göd was a tiny Hungarian town. I showed Angela the moving map, which was pointing at the upcoming town. She peered at the screen and laughed. "We smash a beer bottle in a church," she said, "and then get to see Göd. There's something wrong, there."

Göd, we later learned, wasn't actually that small and was home to almost 20,000 people. The town stretched along the eastern edge of the Danube and enjoyed a proliferation of thermal spas. Mostly, though, it was a sleeper town for commuters working in Budapest. As we got closer to Göd, both of us stared at my phone's screen, not wanting to miss the moment we passed through such an entity.

And then we did.

And Göd looked nice.

Very nice indeed.

Göd was full of large pointy-turreted buildings, numerous pleasant homes (a lot of which sported colourful flowerpots on their lawns) and plenty of trees. I couldn't see any of Göd's people, though. Maybe they were all in Budapest at work. But before we could revel in the glory of Göd's presence, we were rattling forward towards the border between Hungary and Slovakia. I nodded at Angela. "Göd looked peaceful, didn't it?

Angela nodded, smiling.

"But," I said, "if we had stopped in Göd ... and maybe caused a bit of mischief ..."

Angela looked at me.

"... such as knocking on people's doors and then running off, or pulling plants from gardens, we would have been Göd botherers."

Angela laughed.

Beneath our feet, the wheels rolled onward across the border without missing a beat. And then, one hour and twenty minutes after leaving Budapest, we arrived in the Slovakian border town of Sturovo. We were the only people to get off the train. We watched as it left, leaving us alone on a deserted, windswept platform.

9

"You said there'd be a taxi," said Angela.

"I thought there would be."

We were surveying the pockmarked car park outside the train station. Apart from an old car that looked abandoned, there was nothing and, according to my Sat Nav app, the town was a thirty minute walk away. Our fun trip to Slovakia was turning out to be a bit of let-down. Perhaps we should've stayed in Budapest.

We left the station and trudged towards a petrol station, the only building of note apart from the row of three-storey townhouses on the other side of the road. The houses looked empty, but the petrol station was open, though we bypassed it in order to get into the town as quickly as possible. Soon, the long strip of grey tarmac took us into open countryside interspersed with the odd farm building. The town of Sturovo was nowhere in sight. Somewhere in the distance, dogs barked.

"Where is everyone?" asked Angela as we marched onward. We'd just passed a large sign advertising a Lidl supermarket. If things got desperate, I thought, we could always hide out there, drinking cheap Slovakian wine until help came.

"God knows."

Just then, a car passed us. The single occupant was a balding man who peered at us as he drove by. I waved and he waved back. Then he was gone, disappearing past a builders' merchant's yard in the distance. Fifteen minutes later, when we passed an abandoned pub, I felt we were nearing the centre of town. Further on, a series of small houses appeared, some painted in pastel blues, greens and yellows. Mostly, though, they were faded shades of white. And that was when we spotted our first pedestrian. It was a woman walking a dog. She was heading towards us on our side of the street and, as she got closer, she nodded and smiled. Then she turned into a small shopping arcade we had not noticed. Two people armed with bulging shopping bags emerged from the entrance. We decided to investigate.

Inside was a jewellery shop, an odd-and-ends store and a supermarket. It wasn't as highbrow as Lidl, but it did sell cheap loaves of bread, packets of cheese and slices of ham: a feast for our return journey to Budapest. Everyone looked friendly enough, too, and so our moods improved. With our food wrapped and safely stowed in Angela's bag, we headed back outside to explore Sturovo.

10

Not far from the supermarket was the busiest part of town, a pedestrian-only area where a few people wandered around a collection of small shops. The town planners had planted a few shrubs to add a bit of greenery and a couple of park benches for restful folk to sit on, but, even so, they could not cover the fact that Sturovo looked like a 1970s village. Angela and I sat on one bench, taking in the town, trying to ignore the presence of a large casino at one end. Though it was before lunchtime, the establishment was open for business, its flashing lights loudly advertising the fact. I stared at the shops: one was a cafe, another sold mobile phones and a third sold pizzas. That was pretty much it.

"That looks nice," said Angela. She was pointing to our left. In the distance, sitting atop some higher ground, was a grand-looking building, maybe a church or a palace, we reckoned. We got up and walked past the shops until we found ourselves at one side of the Danube. The structure was across the other side of the grey expanse, and the only way to get to it was via a green bridge some distance away. I switched on my Sat Nav app, which told me that the river formed the natural border between Slovakia and Hungary. Across the other side was Hungary. The app also informed me the castle was actually a basilica (the tallest building in Hungary, no less). With no way of reaching it, we walked to the river's edge.

"We are staring at another country," I said. "Over there is the Hungarian town of Esztergom."

"It looks nicer over there," Angela commented.

I nodded. As well as the massive basilica, we could see that Esztergom had some fortified walls and a set of grand buildings. It was the sort of place a person ought to visit, unlike Sturovo. The best thing about the Slovakian border town was the view it had of another country.

We went for a coffee in the town centre. Inside were only a few patrons, mainly young couples and one old woman. All of them ignored us as we took some seats.

"Are you looking forward to Dublin tomorrow?" I asked Angela.

Angela nodded. "Course I am. If we hadn't been to Budapest before then I'd have wanted longer there, but as it is, yes, I'm ready for Dublin. But I couldn't do this day after day, like you've done."

A twenty-something waitress came over to take our order. After we'd given it, she studied us. "Excuse me, but can I ask where you are from?" she said.

We told her.

"So why you come here?" Her question was rather blunt, I felt.

We told her the truth: that we had been staying in Budapest but decided – on a whim – to visit Slovakia by train. I said, "We were the only people to get off at Sturovo station."

The girl looked as if she didn't believe us. "So you come for fun. That very unusual. People go Bratislava or Prague. Few tourists come here, and if they do, they mainly Hungarian people."

I asked her what it was like living in Sturovo because, as far as I could tell, there wasn't much to do beyond spending money in the large casino across the road.

"It is what it is." She glanced around to check that the older man behind the counter wasn't watching her. "When all factories closed in last few years, the town went downhill. People lost jobs, they could not pay bills and many had to leave. Some tourists come in summer, for swimming and pool spas, but Sturovo in winter is ghost town. I stay for my mother. My brothers left many years ago already."

We didn't know what to say to that and were glad when the waitress walked away. Twenty minutes later, it was our turn to walk away. Sturovo train station beckoned, as did the promise of a cheese and ham sandwich aboard the train.

11

Our train pulled into Budapest at the allotted time and we alighted with all the other passengers. A woman behind us had a pushchair and, seeing an opportunity to do my good deed, I helped her lift it off the train. She thanked me graciously as I set it down on the platform.

Since we had a bit of time before we had to return to the airport, Angela suggested we did a bit more shopping. I suggested we didn't, which resulted in a standoff. Then my wife sweetened the deal by pointing out that I needed to buy another bottle of Hungarian beer so I could get the label. "So while we look for your beer, we might as well look in a few shops."

It was a bad deal, I knew, but since I had no other suggestions I conceded the point and we set off along one of the main shopping districts of Pest, a street that would have looked at home in Manchester, Berlin or anywhere else in Western Europe. I bought my beer after five minutes; for the next twenty, I trudged after Angela, trailing around shop after shop until she finally bought something: a candle that she said would make a good present for someone.

Back at the hotel, it was time to pack again. "Your bag looks too big," I commented.

"Too big for what?"

"For Ryanair."

Angela stared at her bag and then at mine, comparing their sizes. She judged it to be a fraction longer than mine and quite a bit thicker in the middle. "It might be slightly bigger, but Jet2 accepted it."

"That's Jet2. Today is Ryanair. They're a bit stricter. You might have to pay a fine."

"A fine?" My wife looked alarmed.

"I think it's seventy quid. Maybe more." I was lying, of course: the bag looked fine. I'd seen plenty of other people with bags much bigger. But I was enjoying myself, getting my own back for the shopping trip earlier that afternoon.

My wife told me to shut up and to stop annoying her. I did, and then cracked open my bottle of Dreher beer. After a couple of slugs, I deemed it good quality ale, but decided not to drink it all. I wanted to save myself for the Guinness in Ireland. After another mouthful, I emptied the contents into the bathroom sink, then began my sticker removal ritual. First, I filled the basin with hot water, then I submerged the bottle in it, holding it down for a good minute or two. Afterwards, the label peeled easily. Another one for my collection.

Finally, it was time to head to the airport. The final country of my trip around Europe was only a few hours away.

*Top row: Panorama of Budapest taken from the Fisherman's
Bastion; Bronze statue of Stephen I with a spire of the Fisherman's
Bastion behind
Middle row: Little Princess statue; Close up of Matthias Church
Bottom row: Esztergom Basilica – Hungary's tallest building;
Wandering Sturovo*

Day 15. Dublin, Ireland

Budapest – Dublin: Ryanair £46

Where better a city to end my trip in than Dublin: capital of the Emerald Isle and headquarters of Ryanair? I'd been before, of course, about fifteen years previously. I'd gone with a bunch of mates, and flown Ryanair then. We didn't take any photos or buy any souvenirs, so all I can recall about those drunken few days is playing pool, eating kebabs (at the excellently named Abrakebabra), and drinking copious amounts of Guinness around Temple Bar. This time, I intended to remember everything about Dublin. But first, we had to get there.

Like at every other airport, the queue for the Ryanair flight to Dublin was long and busy. Only a handful of people were sitting down. Despite my reluctance to join the snake, Angela insisted we did, stating that we would stand a better chance of getting our bags into the overhead bins. I regarded my luggage, the same piece that had caused me untold annoyance and yet had survived the trip intact – even a few hard kicks and dunks in puddles had not caused any lasting damage. It was a miracle the wheels had remained in place.

We joined the queue, even though it was not moving. Twenty minutes later, with still no movement, I started sighing. "We should be boarding by now." I looked at my watch. It was a quarter to five in evening, twenty minutes before departure. "There must be a delay or something."

Ahead of us was an Indian man in a black suit. He was talking into his phone. I assumed him to be a businessman until he turned around to reveal a white dog collar. I'd never seen an Indian priest before. That was when I noticed a Ryanair employee on a mission.

The uniformed woman was walking along the latter half of the queue with a practised eye. She was seeking out oversized bags. I looked at Angela's hand luggage and tutted. "That's for the chop," I said.

"What do you mean?"

"It's too big and it'll have to go in the hold," I said this in a tone that suggested I was an expert in all things Ryanair – which, I suppose, I was. "I warned you about this. Get your seventy euros ready."

Both of us watched the woman. She was checking boarding cards, eyeing luggage and, every now and again, wrapping yellow stickers around luggage that looked too big for the cabin. These were destined for the hold.

Angela manoeuvred her bag so it was behind mine, hoping the vigilant Ryanair woman would not notice it. But she did and she put a yellow sticker around the handle. Then she addressed my wife. "You will have to collect it from the luggage belt at Dublin airport."

"And I've got to pay seventy euros?"

The woman shook her head. "There's no charge."

The woman glanced at my bag, deemed it fit for the cabin and carried on along the line. Angela was glaring at me. Then she leaned towards me and uttered something shocking. "I'm going to pull the sticker off."

My heart skipped a beat. "Really? But ... it's against the rules. You'll be a law breaker."

"Stuff the rules. I'm not having my bag go into the hold when there are plenty of people with bigger bags than mine. Look."

My wife had a point. But the people she was pointing at were at the front of the line. Their luggage would fit into the bins no problem. The issue we had was that we were almost at the back of the queue, which meant by the time we boarded, there would be no room left.

"How are you going to pull it off?" I asked. There was no way she could remove it without attracting attention. She realised this herself and covered it with her hand until most of the sticker was hidden.

Finally, the line moved. We should have taken off ten minutes ago. Outside, the arriving Ryanair 737 was releasing the incoming passengers and our queue was moving into the holding pen beyond the gate. Soon, we were allowed onto the tarmac where a large trolley waited for the yellow-stickered bags. Angela brazenly walked by it, climbed the steps at the rear and sauntered past the cabin crewmember waiting just inside the cabin. With that done, I placed my bag into the overhead bin and then squashed Angela's in too. Job done, we sat down and buckled up.

2

The flight was another full load for Ryanair. When everyone had sat down, the captain apologised for the late departure. "A long delay earlier this afternoon has had a knock-on effect on flights since. But don't worry," he said in an Irish accent, "we should get you to the gate in Dublin only fifteen minutes late."

He was correct. Two and three quarter hours after leaving the heartland of central Europe, we arrived into an overcast Irish evening. For the first time on my trip, the trumpets were silent as we trundled in.

"Welcome to Dublin," said the purser, "where the local time is seven thirty," The young woman's Irish brogue pronounced the time as 'seven terty'. "We hope you had a pleasant flight with Ryanair and hope to see you again soon."

I turned to Angela. "Has it been pleasant?"

"It's been okay. And for the price, who can complain?"

"Exactly."

Twenty minutes later, we were standing outside arrivals, waiting to board a bus to the city centre. The bus was there, but there was no sign of the driver. Then another bus pulled up. A group of passengers got off and so did the driver. The door closed behind him. Where he went, no one knew.

While we all milled around, scratching our heads and wondering whether to jump in one of the waiting taxis instead, a man wearing a coach company jacket approached. Assuming he was our driver, we all waited for him to open the doors. He didn't. Instead, he pressed a button on coach number two. He stepped inside and turned to face us.

"I suppose yar all waitin' for d'coach there?" he smiled, gesturing to the first coach.

None of us said anything.

"Well, the driver'll be here shortly. He's just nipped to the ... ah ... toilet. His stomach's a bit dicky today. He shouldn't be long. But when he comes back, I wouldn't look him in the eye if I were you."

A few people laughed, but a middle-aged couple from the Netherlands failed to see the humour. They regarded their guidebook instead.

"Here he is now," the man said. "Avert your eyes."

The new driver walked towards us and when he reached his colleague standing inside bus number two, they exchanged a few words. The men were clearly friends. The second man realised most of us were staring and so turned to us. "Don't believe a word of dis man. Whatever he's said, he's a liar. Now, who wants to go to Dublin?"

We all trooped aboard the first bus and set off towards the Irish capital.

3

Dublin city centre was awash with touts selling open-top bus tours or handing out flyers for restaurants, bars and tourist shops. Spanish, French and Brazilian accents flowed along O'Connell Street, the city's main drag, mixing with snippets of German, Irish and British dialects. Many tourists were filling their faces inside the proliferation of fast food restaurants along O'Connell's or gawping at the monuments. The largest monument was the Spire of Dublin, a 400-foot dart of stainless steel that was easily the tallest thing in Dublin. It gleamed like a supersized silver missile.

The spire stood on the spot where Nelson's Pillar once was. In 1966, in the early hours of a March morning, an IRA bomb blew it up. The dart that replaced it dated from 2003. Across the road from the Spire of Dublin was one of Ireland's most famous buildings: the General Post Office.

It was a massive construction, which stretched along one edge of O'Connell Street like a granite palace. Why the Irish Post Office needed such a colossal structure to sort letters and arrange parcel deliveries was beyond me. We stood by its grand entrance, a facade of columns and friezes that make it look almost ancient Greek, to pose for photos. As it happened, though, the section Angela and I were staring at was the only part of the vast building that was original. Battles during the Easter Rebellion had destroyed the rest. During April 1916, a group of Irish republicans used the post office as their headquarters and, to flush them out, British troops attacked the building with shells and bombs. Fires soon broke out and spread throughout the building, forcing the rebels to flee and surrender. With the post office gutted and broken, British authorities executed all the ringleaders.

"Smile," I said to Angela as she posed in between a couple of columns. I took the snap and then we carried on with our walk, meandering through the jostling crowds that were heading towards the River Liffey.

4

We stood on O'Connell Bridge surveying the Liffey. It was a brownish-green body of water crisscrossed by a series of spans, including the Ha'penny Bridge (named for the amount once charged to use it), the Millennium Bridge (built in 1999 in commemoration of the impending millennium) and the Grattan Bridge (a cast iron span older than the other two and modelled on London's Westminster Bridge).

The river looked calm, just as it had on a July evening in 2011 when a man jumped into it to save his pet rabbit. The man, John Byrne, had been living rough on Dublin's streets with a rabbit called Barney. On that particular day, Byrne had been sitting on O'Connell Bridge, minding his own business, when an eighteen-year-old youth rushed up, grabbed his rabbit by the ears and flung it into the Liffey. Without pause, 38-year old Byrne dived off the bridge and saved the drowning creature, much to the amazement of the watching crowd, some of whom had filmed the incident on camcorders. With the local Garda on the tail of the culprit (eventually charging him with animal cruelty), Byrne gave the kiss of life to the floppy-eared creature, and managed to revive the rabbit. Afterwards, the people of Dublin praised Byrne's actions, awarding him for his unthinking bravery and giving a large bag of carrots to the rabbit. An animal charity went one step further and offered Byrne a job in their shelter.

No one was in the Liffey right now, but plenty of people were on the bridge. A hen do walked past, cackling and clattering in their heels. The bride had the ubiquitous L-plate attached to her back. "Right," I said to Angela. "We can either visit the National Leprechaun Museum – which is a real place – or have some Guinness in Temple Bar."

"As if you even need to ask that question."

"To the leprechaun museum it is, then."

We crossed the bridge and headed in the direction of Temple Bar.

5

Temple Bar is *the* tourist hub for anyone visiting Dublin. It's where the liveliest bars are, it's where the stag and hen parties go, it's where people go to eat their potatoes, scallions and Irish stew, and it's where tourists go in their thousands to browse souvenir shops selling the same things: Guinness memorabilia, Celtic crosses, leprechaun key rings and 'I love Dublin' T-shirts. Also, it's where street performers set up shop. One band was already in full swing, belting out a fast tempo Irish jig. They were called Mutefish, a six-piece band who described themselves as progressive techno folk, whatever that meant. They were good, though, getting the crowd to stamp their feet and bob their heads in time to the beat. The fiddler, a dreadlocked man who also played a tin whistle, led the band through another high-voltage track that brought a new crowd in to watch, but hunger called us and so we went into a nearby bar to get some food.

As soon as we stepped inside, the homely sound of an acoustic band met our ears. The guitar, banjo and tenor vocals were teasing the Guinness-supping punters until they kicked into a traditional Irish number that had the crowd roaring with delight.

"Here's to Dublin," I said. We were sitting at a tiny table, the only place available in the packed pub. Everyone around us was drinking pints of Guinness or Dublin Porter, raising their glasses as the band finished their song. "The final stop."

Angela nodded and smiled.

I took another sip of my stout. Once upon a time, people claimed that Dublin's Guinness was the best in the world, but that had been in a time when it supposedly hadn't travelled well. The Guinness I was now drinking was the same as the stuff back in England. It was still lovely, though, and after we'd eaten our lamb and potato stew, we decided to find another bar in order to sample more of Ireland's finest.

6

The pubs of Temple Bar were deliciously pretty from the outside. One, appropriately named The Temple Bar, was painted in red and black, and dated from 1819. To us, it looked authentically *Irish*, even though it probably wasn't. Stuck to one of its windows was a notice explaining that anyone who drank there on a Thursday night was welcome to try some complimentary black pudding. Across the cobbled street from it was The Quays Bar, this one elegantly covered in brown and green tiles. Both pubs featured heavily on the postcards in every tourist shop.

From somewhere came the sound of raucous shouting and jollification. It was, of course, a stag party. As they descended upon Temple Bar, we could tell they were British, about twenty men, all wearing identical Guinness-themed T-shirts emblazoned with the immortal words: Heatman's Stag.

Unusually for a stag do, their ages ranged from twenty-something to fifty-something. The younger men looked in worse shape than their elders, already inebriated, and the source of much of the noise. As they staggered past, we caught glimpses of their black T-shirts. Printed in bold white lettering on the back of each one were their names. Milky, Spammers, Big Al and Fairy passed first, closely followed by a wiry man called Eggy. The Stagg and the oddly named Left Arm Glasses ambled by next, followed by a larger group. Underneath each name was an empty glass of stout, and within this space were stickers representing how many pints of Guinness each man had consumed. A ruddy-faced man in his twenties called Pleck was in the lead with twelve stickers. In last place was a bald man called Flaming Torch with only three.

Dublin is the number one hotspot for Brits on a stag or hen do. Cheap flights and copious amounts of Guinness attract them in their droves. Most groups are well behaved, but some are not. In 1997, a British stag party made the news when they attacked some Irish policemen. Because of this, Dublin banned stag groups for a short while. Mind you, British tourists are not the only cause of trouble in the city; sometimes it is home-grown thugs. In April 2012, a group of local hard nuts were in the process of mugging a man in the Temple Bar area when two brothers from New York stumbled across them. Being good citizens, the young Americans told the group to break it up or else they would call the police. The gang of robbers told them to mind their own business. The Americans didn't and so the gang turned on them

While the tourists of Temple Bar watched with alarm, the Americans made a run for it, heading towards some parked taxis. With the gang in hot pursuit, throwing bottles at them, the brothers tried to jump in a taxi, but the driver refused them entry. The next driver refused too. In desperation, they ran through the narrow streets of Temple Bar, hoping to lose their pursuers in the thick crowds. But then, just like in a movie, the brothers found themselves in a dead-end alleyway. The gang caught up and began attacking them with bottles and broken glass. During the assault, the gang slashed at them and knocked the men unconscious, leaving them for dead.

Ambulances rushed the pair to hospital while the police went in search of the gang. It didn't take long to find them: they were all known troublemakers. The ringleader, a 23-year old Dublin man called Anthony Clifford, was eventually sentenced to six years in prison; his accomplices received between three and five. As for the Americans, both made a full recovery, although one is now permanently scarred below the eye.

7

The next morning, a woman working in our hotel's reception suggested we catch a bus to the Guinness Storehouse. "Bus number one-two-tree goes from across the other side of the road."

"123?" I asked.

"Yes. One-two-tree."

We told her we wanted to walk.

"Walk? Are you sure, now? I don't know anyone who would walk from here. But if that's your plan, then just follow the Liffey. It might take a while, though."

The forecast was for heavy rain, but when we stepped outside, the sky looked fine, blue with just a few clouds. Before undertaking our walk to the Guinness Storehouse, however, we found a souvenir shop. Angela was hoping to buy more gifts.

"What is it about you and gifts?" I said as we entered the large green Paddywagon Tourist Store, which promised to sell us *Gifs and Souvenirs Galore!* The shop featured a large picture of a pipe-smoking leprechaun surrounded by clover. He was laughing uproariously at something.

"You're such a miser. What wrong with buying presents for people? It's not as if I'm spending hundreds of pounds on them. It'll be a couple of euros at most."

After browsing a few aisles, mostly of joke-shop items, Angela stopped to look at some gaudy Dublin mugs. Most featured representations of Temple Bar or leprechauns. I stood next to her, wondering why leprechauns were such big business in Ireland. Angela picked one up just as a thin man approached. He was holding a red tube. Angela hadn't noticed him.

"Do you want some ketchup with that?"

Then, before either of us had time to react, he squeezed the tube, sending an arc of red towards my wife's neck. Angela screamed even before it touched her; while she did that, I stepped back to avoid any splashback. But none came, because the ketchup was actually a piece of red string. Angela laughed in relief and so did I.

The assailant, who turned out to be the proprietor of the shop, grinned as he threaded his red sting back into the bottle. "It's the small joys of life which keep me going." He returned to his counter.

As Angela continued with her perusing, a young woman walked up to the counter. I watched the man surreptitiously reach for his red bottle, and then, while the woman was opening her purse, he repeated the trick. The woman screamed and recoiled, but then laughed when she realised it was a piece of string. I searched the shop and found an identical ketchup bottle. When I placed it on the counter, the man nodded knowingly. "A fellow prankster, I see."

Outside the shop, when Angela saw my purchase, she shook her head. In the end she hadn't bought anything. "Why did you buy that?"

"Because it's funny."

My wife looked unconvinced and declared she wanted a latte. We found a Starbucks and ordered some coffees. When they came, I began reading a free copy of the *Irish Daily Mail*. It led with 'the most heart-warming story of the summer'.

A handyman from County Mayo had won 6.3 million euros on the lottery thanks to his faithful dog. The shaggy dog story, as the reporter described it, introduced us to Ger Murphy, a grey-haired man whose two loves in life were purple pullovers and boxer dogs. Before his big win, he had been on the verge of moving to England. What stopped him was his 11-year old dog, Katie, who vets deemed too old to travel. So Ger stayed put and then, to drown his sorrows, he bought a lottery ticket, which ended up being the winning one. He claimed this good fortune was down to his boxer dog. "If it wasn't for her, I wouldn't have won."

I closed the newspaper and looked outside; Angela looked too. Quick as a flash, I raised my hands and squirted her with the joke ketchup bottle. She screamed as if I'd attacked her with a knife. Everyone in the cafe turned to look and I hastily returned the red bottle to its bag.

8

The Guinness Storehouse disappointed us. For some reason, we'd expected it to be an actual working factory, with real workers toiling over pipes, pumps and barrels of stout. In my mind, I'd pictured a sort of Guinness-themed *Charlie and the Chocolate Factory* manufacturing plant, with rivers of black stout surrounded by waterfalls of pale ale. Instead, the Guinness Storehouse was a well-oiled machine of mass tourism that had ceased being a place of fermentation in 1988.

Because I'd had the foresight to buy our tickets online, we bypassed the lengthy queue inside the entrance. We couldn't avoid the mass of people heading up some atmospherically-lit escalators towards the first part of the storehouse, though. We joined the back of them, and then arrived in the massive Guinness Shop. It sold every Guinness-related object imaginable, from Guinness golf tees and Guinness truffles to Guinness rucksacks and a ridiculously large range of Guinness themed T-shirts.

A Guinness pint glass tempted me but after I spied a box full of Guinness crisps, I decided I had to try them instead, even though they cost two euros for a small packet. After paying for them, I showed Angela my purchase. I opened them, and we both peered inside at the darker, but otherwise normal crisps. Angela tried one first, popping it into her mouth. I waited for her verdict. She scrunched her face and said nothing. I grabbed one myself and crunched away, hoping to detect a taste of Guinness on them. I was disappointed. They tasted like normal crisps, with maybe a hint of beer; nothing like my favourite brand of stout.

We entered the storehouse proper. It was full of exhibits, videos and placards explaining the history of Guinness in Dublin, the ingredients that are put into it and how the drink is transported around the world. Then we came to a floor dedicated to Guinness advertising, which turned out to be the best part of the whole experience. There was the famous fish riding a bicycle that was used in the Guinness advertising campaign from 1996, and the original black and white footage of the first ever Guinness TV advert from 1955. It featured a sea lion balancing a pint of the black stuff on its nose. Even more impressive was the huge wrap-around cinema screen that played continuous loops of the more famous Guinness television advertisements. Watching the black horses erupt from the swirling torrent of white surf on such a large screen was mesmerising, so much so that we waited for it to show again a few minutes later.

At the other end of the floor were a series of photographs showing famous people enjoying pints of Guinness in the storehouse. Tom Cruise, Barack Obama and the actor who played Hurley in *Lost* were on the wall. "Right," I said, pointing at a photo of Philip Schofield, "if it's good enough for him, then it's good enough for me. Let's head upstairs for our free pint."

Angela looked at her watch. "It's not even lunchtime."

"I know. That's what makes it special."

9

Upstairs, we had two choices: either we could learn to pour our own free pint of Guinness or we would make our way to the Gravity Bar, so called due to the 360-degree views of Dublin it offered, and have an expert pour one for us. We decided on the latter.

Despite the relatively early hour, everyone (apart from a few children who, in my opinion, shouldn't have been there in the first place) was supping on Guinness. One Chinese couple looked like they were going to retch after every sip. A young woman behind them took a small sip and shook her head. The man with her laughed.

Angela and I walked to the circular bar in the middle. It was a production line of stout, with endless pints in various states of completeness. Despite the hectic activity going on, a young man quickly came over to serve us. I asked for two pints of Dublin's finest and he nodded and set to work, finishing off two glasses that had been settling for some minutes on the side. When he was done, he passed them across the bar. "Can I have your tickets please?"

I looked at Angela. She started rummaging around in her handbag. The tickets had come from the self-service machine when we'd first arrived in the Guinness Storehouse. I was sure I'd given mine to Angela but, just in case, I checked my pockets and wallet. No ticket anywhere. Angela finished rummaging and produced one ticket – hers. Behind the bar, the man waited patiently.

"Where's mine?" I whispered to my wife.

"How am I supposed to know?"

"I gave it to you!"

Angela sighed and checked her handbag again, while I searched my pockets for a second time. The Guinness was waiting on the counter, and I could almost taste it. Droplets of condensation were forming on the side and the head looked creamy and smooth. To be thwarted now would be the cruellest joke of all. Frantically, I rifled through every pocket, every nook and cranny of my wallet but came up with nothing. I felt like grabbing Angela's ticket and running off with one of the pints. When Angela came up empty handed, I almost did just that.

"Look," said the barman. "Just pass me the ticket you have. Don't worry about it. But if you do find the second one, just hand it to me."

We thanked him profusely and took our drinks to a section of the bar near the window.

I took a sip, finding the stout no different from any other pint of Guinness I'd ever had, but still delicious. It was filling too, rather like a meal in a glass. I'd once read that a single pint of Guinness, together with a banana and a Mars Bar, contained all the nutritional goodness a person needed to survive for a day. It sounded unlikely but, at the same time, plausible. I mentioned it to Angela who still hadn't tried any of her Guinness.

She thought for a moment. "Maybe it's true, but I can't imagine it being healthy for long. And besides, who would want to try it out?"

"Students who have no money. Alcoholics who like bananas. People who want to lose weight." I took another sip of my drink. Around the rim of my glass, a white and creamy mark remained. I smacked my lips in appreciation.

Angela finally took a small sip. She grimaced slightly.

"What's wrong with it?"

"I'm not a big Guinness fan," she admitted. "And it's only half past eleven in the morning. There's no way I'm going to finish all this."

Outside, a listless series of grey-slated roofs and uninspiring redbrick buildings made Dublin seem like a Victorian painter's version of England: some smoke-spewing chimneys and the LS

Lowry painting would be complete. Angela read my mind. "It's not a pretty city is it? Not like Budapest or Prague. Apart from the nice parts of Temple Bar, it's quite nondescript."

My wife took another sip of Guinness and then placed it on the table. She said, "So how do you feel?"

"About what?"

"Finishing your trip?"

I was watching a barman balance a three-quarters full pint of Guinness on top of another similarly filled glass. It was hanging half over the rim of the first one. And then he added a third. It was a miracle his structure didn't topple over. "I'm glad," I finally said. "Glad it's finished. Sixteen days is definitely my limit. I'm ready to go home tomorrow, that's for sure."

Angela considered this. Her pint of Guinness was now forgotten, most of it left untouched. "So what was the best and worst place you visited?"

"I think you know the worst: Charleroi. I never want to go there ever again. It was horrible."

The best place was harder to come up with. Northern Cyprus had been fun, and so had Nyköping in Sweden. I had enjoyed them because they were so unexpected. But I'd also enjoyed Belgrade and seeing the castle in Carcassonne. Talking to the businessman in Bratislava had been enjoyable too. But there was one place better than all those.

"My favourite place was Riga." I said, draining the last of my Guinness. "It has everything: history, Soviet monuments, nice bars and restaurants, and it's so pretty, as well. You would love it there. We'll have to go."

"I'd like to."

"Well Ryanair have great deals from Manchester."

I put my empty glass and Angela's half-finished one on the bar in the middle of the large room. Then we made our way down to the streets of Dublin.

10

With a couple of hours to kill before heading to the airport, Angela suggested we visit the Famine Memorial. She and a friend had seen it on a trip to Dublin many years previously. "I think you'll like it,"

I asked her what it was.

"You'll see."

It took twenty minutes to walk back along the Liffey to the O'Connell Bridge, and then another ten until we reached the memorial. Not knowing what it would be, I expected a statue or maybe some sort of museum. And then I saw it, on the other side of the road, adjacent to the river.

Six corpse-like bronze figures, each with hollow features and ragged clothes, were 'walking' along the riverfront. Two of them, both skeletal men, were carrying bundles, possibly children in their arms; another carried what looked like an emancipated lifeless body across his shoulders. A stick-thin metal dog followed close by.

It is hard to imagine the lives of people living through the Irish Famine of 1845, but these sculptures helped. Each face was gaunt, as if taking in fetid air. Back then, with most of the population of Ireland heavily dependent on potatoes as their staple food source (it was easy to grow, hardy and flourished in great quantities), the humble potato was the wonder crop of Ireland, putting food on the plates of even the poorest people. Then the blight arrived in cargo ships from Central America. Quickly, it infected the country's potato crop, destroying three-quarters of it. The result was devastating for Ireland. When people started dying of starvation, those who could do so emigrated. Some sailed across the Irish Sea to Liverpool, but many journeyed further afield to the Americas. They were the lucky ones. Those they left behind faced a bleak mixture of cholera, dysentery and starvation. By the end of the famine, a million people had lost their lives.

"It's worth seeing, isn't it?" asked Angela. I nodded absently as I studied the face of one sculpture. It showed a painfully-thin woman wearing a headscarf; her hollow eyes fixed forward, a small bundle clutched to her chest. And yet, she was one of the lucky ones. She, and the other figures behind her, was on her way to the emigration boats, heading to a new life across the water.

"Some of the boats left close to here," Angela told me. "Each passenger paid three pounds for the ticket to New York."

I looked at my wife. "How do you know all this?"

"I read about it when I last came here."

I turned back to the sculptures. If these were what the lucky ones looked like, then God help the rest.

"I know something else too. See over there..." She pointed across the river, towards some glass-panelled office buildings. "Just behind them is a small hill called Misery Hill. There was a hospital there at one point, a hospital for lepers. It's gone now; I think it's a theatre now. Anyway, whenever a leper was taken to the hospital, a man would go with them, ringing a bell to warn people that a leper was coming through."

"Nice."

"Yeah. And another man carried a forty-foot pole to keep everyone away. That's where the saying 'I wouldn't touch him with a forty-foot pole' comes from."

"Wow. You're a font of knowledge today."

On the way back to the hotel, I insisted we have one more drink to celebrate the impending closure to my European adventure. And of course, it had to be a pint of the black stuff. We found a quiet bar near O'Connell Bridge. Angela opted out of the stout celebration and went for wine instead. Half an hour later, with my final slurp of Guinness, it was time to pack for the final time.

Top row: A view along the Liffey; Paddywagon store
Middle row: The Temple Bar in Temple Bar; Enjoying the craic in one of the bars of Temple Bar
Bottom row: Me, standing outside Dublin Post Office; The Spire of Dublin; Famine Memorial

Day 16. Manchester, United Kingdom

Dublin – Manchester: Ryanair £8

My sixteenth and final flight left the gate dead on time. We took off on a blustery and overcast evening, tracking the runway heading for a few minutes before turning eastwards. Soon we were leaving the coast of Ireland and heading over open water towards the United Kingdom. When the scratch cards came by, I almost bought one for old times' sake.

So this is it, I mused. The end of the line, the final furlong, the closing chapter of a low-cost extravaganza that had taken me to fifteen different European countries, not including England, in just sixteen days.

So what had I learned? One of the main things, I suppose, was not to disparage Ryanair's often maligned policy of landing at city airports miles away from the actual city. Ryanair, of course, did it for financial reasons: out-of-the-way airports had lower landing and handling charges than main airports. But sometimes, these quieter airports were near towns worthy of a visit in their own right. Nyköping was a prime example of this, and so was Bergamo. If it had not been for Ryanair, I probably would never have visited either of these places. Mind you, I would not have visited Nowy Dwor Mazowiecki or Charleroi, either, which would have been no bad thing.

Another thing I learned was that low-cost airlines are great value. Sure, you might not get a free meal, and check-in staff might charge you if you forget to print out a boarding card, but for anyone with a semblance of intelligence, these things are known factors and not an issue. I know I would rather pay £25 for a flight with Ryanair or Wizz Air than £125 to have a free croissant and cup of coffee with Lufthansa or British Airways.

It's a no-brainer, and that is why many legacy carriers are changing their operating principles; if they don't, they will see a diminishing return of airfare income. Almost every North American airline has already abandoned complimentary food for passengers flying in economy. This has spread to carriers in Europe. Iberia, the national airline of Spain, and Aer Lingus, the national carrier of Ireland, both charge for food on their flights. Even British Airways, always a stalwart of things that are good and proper, has introduced a low-frills economy ticket choice, whereby passengers travelling with only hand luggage can buy the cheapest ticket possible. If they hadn't done this, people would simply fly with EasyJet.

Another great thing about the likes of Ryanair is their punctuality. Because they are in the business of making as much money as they can, they utilise aircraft in the most efficient way possible. An aircraft on the ground is draining money, and so they have quick turnarounds to get their planes back in the air as soon as they can. Before booking my trip around sixteen different European countries, one thing had worried me above all others: what would happen if one of my flights were cancelled? The answer was simple and stark: I would be well and truly stuffed. The rest of my itinerary would fall like dominoes – and I wouldn't be able to do a thing about it. I'd have to take the hit and rebook everything from scratch, most likely sacrificing one of my destinations and paying top dollar for a series of last-minute flights.

But this didn't happen. And that was one more thing I learned: low-cost airlines run their businesses well. If they didn't, no one would fly with them and they would go bankrupt. Every one of my flights except one had arrived on time or earlier, and the solitary late flight was only fifteen minutes late. Everything had gone swimmingly. Each of the airlines I'd flown with had delivered me to my destination despite rain, thunder and mad passengers.

2

Ryanair 558 landed on a rain-drenched runway at Manchester Airport less than forty minutes after taking off. It had been the shortest flight of them all. When the trumpet sounded, I nodded in appreciation. So this was *really* it: the definite end. As the captain manoeuvred the Boeing towards the gate, and the cabin crew prepared themselves for another swift turnaround, I thought back to the places I had been: Norway, Poland, Sweden, Germany, Latvia, Italy, Slovakia, Belgium, France, the Netherlands, Serbia, Greece, Cyprus, Hungary and Ireland. I was amazed I was still sane after so many airport security lines, boarding queues, hotel check-ins and terrible cups of airline coffee.

I had survived it, however, and though I'd found certain days harder than others, I had enjoyed the experience of seeing Europe at such great speed.

"Welcome back to Blighty," said Angela. We were walking inside the start of Terminal 3. "Back where you belong."

I nodded. "Back where I belong."

Fifteen minutes later, we were standing by the car. I lifted Angela's bag into the back, then placed mine on top. Both wheels were now hanging on by a thread. No more foreign trips for you, I said silently to my travelling companion of the last sixteen days, just days of rest. I closed the boot and closed the door on my low-cost adventure around Europe.

If you have enjoyed this book by Jason Smart, then perhaps you will also like his other books, which are all available from Amazon.

The Red Quest

Flashpacking through Africa

The Balkan Odyssey

Temples, Tuk-tuks and Fried Fish Lips

Panama City to Rio de Janeiro

Bite Size Travel in North America

Crowds, Colour, Chaos

Rapid Fire Europe

Meeting the Middle East

Take Your Wings and Fly

Visit his website **www.theredquest.com** for more details.

Printed in Great Britain
by Amazon